CW00520609

Sailing Round Russia

Wallace Clark

'A voyage conceived as something far more profound than an exotic pleasure trip'
— *Telegraph*

'As an example of seamanship and enterprise this journey is outstanding'
— *Royal Cruising Club*

SAILING
ROUND
RUSSIA

The Story of Miles Clark's Unique Voyage

Compiled and Edited by his father
WALLACE CLARK

With a Foreword by
LIBBY PURVES

ISBN 0 9509042 1 X (hardback)
ISBN 0 9509042 2 8 (paperback)

Copyright © Wallace Clark

Published by Wallace Clark
Booksales

OTHER BOOKS BY WALLACE CLARK

Sailing Round Ireland

Rathlin – Its Island Story

Linen on the Green
– The Story of an Ulster Mill Village

Upperlands Visitors Guide

Printed by Leinster Leader Ltd., Naas, Co. Kildare.

Contents

Foreword by Libby Purves 7
Editorial Note 9
Glossary 10
Maps and Wild Goose Plans 11
Characters of the Crew 17
Introduction – *Breakers Ahead* 19

CHAPTERS

1	*Forbidden Waters.*	By Miles Clark 31
2	*Archangel to the Gulag.*	By Libby Purves 42
3	*The White Sea Canal.*	By Libby Purves 54

Following Chapters
Edited by Wallace Clark
from Miles' Logs and Crew Memoirs.

4 *Over the Hump* 66
5 *Mologa Triangle* 78
6 *The Golden Ring* 91
7 *Four Towns and a Romanov* 100
8 *Gorky for a Crew Change* 112
9 *Makarieff by Moonlight* 125
10 *The Locks of Cheboksary* 136
11 *Three Days in Kazan* 147
12 *Green Scum* 155
13 *Round the Bend* 167
14 *The Longest Bridge and Shortest Canal* 175
15 *Cossack Kindness* 187
16 *Turkish Delight* 203

EPILOG 210

Acknowledgements 213
The Mary and Martha Orphanage 215

APPENDICES
One: Fit Out and Spares 216
Two: Charts, Air Maps and Navigational Aids 218
Three: Times and distances 219
Four: Agreements with Moscow Adventure Club....... 221

To
all the friends who have made
Wild Goose
a
a happy ship
on many a passage
during the last forty years.

Foreword

By LIBBY PURVES

In 1992 Miles Clark – godson and biographer of the great sailing voyager Miles Smeeton – set out on his own voyage of exploration. Against all odds – bureaucratic, logistical, meteorological – he completed a unique circumnavigation in his family's veteran yawl, Wild Goose.

Other intrepid sailors have travelled to the North Cape and into the Barents Sea; few Western yachts before him had visited the infamous Solovetsky islands part of the Gulag archipelago, and none had entered the White Sea Canal, which Stalin built with slave labour at a cost of 200,000 lives. With Russian crews, in cramped and trying conditions, he navigated the locks and the lakes to the Volga and emerged at last into the freedom of the Black Sea, his curious enterprise complete.

Those who knew about it, and particularly those who had read Miles Clark's distinguished biography of the Smeetons, *High Endeavours*, were eager to read the full story. He planned to write a book; by now, it would have been out for five years, and probably be a recognized modern classic of the sea. Indeed, he began it, writing a powerfully atmospheric chapter which took Wild Goose to the threshold of Russia. That chapter ends at the sad submarine-haunted port of Murmansk, where welcoming officers searched through their phrasebook for proper greetings, among such striking phrases as YOU ARE ARRESTED and I AM SEARCHING FOR THE SPACESHIP IN DISTRESS.

Then, before the next spring came, Miles died, aged 32. Nobody had expected it; he left a wife, young son, brother, parents and countless friends. The shock of this loss was immense, and it took some time for it to become clear that this book must, somehow, be finished even though it could never be the one he would have written.

For one thing, he left clear logs, and the voyage itself is important; an honourable footnote in the history of small-boat voyaging and a sidelong insight into Russia at a time of momentous transition. And it was a remarkable achievement; not only for Miles Clark himself but also for his brother Bruce, former Moscow correspondent of *The Times*, who helped him navigate the thickets of bureaucracy and interpret the country; for the spirited young

Russians, sons and daughter of a country in economic and social crisis, who accompanied him on various legs of the journey; and for his father Wallace Clark, too, who had so lovingly preserved Wild Goose for forty years, and passed on to his son his own love of adventures under sail.

So somehow, the story of Miles Clark's last voyage had to be told. The difficulty facing his family and friends was that there seemed no way of telling it that was both honest and coherent. Nobody could adequately follow on from the vivid, personal tone of that first chapter, because nobody but him lived through the whole trip. This book, therefore, at times, changes tone and changes authors; maybe this is how it should be, because the untimely death of a promising spirit inevitably brings a continuing sense of dislocation and loss.

The book's moving spirit and main writer is Wallace Clark, Miles' father. He tells of the months of preparation; then Miles' own first chapter is here, followed by two short chapters which I wrote myself from studying the unusually detailed and moving logs of the journey to the Solovetsky islands and the entry to the White Sea Canal. Then Wallace, who was in constant touch with his son throughout the trip, carries on the story from the logs and his own notes. The story is supplemented by the work of Bruce Clark; a fluent Russian speaker himself, he conducted detailed, very valuable and often sharply entertaining interviews with the various crew members, whom he sought out during the year after the voyage ended. Finally Wallace can tell first-hand of the moment when he rejoined his boat and his son as they emerged into the cleaner, simpler waters of the open sea at Rostov.

So this is the nearest we can get, between us all, to telling the story that Miles could finish. It is offered as a tribute to him, and we hope that from it will emerge an accurate portrait of a remarkable young man; dogged, sensitive, patient and brave. Miles put on no airs, and made no mystery of his skills; he was a very British figure, practical, humorous and immensely competent yet with the heart of a true romantic traveller. A secular pilgrim, driven to go

> *'Always a little farther; it may be*
> *Towards that last blue mountain barred with snow,*
> *Across that angry or that glimmering sea.'*
>
> *Flecker*

Editorial

In this book I have aimed to assemble from varied sources an account of a unique voyage of some 5000 miles. Sadly it indirectly led to the death of my son Miles who conceived and led the expedition.

His departure in April 1993 nine months after the voyage ended is a loss neither I or any of his family will ever get over. We do however wish the voyage to be recorded as an inspiration to others, just as Miles was inspired by the voyages of his Godfather, Miles Smeeton. There are signs that it has already done so, judging from increasing inquiries I receive from yachts planning visits to western Russia.

Miles left a log, 1500 photographs and seventy pages of recorded conversations but inevitably there were gaps. His brother Bruce edited memoirs from the four Russians who joined by turns as crew.

To tie together this mass of anecdotes, navigational hints and observations has been a labour of love but a difficult one at times. If the knots show in places I ask the forbearance of readers. Hopefully they will share in what has been for me, in places, something of an exercise in detection.

Included are records of the kindness of many Russians met along the way. Travelling in an elderly wooden boat combines independence with an intimacy with the shoreline and its inhabitants in a way no other form of travel can equal. The account will, I hope, add a little bit to the store of knowledge of waters which were closed to non-Russians for generations, and act as a guide to those who may follow.

Narrative by Libby Purves and me is in regular 10.5 point [thus];

Quotes from Miles' log in *italics* [*thus*] and quotes from crew members in 9.5 point indented [thus].

The authors and sources are named at the top of each chapter in the appropriate type.

9

Glossary

Baklan	Cormorant
Burlaki	Manhaulers, walking in teams along shore to pull barges. The original Volga Boatmen.
Chaika	Seagull
Dacha	Holiday House
Dom Odhika	House of Rest
Gorot, Garadot	Small town
Guba	Cove
Isba	Wooden peasant hut
Jon boat	Americanism for small river runabout of any variety. In Russia it appears to be confined to inflatables. See also Survivor
Laht	Bay
Maa	Island
Meteor	Smaller Hydrofoil
Oblast	Province
Ostrog	Fort, Blockhouse
Ostrov or On.	Island
Ozero	Lake
Ulitsa	Street
Pasiolak	Big village
Raketa	Larger hydrofoil from Russian word for rocket. In *Russia's River Shipping* this term is used for an early motor pasenger ship (page 67)
Rechevah	19th Century wooden vessel propelled with a capstan turned by live-aboard horses.
Reha	River
Sobor	Cathedral
Solhoz	State Farm
Soudak	Pike
Survivor	Fisherman in Jonboat.
Vain	Strait
Volochek, Voloki	Portage
Vodokhranilishche	Reservoir
Zaliv	Bay
Zarias	Water Taxi

Wild Goose

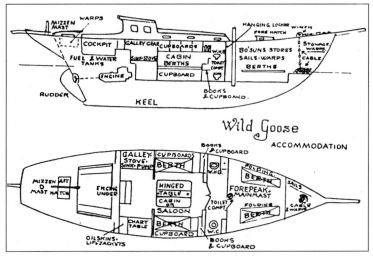

35' O.A. x 10' beam x 5'3" draft. Built in 1935 by Kings of Pin Mill to designs of Maurice Griffiths, G.M., AINA.

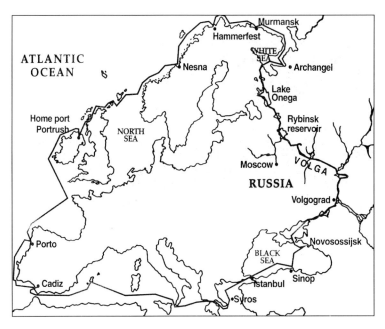

One: *Ireland to Istanbul and return voyage*

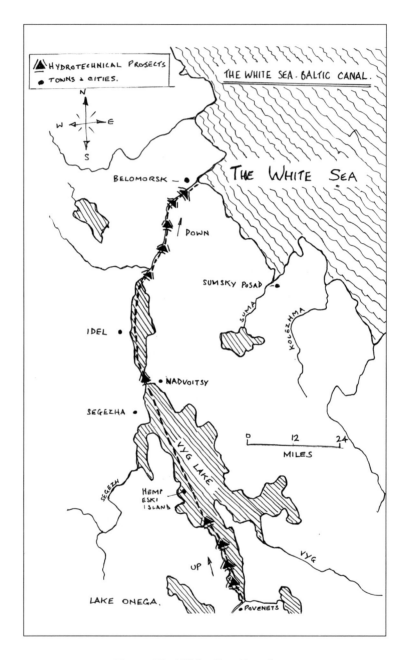

Two: *The White Sea Canal*

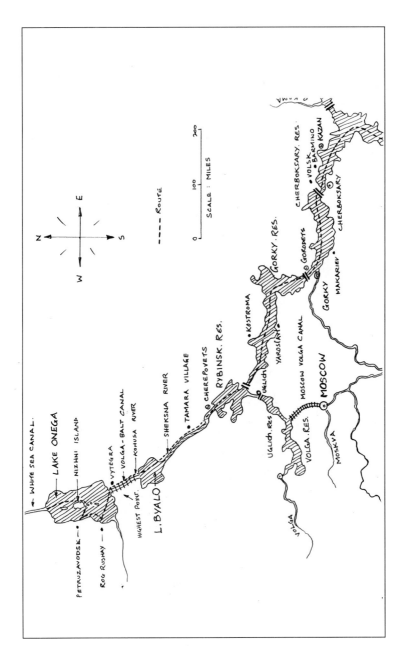

Three: *Lake Onega to Kazan*

13

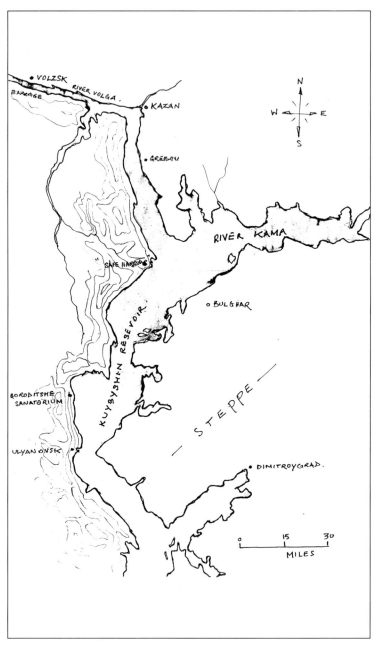

Four: *Kazan to Ulyanovsk*

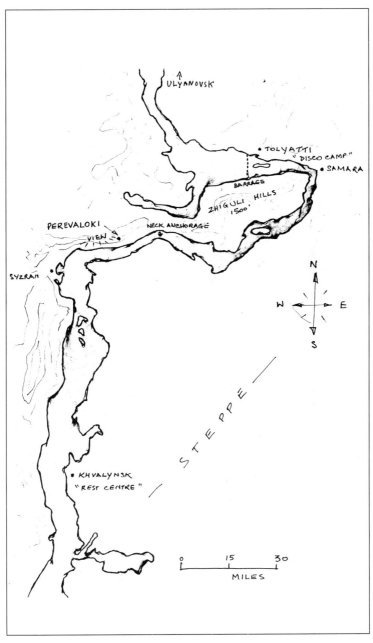

ULYANOVSK

TOLYATTI
"DISCO CAMP"

SAMARA

BARRAGE

ZHIGULI HILLS
1500'

PEREVALOKI

NECK ANCHORAGE

VIEW

SYZRAN

N

W   E

S

S T E P P E

KHVALYNSK
"REST CENTRE"

0   15   30
MILES

Five: *Samara to Balokovo*

15

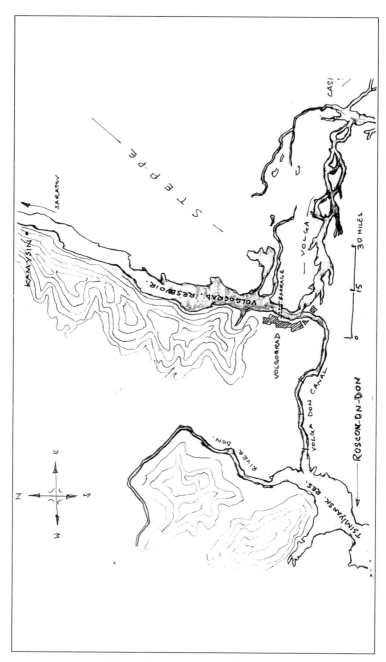

Six: *Kamysin to the River Don*

16

Characters of the Crew

VITALI CHANKSALIANI
Red haired 28 year old from Omsk in Siberia, of half Georgian origin. Married to Larissa with two children. Experienced traveller having been on a Canadian Arctic expedition and done military service in East. A skilled interpreter who enabled Miles to have many in-depth conversations with Russians met along the way. Found difficulty at times meeting the frequent demands of Jim Blair, the National Geographic photographer, as well as carrying out his main object of helping Miles as much as possible.
On board for whole trip.

NIKOLAI LITAU
An experienced yacht skipper aged 38, from Moscow. Handsome, capable and energetic, a good engineer and excellent shipmate. Married to Ludmilla with whom he had done extensive canoeing. Born in Kazakhstan where his parents of German origin had been transported by Stalin. Head of Transport in a Moscow Construction Company. Among the Russians stood out as a model of affability and common sense with a distinct twinkle in his eye.
Belomorsk to Nizhny Novgorod.

ARKADY GERSHUNI
Experienced sailor from Nizhny Novgorod, friend of Nikolai. Married to Tatyana from Georgia. Son of that considerable rarity, a Jewish officer in the Russian army. Hard upbringing after transportation and a leg injury as an infant during the second world war. A metallurgical engineer with a State sector job in Moscow. A most kindly and diplomatic character who smoothed the way for Miles on several important occasions.
Nizhny Novgorod to Novorossisk.

GALINA KAZARNOVSKAYA
Witty, mid-30s, winsome and intelligent yachtswoman. Married with one daughter. Herself a daughter of an engineer who worked on secret rocket development. A widely read and experienced tour operator and radio ham. A very Russian mixture of steely resistance, omni-competence and coquettishness.
Nizhny Novgorod to Kazan.

17

An exciting moment below Gorodets Barrage. (See page 113).

18

INTRODUCTION

Breakers Ahead

By WALLACE CLARK

'How about sailing Wild Goose round Russia, Dad?'

Milo asked the question as casually as he could manage across the round yellow breakfast table in the bow window of our Irish home . I almost choked on my porridge.

It was October 1991. Miles (known to his family as Milo) and I had very recently enjoyed a superb six weeks together rowing from Sligo to Stornoway as mate and skipper of a 16 oar Highland Galley. And I knew that Milo and his brother Bruce had been brainstorming for a new challenge worthy of our old family yawl Wild Goose.

But Russia! My instant inner reaction was the same as would have come to almost any one at that era. 'Niet; Impossible'. But if there was any way of getting the necessary Visas Bruce would surely find it, since he had been a senior journalist in Moscow for almost two years, and with his gift for friendship possessed contacts in almost every field. And if there was one man who could plan and lead such an expedition it was Milo.

And I remembered the mantra that hung in Bruce's office:

> *'Unless an idea is so way out as to be considered derisory when first proferred it is unlikely to be of any importance.'*

It was a bright, frosty autumn morning, the sort of day to make you long to be up and out on Hiawatha's *'shining big sea water'*. Milo filled in a few details about how he saw it as possible. Twenty minutes later over congealed bacon and eggs I was fully sold on the idea.

No Irish boat had done it before. Probably no boat of any sort had done it before, at least not without many portages. It was a fine challenge and looked like a big adventure but within our combined

19

capacity. Just the sort of thing Milo wanted to do before settling down to raising a family and writing about other people's adventures.

We pushed the cups aside and got out the Atlas.

He showed me how, with the split up of the Soviet Union, the north and eastern boundaries of the remaining state of Russia would be a series of lakes, canals and streams, chiefly the White Sea Canal, Lake Onega, the River Volga reputedly set with shoals and shifting channels and the more placid Don. The eastern part of Russia would also mark the not very clearly defined division between Europe and Asia.

Stage One would be 1500 miles of exposed high latitude sailing to get from Ireland round North Cape and Archangel – almost as long as an Atlantic crossing. When I suggested that honour might be satisfied by entering by the Baltic and St Petersburg Milo discarded that route at once.

'We want to do the thing thoroughly, Dad. Get right round everything.'

At this time Milo was a tall fair haired man aged 31 of proven courage and sailing ability, married to Sarah, a stunning slim blonde with a successful career in Public Relations. They had a son, Finnian, aged three and had recently moved from our home village in County Derry, Northern Ireland, to Salisbury in Wiltshire. Full of fun and a natural mimic, Milo could inspire confidence in any crew and keep them in laughs all the way.

In the gap year between public school at Shrewsbury and Downing College, Cambridge, he had learned how to survive in tropical rain forests as a Young Explorer with John Blashford-Snell's Operation Drake. He was a climber who could lead on routes labelled Very Severe. At Cambridge he had read geography and rowed in the Boat Race. As Chairman of the University Explorers Club he raised funds for and led a four man expedition to the Aleutian Islands to search for one of the rarest of marine creatures – the Sea Monkey. It had been sighted by Stellar in the 18th century and again by his godfather Miles Smeeton in 1960.

Then came a commission in the Green Jackets, perhaps the finest infantry Regiment in the British army, and two voyages in replica galleys of old. The first while still a soldier was in 1988 when Milo pulled an oar in The *Argo* up the Dardanelles on the Jason Voyage with Tim Severin in search of the Golden Fleece. The second one, as already mentioned, was as lead oarsman and photographer on The Lord of the Isles Voyage with me as skipper. He had no formal yachting qualifications but having taken Wild Goose to sea as skipper since the age of 17, was becoming a rich collector in experience.

20

You might then agree that it would have been hard to find anyone more suited to captain a yacht on a voyage requiring diplomacy as well as guts, meticulous planning as well as practical seamanship.

There was an odd moment when he doubted the possibility of it all; I encouraged him by saying: 'You're only young once.'

'Good job', said Milo. 'I never could afford to be young twice."

A little too prophetic had we known, but after that there were no more doubts. Wild Goose had at that time owned the Clark family for nearly 50 years. She is a strongly built wooden ten tonner, 35 feet long, with a lovely sheer and an upward pointing bowsprit which with a barnacle goose figurehead below it, looks as if it's sniffing the breeze and longing to be off.

Craftsmen of the breed that took no shortcuts, built Wild Goose at Kings of Pin Mill to the design of Maurice Griffiths in 1935. She had taken my wife June and me through the Midi Canal to the Mediterranean, several times round Ireland and often to Scotland and Brittany. If we go off in other people's yachts, she pretends to sail badly and drops bits of gear overboard. When really upset she refuses to let her engine start; As much as to say, 'You can get me out of this situation under sail. Come on now. Smack it about.'

Over the years she has gradually been modernised – her original bowsprit reduced from eight feet to four and a doghouse built on over the main hatch, winches added for sheets and halliards and an electric capstan for the anchor. Interior alterations have included moving the loo from right forward to amidships and the galley cooker from amidships to below the new doghouse to port, with a large chart table to starboard. We also built in twenty lockers to hold stores and spares for extended voyaging.

I knew she'd approved of the Russian idea as soon as I walked across the yard at the back of our cottage to her private boat shed. She rests there when she hasn't decided to stay abroad. We've said goodbye to her at various times in Spain, Portugal, the Greek Isles, France and many parts of Ireland and Scotland.

Perhaps it was just the springs on her massive road trailer that jerked as I jumped onto her dusty deck but I fancied it was Wild Goose herself that gave a little frisson of excitement as I fondled her goose head tiller.

That was enough.

ACTION

Once we'd decided on the voyage the challenges immediately ahead were urgent and fivefold.

21

1. 'Ships are all right', as Uffa Fox pointed out, 'It's the men in 'em!' So to book a good crew with Arctic experience was the top priority.
2. Then the political side. Get permission from the KGB and other authorities. Bruce would initiate this from Moscow.
3. Raise the necessary finance by sponsorship or whatever. Miles shouldered this one.
4. Get Wild Goose prepared and rigged as thoroughly as we could devise and loaded with the right spares and consumables. Miles and myself plus the team of craftsmen around our home in Upperlands all got involved in this.
5. Prepare a detailed schedule and stick to it. Be ready on time!

TIMING would be critical. The White Sea is choked with ice most years until mid June. The Black Sea which we'd have to traverse to reach Istanbul brews frequent storms after mid September, lethal for small craft of low freeboard.

That would leave a bare three months to cover three thousand miles of lakes rivers and canals, ill- charted for all we knew.

To enter the White Sea on schedule we would have to sail from Ireland by mid-May 1992. That left a bare six months to get everything done.

CREW

Two can handle Wild Goose easily inshore. For a long voyage three is best. The Wild Goose manning principle has always been to ask four, then it's OK if one drops out at the last minute. The obvious sources were our fellow members of the Royal Cruising Club and Irish Cruising Club. Their well manned boats have at one time or another penetrated most of the uttermost parts which can be reached afloat. But none at that time had entered the White Sea.

John Gore-Grimes, the Novaya Zemlya icicles scarce melted on his beard, told us that getting to North Cape was a doddle, then lent charts to prove it.

Two other Arctic hands Willie Ker and Hugh Clay agreed to join for the riskiest leg from Hammerfest in Norway round North Cape to the White Sea. They knew what the tinkle of ice along the hull meant and how best to keep out of the way of growlers and bergy bits, so they would contribute the experience Milo lacked of ice navigation and survival in low temperatures. Willie had sailed a 32 foot Contessa to the Falklands and Antarctica the year before, making most of the passages single handed. Hugh had sailed and rowed the Eel an open double-ended boat with his brother through the Norwegian skeargard of islands from Bergen all the way to North Cape.

The appeal of a first ever yacht passage to the White Sea was what lured these mighty men to leave their own boats for a spell and join a younger man who they must have reckoned would succeed.

Wild Goose has never had any problem in attracting crews, and most years we could have filled her three times over, but these *'ice eaters'*, like the voyage, were special. These arrangements had to be tentative for 1992, pending success in the other key areas.

FITTING OUT

Milo would have to continue to earn a living as a journalist right up to departure. I was retired from my career as a linen weaver so had a little time to spare.

Once we'd listed what needed to be done and a crew secured, the bulk of the overhaul of hull and gear fell to me. That's what sailing fathers are for.

Milo often remarked that the only thing that frightened him about Wild Goose was Dad with a paint brush. I managed still to maintain my carefully nurtured reputation as a ham fisted painter and a worse cook – two jobs I try hard to avoid.

Engine reliability would be paramount for the three thousand inland miles so we decided a new one was essential.

If you're interested in the details of what we did during that hectic four months turn to Appendix One.

Aubrey Denton of Watermota and his manager John Potter plus their excellent backup team at Newton Abbot soon became our true friends. They saw to it that we had spares for all vital engine components.

Another tried friend Jim McGarry from Crumlin Boatyard on Lough Neagh drove long distances day after day to shoe horn that engine into place in our boat shed ... 'Nothing fits easy into a boat except water', was on of his memorable comments as he groped doubled up to fit piping and holding down bolts.

I remember him, in the grandfather class like me, lying flat on his back and drilling upwards into the iron keel. 'Keeps you young', he said

Meanwhile handyman Archie Devennie was fitting extra heavy oak belting round the hull and a new rail cap. Bill Harrison rewired our 12 violt electrics. He talked non-stop the while, with his mouth so full of cable clips that I guess he swallowed quite a few. But he knew just what he was doing. And the radio worked a treat.

Almost all the new gear needed was supplied on most generous terms by David Guthrie of Simpson Lawrence, Glasgow. It was shipped under the canny eye of Keir Graham. Their one stop shopping was one of the major factors in making the fit out possible on schedule.

'As the efficiency of the boat goes up, the efficiency of the house comes down', is a well worn comment at Gorteade Cottage where all these things took place. In that hectic four months before May 1992 Milo's mother, June, put up with uncut lawns, washerless taps and hingeless doors with her usual good temper. Smilingly she supplied a thousand or more cups of tea, multiple meals, biscuits, buns and beer to hungry workers.

GETTING THE VISAS

Bruce, Milo's elder brother, although he is not a sailor by inclination, was part of the planning all along.

Resident in Moscow, he knew both the country and the language. Milo knew neither. He was no daredevil but always ready to take the bold course. Bruce had been the first to realise that given perseverance the voyage was politically possible. The diplomatic window for entry to the waterways brought about by a relaxation of Russian xenophobia was what Bruce had correctly foreseen in early autumn 1991. This stemmed from his correct analysis of the failed coup against Gorbachov of August that year and the emergence of Yeltsin as the master of Russia with liberal ideas.

'Does Yeltsin speak English?' I asked Bruce after he'd had a rare private interview. 'English?', came the reply, 'He can hardly speak Russian!'

Bruce saw this window of opportunity as fragile, and liable to be put into reverse at any moment. But he correctly predicted a period of peace long enough for the transit. For the voyage it was now or never.

Bruce then gave Milo what turned out to be the vital introduction to Nikolai Shparo, President of Moscow Explorers Club. On a first visit by Aeroflot to Moscow in December Milo obtained Schparo's interest and a quotation of $20,000 for his assistance. He was tempted to reply that he could buy half a dozen prime eunuchs for that price in Smyrna, but kept his counsel. KGB permission to use the canals could only be granted on the basis that Wild Goose would be on charter to the Explorers Club. Schparo thought it unsafe to go without at least two armed Russian as crew, one of whom would, on paper, be the skipper. Milo would, for officialdom eyes, be listed as a guest.

Rory Peck, who had photographed the war in Afghanistan as a front line journalist, a neighbour of ours in County Derry, offered to act as courier for cash and spares.

On a second trip Schparo, having taken the measure of Milo as a likely lad, settled for $5000. Most important were the terms, one third payable on getting the right documents signed, and one third

24

on Wild Goose getting cleared into Russia. Then the final, and perhaps most critical third, on getting her, plus crew, cleared out at the southern end!

For Russian shipmates, Gallina Kazharnovskaya, a lively member of Schparo's staff introduced Milo to several fine fellows from whom he selected Nikolai Litou, Arkady Gershuni as successive skippers, and Vitali Chankselliani as interpreter. This stout trio will be introduced fully in due course.

Why did he have to go so often? The anwer is best illustrated by the old WWII joke about naval officers writing to the Admiralty. This process was said to resemble making love to an elephant. The pleasure derived was negligable, the danger of being crushed was enormous and you didn't see results for four years anyway.

Writing to Russian officials was even less rewarding.

Moscow visits were things for which Milo could ill afford time or money but he judged each essential – the last to double check details, collect the actual entry documents and above all to confirm the timing and venues for crew changes.

FUNDS

A generous uncle had recently left me his pair of Boss 12 bore shot guns. Milo and I like snipe shooting which in Ireland involves much scrambling over stone walls and negotiating thorn hedges, hardly the place to be carrying an expensive gun. So it was not too hard a decision to put them on the market and shoot instead with my ancient BSA bramble poker. Sale of the Boss produced nearly £20,000 which covered most of the work.

For running expense on the voyage more funds were essential. Advance royalties from a publisher on a book to be written about the voyage produced some thousands more. Miles, let it be clear, did not make the voyage just to write a book. But to make the voyage income from a book was also needed. And that was soon arranged with the amiable Richard Johnson of Harper Collins. Needed too was Magazine or TV sponsorship. An Independent Television Company and the BBC took a lively interest.

The BBC scheme involved Tim Slessor being on board, a most agreeable and experienced yachtsman. Money aside, he would have been the greatest support. So it was a double disappointment when after endless shilly shally they withdrew. TV is much the most fickle of the media.

That left the *National Geographic Magazine* who had been dithering since November. We had to be off, you will recall, by mid May latest. By March there was still no word. We were then so committed that I guess we'd have gone anyway and funded things somehow. But it was an enormous relief when at the eleventh hour in mid March National Geographic said 'Yes'. Their contribution was generous and they paid the compliment of nominating Jim Blair, a senior staffer instead of a contract photographer, to be the on board cameraman. Of him more anon. He would join at Archangel. By the time all the correspondence and cajoling that these efforts had demanded was over Milo realised once more that the toughest bit of any expedition is the fundraising. After that almost anything seems easy.

By late April we began to feel almost ready for off!

THE REASON WHY

Why did Milo want to go?

As with most major problems there were several reasons which attracted Milo to attempt to round Russia. His love of adventure by sea was perhaps the biggest.

Those who have experienced the unique satisfaction of a landfall after strenuous effort afloat continue to want more. In other words sailing is a disease; you have it until you die.

The career of his godfather Brigadier Miles Smeeton was another … Milo was showing promise as a writer and had recently finished *High Endeavours* (Grafton Books 1991) a deeply researched and sensitive biography of Miles and his redoubtable wife Beryl. This attractive couple had sailed twice round the world in a boat of the same vintage as Wild Goose and not a lot a larger. In Tzu Hung they had survived two dismastings off Cape Horn.

Miles Smeeton, the most modest and amusing of men, had converted from being a professional soldier to become a superb ocean navigator and made his landfalls with aids no more complex than a sextant, compass and a tiny domestic radio. They were arguably the greatest of all the early post War oceanic sailors Their deeds stimulated Milo to venturesome voyages, and he was attracted by the Smeeton view that life without the prospect of adventure would be unsufferably dull. Much of the time I feel the same myself.

The idea of sailing round Europe may have come earlier from the Saga of the Ynglings.

In it *Snorri Sturlusson* the 13th Century Chronicler of voyages wrote:

North of the Black Sea lies Svithjoth the Cold. … In it there are many races, languages, giants and dwarfs. Out of the north, from the mountains a river runs through Svithjoth whose name is Tanais. Its mouth is in the Black Sea. This river divides the three continents. East of it is Asia, west of it Europe.

Miles read that Saga about the time he was starting to sail Wild

Goose as skipper aged seventeen. Perhaps the Irish/Viking blood in his veins turned the account into a challenge. The Vikings for centuries crossed Europe by water but always had to make portages. Like Mount Everest, the challenge of a voyage round Russia was because it was there.

And Captain Sam Wallis, an early Pacific voyager who discovered Tahiti, was also a forbear.

Exploring was in Milo's blood as well as his environment.

Adventures are to the adventurous and one need look no further for explanations.

The Smeeton and Viking connections were more than enough to whet Milo's appetite for ventures and voyages.

A Dublin friend of mine, Robert Barr, neatly sums up why sea voyages satisfy:

'Cruising has been the love of my life. I find that apart from the venture itself there are two other associated joys. First the planning when past experiences in the same or similar waters come crowding into the mind's eye, then as a postscript the log which tries to recapture the joys and tribulations and flavour of it all. For me there is nothing more satisfying in life than a good boat, congenial crew and a wide expanse of sea with perhaps a bon table in prospect on arrival in port.

This voyage would be one in which all the family could all take part: Miles at the tiller, his wife Sarah as base for communications, sponsor contacts and crew changes, his mother June helping to obtain pack and forward food and comforts. Bruce taking care of diplomatic affairs in Moscow, the writer as stand by crewman and base rat.

By 1991 long ocean voyages had become a common place as had Russian photographic journalism.

And so Milo sought out a voyage which no one had done before and which seemed a genuine challenge. This one had the convenience of a circular voyage on which one doesn't have to 'bout ship at a midway point. It was McMullen the 19th Century singlehander who remarked that 'There is a wonderful difference between being outward bound for pleasure and homeward bound for necessity'.

Our reckoning of the chances of success before the start were less than one in three. We listed the hazards: Foundering in a survival gale off North Cape, being holed by an iceberg, barged by an aggressive fisherman or wiped by a ram-you-damn-you steamer in a White Sea fog, a hold-up from broken lock gates in the Canals or withdrawal of political permission, civil war along the way, looting by a starving population, a major engine failure, collision or severe grounding. A delay of more than a week or two for any reason could in itself jeopardise the trip as the timing was so climatically critical. Miles and I agreed that if he had to abandon her in Russia, so be it. We'd had plenty of fun from the old girl and she would rather die game than fade away.

None of us spotted the worst danger.

It is seldom wise to weigh up the risks of a voyage too closely before starting; in fact I've never done it by rote before. But this one was so exceptional that it merited particular study, and plans to cope with each of them.

Bill Tilman, the famous mountaineer and high latitude sailor, remarked, 'A sea voyage is not of much interest if you are certain of getting to the far end'. Miles and I agreed.

By that standard rounding Russia certainly ranked high on the interest list.

SAILING ORDERS

On 5th May I did my two favourite fitting out jobs – best because they are the last ones in the shed – rolling on the International Anti-Foul paint and enjoying its tarry and briny odour. This is followed by knocking out the wedges which have held the hull secure in winter and leaving the Goose supported just by the legs of her road trolley.

A smiling Walter Leacock arrived to tow her to the sea. An hour on the road and we were slung off our road trailer onto the boatlift at Coleraine Marina. This is five miles inland on the River Bann on the north coast of County Derry.

A week later on 12th May 1992 Milo and I, with cousin Stephen Clark, prepared to sail from the fitting out berth. We had been loading and stowing all day. At 8pm we drove the twenty miles home to collect one last trailer load of gear. Returning after midnight Milo who had had less than five hours sleep in the previous two nights, failed to arrive. I had been leading in another car and returned to find him coolly changing the front wheel after having gone to sleep at the wheel and kerbed half a mile short of the Marina. Lucky it was no worse.

The cabin sole was still up as Bill Harrison from Bangor wired up the complex earth mat of copper strips for the SSB Radio. He finished at two am. We turned in at three am. The alarm went at five to remind us to catch the ebb tide down river. An unexpected good omen was the appearance just then of another cousin to tend our lines. No one could have been more welcome to wish us Godspeed than Vice Admiral Sir Arthur Hezlet, a World War Two submarine ace of great Arctic experience.

His practical help was welcome as well. Flood water and a spring ebb was forcing us into our berth. Coming out astern before cutting across close upstream of expensive looking yachts in the outer row

28

we were glad of his hand to man a safety line and let it go at just the right minute. We were OFF!

The anchor went down half an hour later just inside the bar mouth to have a short sleep, large breakfast and clear up some of Bill Harrison's electrical leavings. By ten am the tide was right to head north west for Islay. A 'tremendjous lep' as Wild Goose breasted a big roller at the outer end of the training walls, a dram for the harbour heads when clear and the voyage had really started!

By dusk at 2200 we were twenty miles west of Islay and it was blowing Force 7 from astern. The cabin sole was still two foot deep in unstowed gear. Diesel was leaking into the bilges, and worse still the load of fuel in our newly installed long range tanks was clearly putting her down aft. She was not lifting in her usual easy way to the following seas. But nothing much came on board.

At 5 am dawn I observed from the tiller that a lee shroud was swinging loose, having jumped out of its niche in the spreader. Stephen and I were working out the best way of getting it back in, when Milo, who had been asleep below, exhausted after sustained effort, shot out of his bunk, and was violently seasick.

Then quick as a cat he was up the mast steps and had the wire flicked back into position before we had time to speak. I've seldom seen a more gutsy effort.

Barra Head, a 600 feet green massif, was abeam to port at breakfast time in the brilliant sun of a perfect West Highland morning. Stephen quickly traced the fuel leaks, while we had a splendid sail in the lee of a string of islands to Vatersay and Castle Bay, Barra.

There Milo landed the mizzen mast, its boom, bumpkin and rigging and stowed it behind a nearby shed. The stern lifted a satisfying three inches.

An unpredicted Force nine that night almost ended the voyage before it had properly begun. We were on a Guest Mooring provided by the Highlands and Islands Board at the north edge of the bay with our stern about two lengths from the rocks when we woke up to find Wild Goose kicking over the traces in shrieking gusts and six foot waves. The mooring was overdue for inspection and if a link or shackle had gone nothing could had saved us from serious damage.

Serious damage might also have happened to Stephen as he exposed the most valuable portion of his body to the sharp cranse iron while leaning over bowsprit to attach an additional chain to the mooring buoy.

At Stornoway two days later Bill Spiers, retired surgeon and Royal Cruising Club mate, filled us with drams and supplied some missing bits of gear. Stephen left there to return to work and Alastair Scott joined. He had driven huskies hundreds of miles in

Alaska and we knew his staying power as a bench mate rowing our 16 oar galley the previous summer.

Another new chum was Justin Smallwood who had done a tour of duty at the marine base at Harstad, North Norway and acquired intimate knowledge of the fjords and personalities, specially, I am told, the female ones. Local know-how that would be invaluable in the event of trouble while making our northing.

A wind blew us round Cape Wrath to sight Sule Skerry and pass west of the Orkneys. Yorkshire yachtsman John Hodges joined us two days later at Lerwick in the Shetlands. He combined bursting enthusiasm with great charm, and skill as spannerhound and GPS navigator.

This was my cue to make room by jumping ship. 'It's a big adventure, Dad,' said Milo as we parted, with shiny eyes and some pangs. But I knew I was leaving him prepared as thoroughly as our combined efforts could devise and in the best of company.

The voyage was Milo's in conception, planning, preparation, execution and by personal leadership. But it was also a family affair in the best sense so that we all supported and helped Miles in every way that we could. With him we accepted the risks and took pleasure in progressive success.

Miles, aged 6, with his godfather, Miles Smeeton, who inspired him to travel adventurously.

CHAPTER ONE

Forbidden Waters

By MILES CLARK

'It may be that the gulfs shall wash us down,
or maybe we shall touch the happy isles.'...
Tennyson

There was still something imaginary about the lost grey land which
began to emerge from the sea. The sun had descended from yellow
into pink before climbing into yellow again without bothering to set.
For a time it grew brighter, floodlighting the underwings of a skua
which had wheeled for several hours around the ship. The cold began
to lose its grip, and as it did so, the horizon seemed to break up and
evaporate, unravelling along its length like a slowly breaking wave.

As far as I could see, there was nothing else. Only the rolling black
sea; the low snow-scarred hills; the shadows and highlights of twisting sails; the single wandering bird ... and then, as though by the flick
of a switch, the floodlight was extinguished. The sun was swallowed
by a layer of grey cloud and the land took on the same sense of weary
hopelessness that I had felt in the winter forests around Moscow.

In that moment, the notion of drifting south across the vast
impenetrable country seemed nothing less than absurd.

Then the encouraging thought that I wasn't the first person here
to question his sanity. Not historically at any rate. For a thousand
years, until the dawn of Imperial Russia, traders, raiders and
travellers had navigated the great waterways of eastern Europe,
laboriously portaging their ships through the maze of lakes and
rivers which stretches from the Arctic to the Black Sea. The interior
was a miracle of waterways and watersheds, a kind of fluvial
Snakes and Ladders. From the forested Valdai hills in the heart of
the continent, raindrops falling only a few feet apart began journeys
in opposite directions, gathering into shallow brooks which fanned
outwards into streams which emptied into rivers which led to
different seas. In summer, they had carried almost anything that

would float, from simple wooden rafts to strong swan-bowed ships which smelt of stale sweat and rancid fur. In winter, they became a highway for horses' hooves.

The way through was often opposed. There was always some-one. If it wasn't the settling Slavs and Vikings, it was the Bulghars, the Khazars, the Mongols, the Volga princes or the Tatar Khans. They were, between them, the guardians of the watersheds: for just as the isthmus was the key to dominating maritime gains, so the voloki or portage points became the bastions of the inner continent. In peacetime, crossing from one headwater to the next involved lit-tle more than good old-fashioned labour. All you had to do was pay your respects at the local kremlin on the watershed or leave a bag of squirrel skins at the door. The system of tribute was universal.

But just imagine the sweat. If hauling ships up mosquito-pestered hills was character-building in peacetime, how much worse must it have been in times of war? Every man that ever strained at the ropes must have dreamt of a corridor of water from one river to the next. Peter the Great showed his greatness a thou-sand years after the trade began, by being the first to try to create a whole empire linked direct by water to its five surrounding seas. That dream had a dreadful price, one which thousands of his sub-jects paid for with their lives. Compared with building with forced labour, portaging ships must have seemed almost a happy memory. By 1725, Peter's canals had joined the Baltic to the Volga and the Caspian, but the remaining watersheds were more formidable obstacles. It wasn't until this century, at an even more terrible cost in human suffering, that the final links were built in a 2,000 mile waterway from the White Sea to the Black Sea but by then the way was completely closed to non Russians : this time by the Cold War and Soviet xenophobia.

From the earliest imaginary journeys across *The Times Atlas of the World*, my finger had followed this thin blue line which expanded and narrowed across the unimaginable wilderness of cen-tral Russia. I couldn't picture it, the water, the trees, the shape of the land. It was simply an unfocusable image, one of a hundred mysterious journeys that could only be reached from the sea – the same real, wet touchable sea that pounded ashore near my home in Ireland.

By itself though, the sea would not have been a strong enough spur to imaginary travel. It needed a conveyance of some kind, a moving spirit. Before I was born, my father had bought Wild Goose, a 34ft wooden yawl built for neither speed or endurance, but with all the gently curving grace of her day. Her decks were so close to the water that I could trail a hand in the sea. I often sat astride her bowsprit so that my legs plunged in up to the knees as

Wild Goose as she left Coleraine with mizzen mast stepped.

At Hammerfest, Norway, to collect large box of foodstsuff for Russian transit.
[Hugh Clay]

Alastair Scott doesn't seem to be missing his Alaskan Huskies as he steers by Norway's icy mountains.

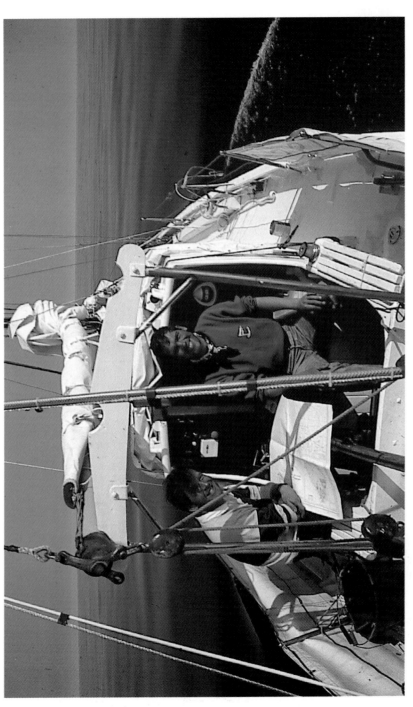

Northward bound on the Swan's Road from Shetland. John Hodges (left) and Justin Smallwood.

Hoisting the Russian courtesy flag in the Barents Sea.
"The owl, for all his feathers, was a-cold."

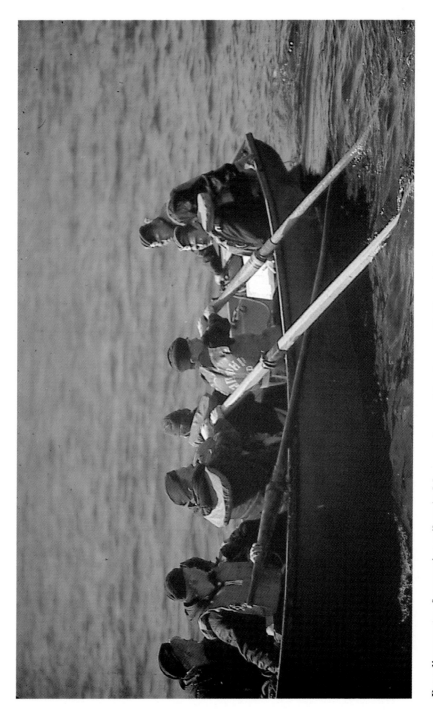

Boarding party of conscript sailors in Murmansk guard boat row with ill-matched oars.

Under tow after arrest by Russian light cruiser.

'Your peppers are in order. Have a best voyage!'

Alongside the yacht club at Archangel where members were most helpful. [Hugh Clay]

The Church of Golgotha, Anzer Island. Vitali makes a risky ascent to the dome of building used for years as a political prison.

A room with a view, Anzer. Collapsed prison hut showing like a wreck in seascape.

The Kremlin on the main Solovetsky Island has walls eight metres thick and a perimeter of five miles.

Willie Ker enjoys a dram in what Miles called 'the most memorable anchorage of my or Wild Goose's lifetime.'

Nikolai Litau, Russian 'skipper' who joined as we entered the White Sea Canal.

Alongside in the White Sea Canal. Jim Blair watches as Nikolai vaulted.

Bearing off in a White Sea Canal lock. [Vitali Chankseliani]

Spikes and splinters in a White Sea Canal lock could have caused serious damage.
[Vitali Chankseliani]

A visit from Alexi and Anastasia, sole inhabitants of Hempeski Island, Lake Vyg.

Fish drying huts around Hempeski Pier. [Vitali Chankseliani]

The unique Transfiguration Church on Kizhi Island, Lake Onega. [Jim Blair, National Geographic Society]

she rose and fell on the breast of a wave. I was never remotely interested in how fast she could go: only in Where and How Far. She took us to islands which seemed to be on the other side of the world – Ushant, Ile de Sein, St Kilda, the Flannans. She rocked us to sleep and as I got older, nothing gave me a clearer sense of my size under the sun than to watch Ireland dip below the horizon and Scotland gather from the gloom. Together, sea and boat were a frictionless conduit to my two-dimensional destinations. No roads. No tracks. No runways. No timetables. Not even a predetermined course.

In winter, when the boat stood in an open shed behind the house, the imagination had to work a little harder. Beech leaves, wood shavings and pigeon feathers pirouetted across the foredeck.

Anchors lay hidden under wheelbarrows and lawnmowers, and the sea seemed very far away. Somehow, though, Wild Goose was never completely motionless. The wind came to her across an ocean of green hills, buffeting her hull and sending cats paws racing across the lake beyond the beech trees. Even the sounds around her were easily transformed. With my eyes closed, a flapping tarpaulin became a fluttering headsail, a swaying branch the creak of bowsprit and boom.

These daydreams were a very private affair, never shared by Bruce my elder brother, whose mind was filled with other things. When he wasn't teaching himself Dutch or Greek or Esperanto, he was making up a language of his own, complete with an alphabet which only he could understand.

Quite what the White Sea looked like, I could only guess. At seven, I imagined it as home to a White Queen, a long-nailed exile from Nrnia who lived in a Palace of ice but whose face I could never quite picture.

Yet even when I first began to read about it, the truth seemed no less fantastic. In the 9th century – soon after the first Vikings reached through the waterways to Constantinople – a Norwegian trader called Othere ventured into the White Sea and the northern shores of Biarmaland. In Scandinavian tradition, Biarmaland was the end of the known world. Beyond it were said to lie strange people and fabulous lands. It features in many of the sagas as a place of wild adventure, with sacred areas surrounded by palisades, burial mounds filled with silver, and images of the Biarmian god, Jomali, with a bowl of treasure in his lap.

For six centuries after Othere's voyage, the existence of a route eastward into the Icy Sea remained little more than a fable in the maritime nations.

Willoughby's search for the Northeast Passage in 1553 brought triumph and disaster. The ships were scattered in a storm and the

Edward Bonaventure under Richard Chancellor, continued alone to a place where they found 'no night at all, but a continual light and brightness of the Sunne shining clearly upon the huge and mightie Sea.' By the time she found her way into the White Sea, it was already well into August. Chancellor was forced to winter near the mouth of the Northern Dvina, and 'after much adoe, came at last to Mosco.' There he was warmly received by Ivan IV – a meeting which laid the foundation for three centuries of trade between England and Russia.

They were lucky to have found Ivan in a state of euphoria having just won his first major victory over the Tatars – the intaking of Kazan.

For the 40 years before 1992, the idea of a foreign vessel entering the White Sea, much less Soviet inland waters was as much a fantasy as the country itself. In spite of all that I had read, the Russians who inhabited the bookstalls, the newsprint and the ether were scarcely more real to me than Willoughby or the White Queen. I could picture the domes and bell-towers of the river churches, the deadening sameness of the Soviet city, the triumphant memorials, the Palaces of Culture and the hunched shoulders in the bread queues, but I couldn't grasp them. I could picture the grey cadaverous faces of the People's Deputies, but never the people they claimed to represent. All I could put together was an ill-fitting mosaic of second-hand impressions.

In the 40s and 50s, travel in many parts of the Soviet Union was so rare that simply having been there was reason enough for a book. The shelves of the University Library were filled with them. *I Went to Moscow, I Went to the Soviet Arctic, I Worked in a Soviet Factory, I Was Stalin's Bodyguard*. There was even pairs of books: *Russia Has Two Faces and The Two Faces of Russia; I Married a Russian and Me and My Russian Wife*. I was Stalin's aunt and Lenin's nurse.

The White Sea was the most elusive of all. The crystalline world I'd first imagined was soon covered with a rash of cartographers' symbols – soldiers, airstrips, submarines and inter-continental missiles representing the launch pad of Moscow's front line arsenal. ... The highest concentration of nuclear installations in the world. Throughout the Gorbachev era, the far north remained resolutely barred to foreign eyes, untouched by the political thaw. But in 1991, the failure of the August coup seemed to signal a fragile opportunity. Fragile was the operative word. The Union itself was stumbling towards dissolution and uncertainty, and had it not been for my own personal mole – a brother working as Moscow Correspondent for *The Times* – the odds and the risks would have been too elusive to judge.

In December when I first visited Russia Moscow was impossibly foreign, a warehouse city which seemed to have been built and then abandoned for fifty years before anyone had been allowed to set up home. Everyone looked cold and cross. With Bruce's help, I engaged the services of Oksana Kalovna, a medical interpreter whose round open face delivered a smile that stayed in place for seven days. Nothing was too much trouble. When I needed a car, she called a friend, a surgeon who took time off from a city hospital. 'It will be better for Sasha to drive us for a few days than to work as a surgeon', she said.

Together we walked down the narrow red carpets of the White House, ushered by a chain of officials to broad offices overlooking the Moscow River. And together, we entered brooding faceless buildings where one contact after another listened to my plans with calculating interest. 'Well, I have one or two friends who may be able to travel with you. They speak some English and know the waterways. But of course ...' – and here they added a carefully-timed exhalation of breath – '... I think it will be very, how shall I put it, not cheap for you.'

One afternoon in search of possible crewmen, we left the city, heading north through smoking chimneys, over railway sidings and into brush forest, looking for apparently imaginary boatyards buried under snow. Where life existed at all, it was usually announced by a dog. The smaller the dog, the louder the reception.

Usually, but not always. Beside one frozen reservoir was a tired wooden clubhouse which looked as if it might collapse at any minute. Icicles hung from its eaves. The main door, surmounted by a crooked anchor, led to a dark staircase and the sound of muted voices. As I reached the top step, the conversation stopped. But beyond the door was neither office nor clubroom. Only a chorus of pigeons clattering out through a broken window.

When Oksana and Sasha the surgeon saw me off at the airport, I still wasn't sure about the whole endeavour.

'So what about the next six months?' I asked, as we got out of the little Lada. 'Are you fairly optimistic ...?' ... but even as I spoke, a lump of masonry broke off the airport building and exploded around Oksana's feet.

'How can anyone be optimistic in a country like this?'

One can drop a foreigner into the centre of Parma or Siena, into the old market place at Basle, or into almost any corner of any French town, and in ten minutes the most unsophisticated will have drunk in something of the atmosphere of Italy or Switzerland or France. But there is no corner of Leningrad of Moscow where a visitor could similarly absorb in a concentrated way the atmosphere of Russia. In Russia, the life of the people does not vibrate on the air as it does in the Mediterranean countries, where one does not need to know the language in order to understand much of what is going on. The Russian language does not even lend itself to a simplified or pidgin version; there is practically no halfway house for the foreigner between no Russian and good Russian.

Ten days after my first visit, the Soviet flag came down. It took two more visits to Moscow to research the journey and find suitable crew. By 1992 April the military authorities, the KGB and the relevant ministries had given their approval.

From the start, the voyage seemed to demand a particular kind of ship: strong enough for the Arctic, shallow enough for inland waters and old enough to dispel any suggestion of affluence. In practice there was never really any choice. Wild Goose was sitting looking at me from her shed under the beech trees. In some respects, Wild Goose was not ideal for such a long voyage. Her freeboard was low and her thirties design allowed only two bunks in each of two narrow cabins. But any shortcomings in her accommodation were made up for by the rewards that come with fidelity to an old boat – my father and I had always done our own fitting out, thereby acquiring a knowledge of every plank, porthole, fastening and bookcase and an instinctive feel of her behaviour.

This time the preparations were relentless and for six months in a shed below tall beech trees, Wild Goose was virtually rebuilt around the bunk cushions. A boat with her deck only 18 inches above sea level was going to ship a lot of water if we were hit by a Barents Sea gale so every source of leakage above and below water had to be traced and stopped. Every fastening checked and in doubt doubled. A tight ship is a good ship.

Spares and tools for just about every breakage were somehow found room for below decks When I sailed from Ireland with three British crew on 13 May, she was stronger than at any time for over 50 years.

The outward passage seemed a contradiction, sailing north into Arctic daylight on a voyage to southerly Black Sea.

After leaving Lerwick in the Shetlands a big anti-cyclone hung over our masthead for three days giving blessed time to get into seagoing routine. We motored at five knots over seamless seas. Sometimes the wet half-night was lit by the flame of an oil rig, and for three days in the Norwegian Sea, the eastern horizon was filled with white shark's teeth islands and the emergent peaks of distant hills.

Here were boat and sea, at it again, allowing a kind of travel that was sometimes not quite of this world – and at others, more rudely immediate than the sofas and soap-operas of home. It was only ashore that life returned to a sensible everydayness. When a small filter dropped off the engine in the Shetlands, as islander quickly volunteered to replace it with a 'wee piece of the wife's pantyhose.' The wife herself, Big Muriel, was clearly a veteran of the method. 'I'd better no' give ye the crutch,' she said getting to work with a pair of scissors. 'It's no' affie nice.'

At Aalsund we got warm handshakes and offers of help. A top up of diesel was traded for a bottle of Bushmills whiskey; gifts of fresh bread and timber for Alastair's internal joinery followed.

The northern Norwegians were no less lavish with their welcomes, some of them regarding the return of perpetual daylight as cause for a perpetual orgy. There was more rocking in the harbour at Harstad than in the previous four days at sea. The Royal Marine base there in which Justin had recently spent a couple of years helped sort out some electrical defects. In Tromso early one morning, we were helped to find a berth by the local stud, complete with collarless white shirt, blow-dried hair and a large gold medallion. His own boat went on rocking long after he stepped off it.

'Now dat's a real old basstad of a boat,' he said, as he fastened our sternline, re-adjusting the contents of his jeans with the other hand. It was less a compliment than an identification signal. One which said, 'I'm a salty old basstad and I know an old boat when I see one.' 'Thanks very much. She was built in 1936.' He shook his head. 'No fookin kiddin.' I wondered where he'd learnt such good English. 'Vell,' he shrugged, 'It not's so fookin good really. But yeah, I spend six years on a trawler out of Grimsby. You lookin at Knut Belgrim, the best fookin cook in the North Atlantic.' He glanced at the steamed windows of his still-rocking cruiser, and turned to me confidentially. 'Now listen, if you wanna com and join in, dat's no fookin problem. ...'

I have to admit I was rather flattered. Less by the invitation than the idea that anyone should interrupt an orgy to take our lines.

My outward crew Alastair Scott, John Hodges and Justin Smallwood was a curious blend of culinary Rembrandt and withering robustness – all three had insisted on swimming across the Arctic Circle – but at Hammerfest, their berths were taken by two equally formidable friends. In 1987, Willy Ker and Hugh Clay had reached 76N on the northwest coast of Greenland, relegating the matter of a broken boom in mid-Atlantic to a small paragraph at the end of their account. Willy had just sailed the same 32-footer from England to Antarctic. He was 68.

We were entertained to a meal in the house of the Harbourmaster, an old friend of Dubliner John Gore Grimes and collected the 200 kilo box of food which John Shields the manager of the Shipping Department of our family business had sent off from Upperlands three weeks earlier.

One 2 June, Wild Goose reached North Cape. Its head was hidden in cloud.We anchored in the hope of a chance to photograph our Farthest North.Willie after a few minutes jigging caught three fine cod but the mist remained. Continuing east into the Barents Sea we followed the route of the wartime supply convoys to Murmansk on which five million tons of allied supplies shipping was lost to Nazi planes and U boats

Over the next three hundred miles, the tall treeless hills descended into a wilderness of snow-scarred tundra. Twice we sought shelter from westerly gales and for two days we waited in the toe-hold harbour at Vardo, just as the crew of the *Edward Bonaventure* had waited for news of their accompanying ships.

We cheered on the local female football team and filled every possible container with good Norwegian Diesel

EAST FROM VARDO

Gradually the picture altered as Norway's Icy mountains declined to Russia's Tundra Strand. With every mile of approach colour came slowly into the rocks. The radio crackled with strange international noises and bursts of machine-gun Russian. Still there was no sign of life. At last, the tundra parted at the mouth of the Kola Inlet, and for two hours we ran south past dark sounds and channels which didn't officially exist. Lost for information, the cartographer had simply drawn one headland round to the next in an anonymous yellow curve. The vacuum behind it was stamped in purple with the words ENTRY PROHIBITED.

Navigationally we would have carried straight on for Archangel but this 30 miles leg south was an essential detour, Murmansk being the compulsory Port of Entry.

Murmansk, created in 1915 as supply point in World War One and extensively used for the same purpose in WW Two, now has a population of half a million. This makes it the largest town north of the Arctic Circle.

Due to a quirk extension of the Gulf Stream it remains clear of ice all winter.

Willy was rather taken with the idea of sailing off the edge of a chart into the yellow unknown, but even from seaward, the contents of these dark recesses was perfectly clear. Vast grey complexes were surrounded by white sugar-lump apartment blocks, towers, dams, walls, chimneys and antennas.

As the morning progressed, ships began to emerge from south, many of them still wearing the Soviet flag and some in little better condition than the wrecks which lay at improbable angles along the shore.

It wasn't until we were nearing Severomorsk – the biggest nuclear submarine base in the world – that the reception began. Without warning, a large rusty coaster altered course and steamed dangerously towards us, rising and plunging on the incoming swell. We swung away from her. The coaster followed. We swung away again. Again she followed, each time resuming a collision course. As she closed with us, a small dirty figure threw open the door of the bridge and began frantically crossing his arms above his head. 'schhhhhtop ! ... Schhhhhtop! ...'

The radio began to burble and schpit. The coaster was joined first by one patrol vessel and then a second and in minutes we were surrounded by four Russian warships. Electric voices echoed over the water, davits were swung outboard, a boat was lowered, followed by a scramble net and a swarm of life-jacketed sailors.

The effect was certainly intimidating, and if the ship's boat had then crashed alongside to barked orders and running boots, it might even have been alarming. Instead, one by one, the sailors laboriously pulled out an assortment of long and short heavy wooden oars, and on a word from the bosun, they struck out across the inlet, each man taking a stroke more or less when he felt like it. By the time they made it to Wild Goose, the kettle was on the boil.

It was a strange scene. Six adolescent sailors climbing awkwardly over the rail and shuffling to their allocated positions – two in the bow, two on the side decks and two in the stern. Each was armed with a pistol and their faces all wore the same grey palor and a look of total bewilderment. None could have been more than seventeen. 'Good morning, keptin.'

Lieutenant Popov was a picture of courtesy – grey side cap, neatly trimmed moustache, fawn shirt, black tie, black boiler suit and dirty orange lifejacket.

'Good morning. Meenya zavoot Miles Clark.'

'You spik Russian?'

'Well not yet, I'm afraid ... not till Arkhangelsk. I'm being joined by some Russian crew ...'

'Keptin, these is military zon. You need special permission to come inside. Where are you peppars?'

For an hour, Lieutenant Popov passed details of our special permissions to the cruiser Sapphire on a small battered radio that wouldn't work. In the end, he agreed to borrow mine. He took a tracing from our chart, drawing in our approach track and noting our timings from the log. He wouldn't have a cup of coffee, and No, the sailors couldn't have any either. Not even a biscuit.

Yet there was no hiding his interest. It wasn't a confrontation between illegal immigrant and border guard. Rather, a meeting of enforced formality between two people connected with the sea, both aware of the necessary pageant and both keen to make a good impression.

The radio burped, issued a series of short electric orders and then burped again. Popov responded and said that we would have to accompany the cruiser into one of the uncharted bays on the western shores of the inlet. Willy smiled, Hugh sheeted in the sails and as Wild Goose began to gather way, the sailors at the foot of the mast edged nervously back along the deck, trying to avoid the spray that was curling over the bow. By now the sun had come out. Sailors lined the rails of the other ships. Even the captain of the ram-you-damn-you steamer gave a grudging two-armed wave. We might have been taking them for an afternoon sail.

The cruiser anchored in a small deserted bay. Hugh threw a line to a sailor on her after-deck and we lay astern of her in a blue cloud of diesel smoke. A second officer was ferried on board and the procedure was repeated all over again. More traces from the chart, more checking of papers, more squawking radios. Finally, Lt Popov fumbled in his pocket for something, and pulled out a battered Soviet Navy phrasebook. He studied it for moment, and then handed me the open book. At the top of the page were the phrases:

– YOU ARE ARRESTED
– I AM SEARCHING FOR THE SPACESHIP IN DISTRESS
– AERIAL BOMBING IS BEING CARRIED OUT IN THIS ZONE
– THE SUSPICION HAS YET TO BE PROVED
– WHEN AND WHERE SHOULD I FIRE A NATIONAL SALUTE

and finally at the bottom:
– WE ARE GLAD TO BIG YOU WELCOME TO OUR HOSPITABLE SOVIET SOIL AND WISH YOU EVERY SUCCESS

'Welcome to Russia' he said. 'Have a best journey'.

In my relief I thought back to what I had read of Lamont's voyages, the first 'yachting' in these waters, over a century ago. His navigational problems were greater than ours, but the political ones much less.

In 1875 James Lamont, a wealthy Scotsman, built what he described as a handy little schooner of 250 tons in an effort to reach a suspected major land mass north of Novaya Zemlya. Fifteen years earlier in 1858-59 he had made two successful visits to Spitsbergen and found a way of paying expenses by bringing home polar bear skins, as well as walrus tusks and blubber. Hundreds of Scottish and Norwegian boats were involved in this fishery. Down from the nests of eider ducks and eider eggs were another commercial commodity.

In 1875, a bad ice year, it proved impossible to get east of Novaya Zemlya to where open water had been reported leading northwards. Lamont after six tries to penetrate various sounds returned west to Spitzbergen. His ventures are described in Yachting in Arctic Seas, Chatto and Windus 1876.

But it was not the day for reverie.

I don't remember what I expected to see at Severomorsk – tall secretive breakwaters perhaps or submarine pens – but nothing like the sight that slowly appeared along the eastern shore: a solid grey wall of frigates, cruisers and destroyers, all still wearing a fluttering red flag at their bow – defenders of a nation that no longer existed. 'Actually that reminds me', said Willy, pulling out a small cloth bundle. 'One of the sailors pressed these into my hand when Popov was tracing the chart. They were really meant for you, a sort of welcome present'.

I have them beside me now: a blue sailor's collar and a hammer-and-sickle cap badge – the insignia of the Soviet Navy a reminder of the friendliness and essential kindness of the ordinary Russian matelot, and indeed of most of the people we were about to meet.

Siesta on the starboard bunk.

41

CHAPTER TWO

Murmansk to the Gulag

By LIBBY PURVES

'The fair breeze blew, the white foam flew,
The furrow followed free;
We were the first that ever burst
Into that silent sea'.

The Ancient Mariner

To westerners who grew up through the Cold War years, the symbolic light of Murmansk is awesome and troubling. 'Rusty hulks and warships with long, sleek sheer', says Miles' log. 'Magnificent destroyers, enormous castellated icebreakers'. Wild Goose chugged cautiously past the dour, abundant evidence of ship business and shipbuilding: the echo of hammers among the cranes, the flicker of welding-torches, curt instructions on loudspeakers echoing through the container yard, the sheer scale of it dizzied the crew. Everything the West has so long imagined and feared as 'Soviet': greyness, power, determination, industry. War – still lies concentrated among those clanging, flickering shipyards.

Here in both World Wars came many thousands of British sailors, numbed in body and mind from the cold and the sight of so many fellow countrymen burned or drowned. Their ships came most frequently in the 24 hour darkness of winter, for concealment from U boats and Heinkels, to a bay called Polyarnoe.

In brief intervals they in harbour had to make their own amuse- ments, for the natives they came to help were usually unfriendly. Even fraternising had its problems. One sailor on a British destroyer returned on board wearing a fur coat he had swapped for his service duffle. When the Pusser suggested a re-swap the Russians returned the duffle, saying their sailor had been shot!

Coming alongside a floating dock towards evening, among the heavy-duty ferries with their peeling paint, Wild Goose was boarded by an expressionless team of officials. 'Speak English?'

42

asked Willie Ker. 'A small', they said curtly. All details were taken down – some, rather disconcertingly, jotted on the edge of a newspaper by a quiet man from Immigration. Boris, official representative for the Polar Sea Terminal, in his smart grey suit and white socks, briskly conveyed the rules for Visiting Ships.

Once this official business was over, however, Boris proved the first of many Russians who was anxious to communicate. The average frequency of yachts visiting Murmansk* was, he told them, one in every three or four years. He knew the West himself: had been three times to the US; had friends in New England and Minnesota, and regularly took delivery of the National Geographic. Murmansk, they told them, has always been doubly cut off: from the West, but also from the more southern parts of the Union. 'It has taken', said Boris sadly, 'several years to get my mother to come up here from Volgograd because she was afraid of polar bears who were walking along the street.'

Historically, all effort had been heaped on developing the industry of the great ice-free port, central to Soviet industry and defence, but hardly anything invested in the lives of the people themselves. Life has been harsh. Now it is better. There is more power for local administration. And also not as cold and severe as it used to be. 'I think it is due to global warming, I read much about that. There are milder winters now'.

Money was changed at 85 roubles to the pound (by the end of the voyage, as the economy of the old Soviet bloc deteriorated sharply, it was to be 200 roubles to the pound). The log records a commercial milestone. 'Bought our first vodka from the policeman who was guarding the boat – Russkaya brand, in a stinking fishy bag wrapped up in an old newspaper, handed to me surreptitiously. Cleared all formalities and having a drink – a great day for Wild Goose. Harbour fee $320 reduced to $160. 1700 roubles for Boris. We have specially arranged to leave earlier, to accommodate his birthday party'.

His entry in the Visitors book was effusive. 'Strongly impressed with the courage displayed by the crew who made up their mind to go for the Arctic Circle in a tiny boat like Wild Goose. May your expedition contribute to a better understanding of British and Russian people!'

---

*Murmansk was not always thus. Two years later Mike Coleman from Cork, a master mariner and professional Harbour Pilot, was promised a welcome by letter from Murmansk Harbour Master particularly when he explained that his father had been there on Arctic convoys. On arrival he and his crew were confined on board for 48 hours, then escorted back into Norwegian waters by a destroyer so saw nothing of Russia.

It was still only the second week in June: early to be making the exposed 500-mile passage from Murmansk to Archangel, through the Gorlo, the 'Throat' opening into the White Sea. The mild spring which brought out the sunbathers in Murmansk also brought an early break-up of the ice: but storms remained a danger. The British Admiralty's White Sea Pilot warns that more than 50% of all storms crossing Western Europe track north-east over the Kola peninsula. In a spirit of some caution, the Wild Goose left the shelter of the shipyards in a bracing Northerly wind, at 1850 on the tenth of June. The Harbourmaster (rather to the head pilot's annoyance) absolved them from the need to take a pilot; they sailed past the Severomorsk submarine base, with its all candy-stripe chimneys and mass of grey warships packed as closely as it is possible to imagine. No submarines in sight: they must, reflected Miles, be all at sea. Through the coldish, dullish evening, with one reef in the main, the little boat sailed out from among the great grey ships, east and south towards the Gorlo. The routine of reporting to radio stations along the way began: Vashot Vekiliy, Vashod Salnny, Tyuvagubskiy.

It is hard to convey the problems of this four day high latitude passage – just how cold it was and the potential risks which gnawed Milo with a worry he could not show.

He wore trousers, long johns, long pants and short pants, long sleeved vest and three pullovers. Going on deck to check an aerial without putting on oilskin top and bottoms he was frozen to the marrow within two minutes. The weight and fastenings of such necessary clothing meant that undressing to go off watch or perform the simplest bodily function took many minutes, and when the old ship was rolling fiercely a good deal of energy as well, with the need to support oneself from handgrips at every stage which meant undressing one-handed . A break in the weather – a severe onshore gale – could enforce an attempted entry to prohibited ports on the coast. Of these details were minimal. and entry would be subject to prolonged argument.

At least navigation was simplified by the constant position checks provided by the satellite-fed Garmin GPS. Milo supplemented this with an occasional sextant position line to make use of what he had learned on a short celestial navigation course he had managed to find time for in March.

When the engine was on, the Autohelm kept Wild Goose on course most efficiently and the man on watch did not have to steer. Standing in the companionway to keep warm, the watch keeper could listen to a tape of the 'Forsyte Saga', a story from another world. The wind lightened, and the crew slept fitfully below decks. By 5am the engine was running, the wind very light on the port bow. An oily, rolling sea was fringed by miles of bleak snow-patched tundra; at nine they ate porridge and scrambled eggs, and Miles, flicking through maps, reflected, 'strange, we're in the same longitude as Beirut and Sinai'. By noon the sun was out, but the wind dead ahead; the weather forecast spoke reassuringly of a stationary high pressure area over the East Kola peninsula, keeping gales at bay. The day wore on slowly; the wind went harder into the East, and by dawn on Friday Wild Goose was jogging east under a well-reefed main, staysail and engine, with Forsyte Saga continuing. A whale spouted in Hugh's watch; at 8am punctiliously, the little ship tried reporting to Mys Cherny, but got no answer. The log also notes that there was no sign of an ice floe, and a little disappointment at the absence of 'even a teeny weeny Polar Bear'.

At last, a sunny evening rewarded them, the haze producing extraordinary visual effects, the horizon unfolding and twisting like a breaking wave in slow motion, under great cauliflowers of fair-weather cumulus.

All Saturday they motored against a headwind, weathering Cape Svyatoy Nos ('Sweaty Nose') and behind it glimpsing the shallow inlet where in 1553 the crews of two English ships – stragglers from the first merchant venturers to reach the White Sea – were entombed by the onset of winter, and died together in chilly misery. They fought a strong tide at the entrance to the 30-mile wide Gorlo strait, but enjoyed a bright morning with the sunlight glistening off the snowbanks. 'The land that God forgot', said the skipper. A fine sunny evening saw them sailing well again in a brisk Westerly wind, whales blowing alongside, the horizon still doing its distant, ghostly Mexican wave. At last Wild Goose anchored off Sosnovetz Ostrov island, sparing herself the six hours of strong foul tide in a brown sea full of debris, swirling tree trunks and yellow eddies. At last she was acknowledged on the crackling cold air by Terskiy Orlovskiy radio station, 'who sounded suitably surprised'.

Through Saturday night, still listening to the Forsyte Saga ('What will happen to the Buccaneer, Mr Bosinny?' says the log anxiously), the yacht tramped on, working the tides through the Gorlo, her lookouts still spooked by the false horizon lying a third of a finger high above the sea. For the first time in three weeks they saw navigation lights during the sun's brief midnight dip; by dawn on Sunday could see sandy shores, pine forest, a village surrounded by huge canisters and, to the West and partly hidden in trees, a big building with watchtowers antennae and radar. The log reads:

'Air temperature as well as brilliance of sun is extraordinary. 23 degrees in cockpit. Reported to Vashot Vaprovskiy – no ack. Much slumbering in the marsh. Much washing of hair, armpits, clipping of moustaches and rubbing of sun cream on ears, noses and pates. Couldn't reach Portishead'.

THE DVINA

The outer buoy of the Dvina river was passed at 0130 having averaged over five knots over four days. For six hours the boat motored through the archipelago to tie up at Arkangelsk Yacht Club at 8.15, with a dredger screeching in the channel and a sick seal struggling in the water. Everything in Archangel is wooden: the smell of sawdust overpowering, the whole place built of timber: docks, buildings, green timber houses with white frames, a whole new world for the tired, confused eyes of the passage makers. They had time to register the incongruities of the old Imperial yacht club, built in 1911: deliberately stately, grey with white trim, badly in need of a coat of paint. And not, for the moment, remotely excited by the arrival of such a rarity as a foreign yacht.

'Ropes taken by Ivan – cracked pavement, rusty boats, frayed ropes, filthy office with cracked lino and two men completely enveloped in a game of chess. One smoking through cigarette holder; wearing sandals, brown wrinkled skin. Stove through ceiling, generations of flies stuck to the walls, bits of lino tacked together to make a floor, old television, telephone in various bits which had been put back together again, a dripping tap, cooking ring in one corner and faded picture of yacht on wall. Totally underwhelmed by our arrival'.

They waited politely for the conclusion of the chess game before one participant slowly rose and led Miles to one of the faded doors. Expecting a yacht club official, he found himself confronted by a red-headed figure in purple check shirt and underpants. 'I will come over in five minutes' it yawned.'

This, anti-climactical though it might sound, represented the second triumph – after the smooth entry formalities at Murmansk – or Miles' long winter of planning this unpredictable voyage. Here was Vitaly Chanksalcahc, a young Russian interpreter from Omsk in Siberia, of half-Georgian origin, red-headed, chippy, and cheerful. He was to be a key crew member for the whole journey through Russia. Vocal in his plaints and criticisms – particularly of Jim the American magazine photographer, Vitaly was to become a considerable support to Miles.

Not that he was untravelled; military service in Siberia had taken him to many of the great mountain ranges of Soviet Asia, and a recent Soviet Canadian Expedition to the Arctic had added a disconcerting North American flavour to his textbook Edwardian English as taught to aspiring interpreters. When he had found some trousers he came to gaze down, a little surprised, at the humble sight of old Wild Goose – not, after a tough voyage out, an obvious symbol of Western prosperity. 'So this is it', he said. 'I didn't

46

believe it would happen'. And 'Hey guys, could I possibly have a cup of tea?'

Later he recalled *'I was a little surprised to find that I would have to act as interpreter to two Westerners, not one.*

We were joined by the unmistakably American figure of Jim Blair. The distinguished photographer arrived with a dazzling collection of cameras and enough cosmetic and pharmaceutical products to cure every disorder known to man or so it seemed to my simple Siberian eyes. In those days at least such exotica as Anti-Gas Pills and Intimate Wipes were simply unknown to simple folk from Omsk.

Jim spoke to me very slowly and carefully, and I wasn't sure at first if he just took a dim view of my English vocabulary or thought I was soft in the head. I'll admit I was tempted to grumble at times at having in effect two bosses but I generally held my tongue because I didn't want to make things any harder for Miles.

I thought a little enviously of my Georgian father an ordinary bus driver back in Omsk who met my mother, a geologist, in Siberia where he was sent to labour on a construction project. Life was simpler for them then. They had the old certainties The party could not do wrong.'

When Jim's gear was stowed and the crew below there was little chance of turning round let alone moving fore or aft without the risk of being accused of indecent assault The punishing schedule allowed one clear day, and a morning of provisioning, fuelling and making arrangements in Archangelsk. Miles, all the time, was trying to understand and to see the differences through the similarities. Rapid, impressionistic notes and conversations built up into the beginning of a picture. 'Short skirts, bikinis, rubbing sun tan oil in. Draped on sand just like anywhere else. Smell of wood, tree lined boulevards, but ramshackle. No heart to the town. Absence of comfort'. In a restaurant with a dance floor where crew and guests spent the evening, they ate Beef Stroganov, salad and pickle: dinner for eight cost a thousand roubles, 13 US dollars. Afterwards, rather stiffly, the Immigration officer danced by himself to 'Woo-ooo, you're in the army now'.

Local television did an interview; in return Anna Nurpaysova, the journalist, tried to make the Westerners understand the way things are and the way they used to be. 'I am very glad that my Grannie was die in time, before perestroika'.

Why? 'Because it would be very difficult to understand. They were optimist, they liked their life. My grandfather said that Communists can make mistakes, but party never makes mistakes'. Her grandparents had come to Arkhangelsk because it was an area of economic growth. 'They were satisfied' she said, 'But I know they are afraid of something. They didn't want me to laugh loudly because I am happy. They tried to stop me, and I didn't understand'. Down at the Main District Executive Council for the region, Marina Belogubova tried to explain the difficulties of perestroika. 'Recently we had everything highly centralized, goods, orders, everything sent from Moscow. Now we have to solve the problems ourselves. The most serious problem is that we have so many enterprises which are monopolies, which is why we can't solve the problem of level of prices too quickly'. The price of freedom, already weighted heavily on ordinary families. 'It is very important' said Marina sombrely, 'not to let the level of crisis rise higher and higher. If there is the third jump in prices, the people could just explode'.

Sergei Zvyagin of the Archangelshk Yacht Club was most kind and attentive. Later he wrote most a most charming letter about Wild Goose's visit. On Wednesday evening, after a curry, the newly formed crew – Miles, Vitali, Jim, and Willy – slipped their lines under grey skies and pouring rain, to sail the 250 miles to the Solovetsky islands: a much older, grimmer reminder of the tortured paths of Russian history.

THE SOLOVETSKY ISLANDS

Lying in his bunk, deathly pale beneath his mop of red hair, Vitali hated the short, steep, uncomfortable seas and the motion of the little boat against the strong north-westerly wind. At 1.15am, struggling to get out of the Dvina river, Miles decided to turn back from the brown and breaking seas ahead and anchored for a while south of an old dredger, under a low, thickly overgrown island. Six hours sleep strengthened the crew to motor out against the headwind, and the morning gradually became bright and sunny; by night the skies ahead were again as grey as the Russian submarine cruising nearby. *'Sky different everywhere' wrote Miles at 2am. 'Above divided by bank of white like Tippex, behind us blue with moon rising over the sea. N. and NW, long grey streak like smoke from a pipe. Sailing in Bible blackness'.*

Vitali recalls *'I will not say very much about the passage to Solovky except that I enjoyed it as much as the politically prisoners must have done when they were transported there in the 1920s. I hated those short steep uncomfortable waves and motion of the boat against the strong north westerly wind. Part of me was longing to help Miles and prove my worth as a sailor but I felt queezy the moment I stood up, so the only thing I could do was follow the other advice and lie in my bunk. Willy Ker was the biggest support to me, he kept telling me that Lord Nelson, England's greatest naval hero had suffered terribly from seasickness. Willy didn't speak much but when he did it was solid gold.*

48

Then Vitali began to recover 250 miles out into the White Sea . Next morning, they raised at last a low, forested archipelago, grey and lifeless under heavy black cloud. 'You couldn't ask' said Willy, 'for a more fitting landfall'.

For this has been both the holiest and the most horrifying of places. Cut off for seven months a year by blizzards and drifting ice, the Solovetsky islands were colonized in the early 15th century by monks, who founded one of the most honoured of orthodox communities there. During the rise of Arkhangelsk as a trading town, their wooden chapels were joined by three stone churches, monks' quarters, and a kremlin with walls eight metres thick. By 1850, two thousand young men a year and thirty thousand pilgrims travelled there in its accessible months: the monks staffed a tannery, foundry, brick factory, paper mill, printing works, and even an infantry unit and a gun battery. But the island's isolation was a temptation to tyrants too; religious and political heretics were exiled to Solovetsky from the time of Ivan the Terrible onward. And in 1923, the Bolsheviks arrived, murdered the monks, burned the icons and rare books of five centuries, despoiled the altars, and set up the headquarters of the Northern Camps for Special Purposes.

Special purposes, that is, as in the 'House of Special Purpose' at Ekaterinburg, where the Tsar and his family were shot. It was here that, as Maxim Gorky put it, 'the foundations of labour as a method of educating the criminal were laid'. From 1924 to 1929, counter-revolutionaries and common criminals were shipped here, 83,000 of them, and held in bestial conditions, starving and semi-naked. Bishops, doctors, murderers, princesses, prostitutes – every condition of person came here to be beaten, starved, shot, to die of plagues or be given the 'mosquito treatment' or tied to logs and rolled down the steep hill below the Anser monastery. 43,000 died – and those are just the official figures.

Yet when Wild Goose dropped anchor in a small cove on the north coast of Anzer Island, the sense of triumphant landfall and the tangle of wild flowers ashore raised the crew's spirits incongruously. After grimy city docks, it was a fresh island landing, irresistible, an echo of the Western islands of Wild Goose's home waters. *'Birch, dwarf willow, dog-roses and heather ... bursting out with forget-me-nots, cowslips, dandelions, buttercups, orchids, sages, buzzing with insects, warmth coming out of the ground ... great feeling'* wrote Miles. The four men leapt ashore to the warmth and the flowers. But after an initial moment or two one man by turn remained on board to guard the ship.

Anzer is, officially, closed to Visitors because it is a Nature Reserve . Despite Wild Goose's unique permission to visit the islands, Vitali was momentarily fearful at the sign LANDING

PROHIBITED. The only Russian citizen aboard, he had, after all, grown up in a society where official signs meant what they said and carried terrible weight. Miles, however, robustly uprooted the sign and hid it in a bush. Then he stood for a moment on the warm ground, smelling the herbs, noticing the footprints of animals all around, listening to the birds and the still blustering wind; and walked up to the monastery on the hill.

'Path narrowed down, roots across, moss, leaves, acorns, saplings screaming to get up while they can. Glades and meadows alive. Wind-grey logs across path. Deadfall trees. Small white dog-roses. Small ponds, mushrooms, lichens. Grey granite rocks. The path rises and falls 50ft above the sea, into birches. Flowering weeds suggest an English garden run wild. Troops of ants crossing, recrossing; smell of vegetation quite overpowering. Rash of wild flowers, then huge white building – no, red building painted in white. Tumbledown cell block. Total disrepair'.

Nobody lives on Anzer today; perhaps because here, on this earth bursting with spring, some of the worst of all the gulag atrocities were committed. In the nave of the church to which they walked that morning as the first Westerners in seventy years, frozen bodies of dead prisoners used to be stacked upright to save space, between the peeling frescoes of archangels and doves and cherubs. The atmosphere of the cells where the monks prayed for centuries was too much overlaid, for the Westerners, with the memory of prisoners who screamed there. FORBIDDEN PLACE, said another sign. Silently, an angel in a gold chalice with white wings and blue cape stands next to a crusader with shield and red cape, watching over old holiness and years of death. A young rabbit lay dead on the floor; butterflies flew in and out of the broken stone. For Miles, after so much reading and expectation, after the brief glimpse at Murmansk of the Soviet might built since Stalin, it was a moment he found hard to write about. He counted cells. 'One cell per window, maybe forty or fifty cells, God knows how many in each. 18 windows on each side. Sense of total stillness around buildings that once had so much life. Missing the babble of voices. The still, silent remains. Seem to require so much of the imagination'.

Nevertheless he shinned up a thin rope that dangled from the top cupola. A dangerous ascent. It might have been rotten or secured with a slippery hitch at the top but Milo thought it was worth the risk to photograph a panorama of the island's close-set tree tops with the ruins of prison huts showing like wrecks in a seascape. Vitali followed up then wandered with the rest amid scenes of his own country's worst past. To him, though, the monks were far more vivid than the gulag. He said, months later, to Miles' brother Bruce.

'They must have had a very deep faith to choose such a difficult

50

place. There is something mysterious, sacramental and enigmatic. I wouldn't say there was an atmosphere of evil. It is a place where nature has taken back what is hers. We human beings might remember that this piece of earth has been used for evil purposes ... but the fact is that the buildings which people built were constructed because of a very strong faith. They did not come here with evil intentions. The fact that the place was used for evil purposes afterwards is our tragedy. The original purpose is a manifestation of everything that is strongest in mankind'.

Modern Russians feel little of the guilt about Stalin that Germans feel about Hitler. Their recent history, perhaps, inclines them more to the view that government is something over which ordinary people never have any control, and for which they cannot be held responsible. 'It is a sadness for our country that history developed in that direction, that such things happened' he said, and that was that. Oddly, the guilt weighed more on the Westerners, cast down by what they saw.

Vitali was the one, however, to notice oddities in the official record of the island. *'It is interesting that even after perestroika, groups of voluntary work parties, subbotniki, were still going there to paint the walls white to cover up the inscriptions of the prisoners. The workers at the Solovki museum told us that. It was difficult to believe that the building stopped being used as a prison in the 1930s. It appeared to me to have been decaying only since the 1950s. Attempts had been made to cover things, to mask them, but it was obvious that something was not quite right, not real, false'.*

Subdued, the crew sailed twenty miles south-west to the largest island, Solovetsky itself. *'Best sailing for days, warm and pleasant, scent of pine off land. Two seals rose in water and gave a great thrash. 1700: low coastal woodland rolled back to reveal the most extraordinary sight, of the kremlin and white churches above the outer walls. Guided by British Admiralty Pilot and chart they found the leading marks, and by 5.45 were in among the tiny islands. Sinister rocks on either hand. Anchored in golden light below Kremlin. Certainly the most memorable anchorage in my, or Wild Goose's life. Somehow it seems unbelievable that this link with the past should have survived, close to the largest nuclear submarine base in the world'.*

Thinking of war he might have added that ships of the ubiquitous Royal Navy had come here under sail in the 19th Century and bombarded the islands.

This is Solzhenitzyn's Gulag Archipelago. Writers and scientists were still kept here in 1970s although much of what Solzhenitzyn wrote, the museum guides sternly told Miles, was 'muddled'. Tourists are coming back now, as pilgrims did of old, to the

Solovetsky monasteries. There is a museum, a few hundred crafts-men, a restored chapel echoing again to the hypnotic tones of the Orthodox liturgy. Guided through the island, they saw wooden houses, still built in the old way, caulked with wool and joined with pegs; grey wicker fences, buttercups and cowslips and sandy roads. An old woman, Anna Alexandrovna Tretyakova, told him how much better life was under Communism.

They watched a christening, a long Orthodox service, the baby lowered into the font, the oil crossed on the child's eyes, cheeks, ears, throat, hands, legs and feet; saw old motorcycles and sidecars wrapped in tarpaulin, stray dogs with hackles up, nettles. Miles talked, through Vitali, with monks, who told him of their simple life and tried to express the honour of serving here.

'This is famous for the simplicity of its people. Monks came here and there was nothing. Living on the edge. Maybe it made their life more severe, but people as a result are simple and more reliable'. And Father Petr, slim and calm in a heavy black cowl, spoke measuredly of the dead. 'The land is almost running with blood. And yet, what could offer a more plaintive call to future genera-tions to follow the ways of mercy and peace?'

The same philosophical approach came from a 30-year-old doc-tor, Volodya Anatolyevich Stakhanov, from Moscow. 'A feeling of pity and sorrow; so much horror. But people should remember the good times before, not the sick or ill branch of the historical tree. I sleep well here'.

Back on the boat, down in the bay, the crew sang Yellow Submarine, drank vodka in the cockpit, celebrated Tatyana the guide's birthday, and lived in the present. Streetwise Vitali mused on the extraordinary honesty of life on the islands. 'None of the boats locked up … life seems very tough, not much opportunity for development, but they are trustworthy. The whole thing was a won-der to me, these Solovetsky islands'.

On Monday, Vitali's last, short, open-sea passage came to try his own endurance. With the glass dropping, a full gale blew up dead in their teeth, the White Sea's parting gift. By late afternoon in a steep, wet sea, he was white and vacant, with the air, Miles told him, 'of a man who is wondering whether he has got on the wrong train'.

'I'll steer and look after the boat', said Willie. 'You navigate'. For twelve hours the hardy Major stuck to the tiller while Miles set a series of courses to dodge rocks and shoals. Staunch and sturdy Willy, well into his sixties, was at his best when the going got tough; a Somerset sheep farmer when at home, a professional sur-veyor trained in the army as a Sapper, a man of endless resource and total reliability, who liked solo voyaging because you didn't have to bother talking to people.

He seemed impervious to the icy sleet while Miles kept the plot going to reach a channel marked by scant withies in visibility down to 50 yards at times. In the approach soundings lowered ominously. Where dredging had been inadequate there was less than a fathom to spare at times.

At last the ordeal ended, and the long weeks of flat water began as Wild Goose slipped between the breakwaters of Belomorsk, the entrance to the great White Sea Canal.

Archangel Skyline

53

CHAPTER THREE

The White Sea Canal

By LIBBY PURVES

'Blue days in forests and green days at sea'
Robert Louis Stevenson

Three hundred years ago Peter the Great reached the southern
shores of the White Sea after making the same passage from
Arkhangelsk as had Wild Goose. He had to haul his two ships
ashore and have them portaged – physically carried – south through
130 miles of forest, river and swamp to Lake Onega, the eastern-
most of Russia's great lakes. From there they could, under oar and
sail, reach the Baltic. Peter's plans for a canal failed to mature in
his life time. Over the next imperial centuries, numerous plans for
a canal between Lake Onega and the White Sea were mooted: it
became Russia's Channel Tunnel, spoken of decade after decade,
always postponed – until Stalin. To him, labour was 'no longer a
hateful existence but the rational expression of a happy life', and
the canal seemed the perfect challenge.* No stipulation as to the
happiness of the workers was made; the task was handed over to
the State Political Administration with instructions to use only
manual labour and the cheapest local materials, wood and rock. To
use machinery would have sullied the purity of the final triumph. In

---

*The White Sea Canal completed in 1930, was called at first the Stalin Canal
and followed an ancient portage route. It begins at the Gulf of Onega, the western extremity of the White Sea and follows up the River Vyg. From there it
connects Lake Vyg, the River Telekina, Lake Telekinskoe, Lake Matko, Lake
Volgoe and Vol Lake, reaching Povenets on Lake Onega through an unnamed
stream.

It replaced a route 200 miles further east developed a hundred years earlier
by the Duke Alexander of Wurtenberg. His system enabled goods to be carried
from Archangel in five short canals, several lakes and six rivers for a thousand
miles from Rybinsk to Archangel. But the boats were small and the labour
intense. The White Sea Canal, although small by today's standards, transformed freighting to Russia's northern ports.'

1930, therefore, the Solovetsky labour camps were extended onto the mainland, and through two sub-Arctic winters, the waterway was dug by hand in 20 months.

This was the 'BURMA ROAD' of Russia. It cost over 200,000 lives to make 120 miles of channel. One human dead for every metre advanced. To come from the Solovetsky islands to this waterway could hardly be a starker introduction to the sufferings of 20th-century Russia.

But Wild Goose's arrival also symbolized something. In the sixty years between the completion of the White Sea Canal and the little yacht's unceremonious arrival, not one foreign vessel had ever been allowed within sight of the canal.

And Nikolai Litau joined – as captain. To travel these forbidden waters, Wild Goose – under the Russian flag – took a Russian skipper, and her owner stepped down, officially, from his post as master.

Nikolai, handsome, energetic, a problem-solver and optimist, is a professional skipper and the transport manager of a state-owned construction firm. He remembers the moment of his joining. He had not known that Miles, to save weight, had removed Wild Goose's mizen-mast in Ireland, and was puzzled when a late night report reached him in his hotel of a white yacht with only one mast. 'But', they said, 'Russian yachtsmen wouldn't go out in such weather. It must be some travellers'. So accompanied by Schparo's son Viktor who had come all the way from Moscow to make sure the rendezvous worked (and collect the second tranch of his fee) he went out to look at 5 o'clock in the morning and found Miles standing on the pier at a timber factory.

They made their way towards us rather uncertainly through piles of wood.

Almost at once Willie left with Viktor, bumping away through the dreary dereliction of Belomorsk aboard a timber-lorry to the railway station. Although the departure of such a trusted friend as Willie left the boat feeling empty at first, Nikolai's adult, firm optimism and determination brought a new energy to the operation and made it easier to see the possibility of success.

Even now there were restrictions. The first challenge to his perseverance was the long process of talking Wild Goose into the canal officialdom. The Fire Authorities demanded to see hoses and pumps, and when they couldn't, said, 'You ought to go back where you came from'. Nikolai went to his superior and – he says understatedly – 'made a fuss'. The Health Authorities queried the absence of a sealed sewage system. Everything had to be done by the book, as if they were a big ship. It took much bargaining to get through. Not, however, expensive bargaining. One advantage of bureaucratic fixity was that fines had not yet been adjusted for galloping Russian inflation, so Nikolai solemnly handed over a fine of 20 roubles – about tuppence – to the fireman. He also assured the sanitation squad that the crew would make a point of squatting on the bank. Throughout the voyage, Miles, a firmly 'green' man, went ashore each morning by dinghy to do so – even amidst the worst pollution. Perhaps it was his later undoing. He told Jim at the end of trip who replied, 'I wondered what the hell you were going for'. The others were less scrupulous.

The paper work took two whole days. By the morning of 24th June they were chafing to leave, waiting an hour for the first scheduled opening of the bridge until it swung aside horizontally. At 8.30 they glided through and were on their way down the forbidden canal, the Russian tri-colour fluttering aft.

The canal rises, lock by lock, through forests so thick that the trees seem to be growing from the very surface of the water. The old wooden locks, a working memorial to human endurance and human cruelty, were made so much from the rock and timber of the land itself that it seemed sometimes they had not been built, but grown. After six weeks and two thousand miles of open ocean, it felt strange to be enclosed by trees, only occasionally opening out to show scenes of irreducible simplicity: a flock of goats tended by a figure in a sack-cloth shawl, a cluster of wet cabins, a plume of wood smoke climbing upwards from a hut, lapping as an elk drank in the dusk. On Lock 16, a driver was working, in original Jules Verne diving-gear, with a copper helmet. Each lock along the stretch was operated by a lock-lady, brightly dressed, wearing a lifejacket, shouting a greeting.

The pleasant roly-poly ladies were hard to associate with misery of any kind. One playfully threw flowers on the deck. Another at Lock Nine chatted eagerly about her relationship with the White Commander Admiral Kolchak when she heard that Vitali came from Omsk where he had been born. A year or two back she'd have been jailed for mentioning him. The locks themselves were taxing, faster and wilder than any you would meet in the West, with ever-present risk, in the climb, of getting the yacht's bows momentarily wedged under a crossbeam, and losing her instantly to the flood.

'Water pouring down the side lattices of heavy baulks of timber – like being under a waterfall. Moss and creeper growing either side. Posts every 4ft, cracking and crumbling away at the bottom; big original heavy nails driven into the rock. A few new pieces of bright yellow timbers, but large parts of it simply falling apart. Locks fill incredibly fast. Water starts to boil, thick and brown, like filling three of four huge swimming-pools in five minutes. At the far end, spitting brown water several feet in the air. Gradually, you

climb up into a completely new world, the tops of the birch trees at first. The whole surface of the water is heaving upwards, so it looks as if you are on a slope. Wild Goose surges back on her cable, then surges forward – depth gauge climbing from 3 to 11 metres. Water boiling all around us, far end covered in foam. Immensely strong structures, no wonder they've survived; in brilliant sunshine, with buttercups and birds, hard to picture the misery of building these locks'.

Gliding through the 22 hours of daylight, climbing into Russia, Vitali was torn between horror and admiration for this piece of history. Of course the White Sea Canal meant the death of thousands of people, a high and terrible price. But the very design concept, the thought that one could build such a thing, is still astonishing. 'It delights the imagination!' he cried, months later. But 'Of course, the end does not justify the means'.

More immediate to him – though not to the Westerners, for whom all seemed grimly poor – was the visibly rising prosperity of the people. 'The food markets have become richer, there are fruit and vegetables at reasonable prices … in Rostov handsome two storey houses, even miniature castles, privately owned. Ah, history has turned out to give the south a better living standard than the north'!

The crew began to develop their relationships, their own language. Miles loved the way that whenever a lock-keeper asked them their route, Nikolai said only 'S Belovo na Chornoye' – from the White to the Black. Nicolai developed a taste for Miles' Black Bush whiskey, a memory of home. 'Let's hit the Bush', was his evening refrain. He and Miles, the only two real sailors, could communicate with one word when it was anything to do with the boat. Jim, the photographer, looked after his own gear but had a particular obsession with scrubbing the deck. 'From early morning to eleven o'clock', remembers Nikolai. They worked, with imperfect understanding of one another's words, moods, and wishes, through all the tensions of unlike men penned up together, with oddly overlapping jobs – one owner, another official skipper, a photographer in semi-competition with an owner who was himself a professional photographer, and Vitali, employed by Miles but often given orders by the other two. The Bush and the vodka, helped.

Once, buying vodka, Jim remonstrated with Nikolai about the outlandish Russian system whereby some vodka bottles have screw-tops but others do not. Nikolai lost patience. 'Jim kept asking, what happens if you open it and you don't drink the lot? I said to Jim, that is the root cause of Russia's drunkenness. You open a bottle and there is nothing to close it with and therefore you have to drink to the very end'. The Westerners tried once or twice to buy wine, to Nikolai's disgust. 'They did not understand about Russian drinks. They had to throw it overboard. I was happy enough with vodka'. Nor was wine the only thing thrown overboard after mutual recriminations. Fishermen often gave them fish. Nikolai was all for eating fish. Miles was against, and Jim was also doubtful. There seems to be some sort of Western guidebook entitled 'How to survive in Russia', with an article saying that in Russia absolutely all the fish are infected by parasites'. Nikolai's scorn failed to deflect the timid. 'Obviously all their doctors and insurance companies make a tremendous point of these parasites. We had to pass up such lovely fish, nice little perch. But Jim had absolute faith in the printed word and was against them'. When he was left aboard to guard the boat, which was often, Nikolai would contentedly take out his fish, fry and eat it. 'Jim would get the book and show me statistics on how many people became ill as a result of infected fish. Well, statistics are statistics, but fish are fish'.

Miles' log – he was cook as well as skipper – maintains a dignified silence over the matter of the fish. The Cold War over hygiene, however, blew up again over the matter of spring water alongside the canal. 'For us Russians', said the exasperated Nikolai, 'there is absolutely nothing better than spring water. We don't need anything else. Jim would of course carefully sniff every canister, and torment Vitali – 'Is that canister really clean?' He would insist on putting a tablet in each canister, which gives the water a peculiar taste. Mediation by Miles led to one canister being set aside for Nikolai's personal use, with no tablets in it.

The lakes widened around them, mirror-flat, surrounded by birch forests. One evening they turned into a small inlet to anchor out of the channel, to run hard aground on brown mud. Wild Goose's bows stuck high out of the water, and momentarily it seemed as if she might end her days there, herself another ignored memorial to human frailty. The crew hauled all the deck cargo of diesel, and the heavy chains to the stern, put an anchor out into the main channel, and using the anchor windlass, struggled the boat off. It was a scare, the first of several, an enervating moment for a sea-boat come too far inland. They were fighting for freedom among the killer mosquitoes, under the beautiful but impenetrable forest, surrounded by reproachful ghosts. After that they assumed that any wider point along the canal would be shoal unless there were positive indications otherwise

It was here that the Admiralty Pilot in rare touch of humour remarks that *'The hinterland is infested with bears and wolves. In summer they are hunted by the inhabitants. In winter the process is reversed'.*

This was at the period when an imaginative printer bound the

Red Sea Pilot in crimson, the Irish one in green, and the White and Black Sea also conformed.

LAKE VYG and HEMPESKI ISLAND

One morning, Wild Goose sailed out onto the great 70 mile expanse of Vyg lake, 'A huge edition of Mulroy Bay, though not as pretty,' wrote Miles, loyal to his favourite Donegal anchorage 'Wilderness but not quite. A feeling of hopelessness with the occasional huge aluminium plant'. They anchored with more success off a low, narrow island where a dozen ramshackle huts were gathered in a meadow cleared between the pines. Once it was a small fishing community. Now only one elderly couple live there: Aleksey and Nastasia Antsiferov. Their lives are untouched by today; they do not even own a boat, which meant, at least, that they were no more or less surprised by an Irish boat than by a mainlanders' visit – simply glad of the company. 'There are people everywhere; why can't they come here? Nothing extraordinary in that'.

Nastasia led them into a small, dark room where winter clothing hung on birch-twigs nailed to the wall and mosquitoes crawled and buzzed everywhere. Iron nails and pieces of guttering were pressed into service; spiders webs stretched into the darkness of the corners. Eight or ten old layers of wallpaper, showing through one another's tatters, covered the walls. A filthy plastic tablecloth unmoved apparently for decades, held cracked and filthy old cups. Nastasia, in her buttoned-up dress and blue coat and red and white check scarf, looked at the visitors with watery, unsurprised eyes; behind her a grand bed with a picture of Lenin on it, some pots and pans, and an orange plastic radio wired to a speaker. Apart from a generator and that small transistor radio, 'which we hardly ever use,' said Aleksey, there was little to show what century they lived in. On a rough old green dresser lay postcards from forty years ago. They had no interest in the outside world.

'What's the point? We're old and have no education, only each other. We have been married 30 years, no children. My wife has not been to the mainland for over a year'. For thirty years, they salted and dried pike for local fishermen, and lived well enough. Controlled Soviet prices meant, for them, stability in this simple, undemanding uncertainty. 'When prices were low the fish brought us the little food and news we needed. Now it is difficult. Fishers reduce their activity, fish is very expensive. And food is expensive and they come only two or three times a month. My wife washes clothes and sheets for one of the teams which from time to time stay here, and cleans their floor. Next year we will probably have to leave the island'.

59

'I completely forget about things from the mainland. My husband's sister Segheza, and some other old women I visit there,' says Nastasia, 'say, Come over here, leave this place as soon as possible. Why do you live there?'

'But I don't want to leave'.

The changes in Russia leave them baffled. 'We haven't got good education. I do not hear much,' said Alexey. Miles wanted to know everything about them, asked questions which with simple good-temper they answered, not quite seeing the point. 'What happens if you get sick? Do you have a boat?' 'No boat. Just live here'. 'Do you ever get sick, though?' 'Never sick', said Nastasia gently, 'that is the way we live. It is simple here'. She stroked his hair, suddenly. 'Say our hello to your wife'. From the roof came the smell of a hundred drying fish, hung in the eaves with the wind blowing through. Miles and Nastasia climbed up, she anxious to give him some of the odorous fish, stiff as boards, breaking at head and tail. Vitali, translating, explained, 'They are so thankful for us to visit them, that's why they want to give us everything'.

All Aleksey wanted in return was insect repellent. The smoke of a log, smouldering in a bucket on the floor, was barely effective against the clouds of mosquitoes, and his only recourse for sleeping was to drink vodka. There are no small birds to eat insects so they breed with nil hindrance or control. In the morning after Miles gave him insect repellent, he gesticulated, 'Bug juice very good!' mimicking Vitali until his laughter tripped in a fit of violent coughing. 'But strong, Vodka better'.

Faintly convinced either that he had drunk the stuff, or that he wanted them to think so as a wild, perverse island joke, Miles and crew said their farewells and sailed on.

LABOUR CAMP

Further down the lake, listening to Wimbledon news on the World Service, his thoughts turned rather longingly towards home from this strange wilderness and the increasing bickering between Jim the photographer and sensitive Vitali. Miles was roused from thought by Nikolai, who had spotted the grey timbers of some abandoned buildings at the southern end of the lake. Anchoring, they rowed ashore and followed a path into thickening undergrowth to find, again, the unmistakeable furniture of imprisonment. Among the vigorous saplings were scattered watch-towers and wire entanglements. In one building half-finished wooden spoons and pipes lay strewn among the debris of plaster, with a mouldering hand-painted sign. Nikolai translated: A CLEAN WORKPLACE IS THE FIRST ESSENTIAL OF PRODUCTIVE LABOUR.

Two thousand people worked here, logging the surrounding forests, building the canal, staying on after its completion. This camp was only abandoned in 1977. In the 7ft solitary confinement cells, a boot lay discarded in the corner of a door, and spiders wove webs among the barbed wire. Eyes, becoming accustomed to the gloom of that dark place after the summer sunshine outside, made out the end doors, with dates scratched on them, pathetically padded with quilted green material to keep out winter winds. Quilted green jackets, the symbol of the Soviet prisoner. Twisting onwards through the narrow channels of the watershed that evening, Nikolai fell silent for a while, then said quietly, 'One life for every metre of canal'.*

LADDER OF LOCKS

It was midnight before Wild Goose reached the ladder of locks descending to Povenetz and the 150 mile expanse of Lake Onega. Anchoring above Lock 7 at one in the morning, they spent a cold, sleepless night persecuted by the mosquitoes and came on deck bleary to a beautiful morning, with crying terns. Diesel was, mercifully, available here. Filled up, they were inside the double box of Lock 7, against the bare rock by mid morning, finding it strange to be going down for the first time. In three hours Wild Goose dropped 70 metres, her crew working the lines, sweating in the rising heat, watching the swallows' nests in the gates reappearing each time the locks closed. From Lock 4, built on quicksand, they could actually see the Lake. The canal barge Onega invited the crew on board and made friends. Her captain, Viktor Nikolaovich Gavrilov was striking in his grey jacket, with pinched, high Slavic features and a young daughter who stared uninhibitedly at the strange, small, wooden yacht. As they were ready to leave there was the honour of a visit from the President of the White Sea Canal Company, Vitaly Petrovich Alexandrov, confirming the little boat's odd status. 'You are indeed the first foreign vessel ever to pass through,' he said as he presented a medal.

The White Sea Canal is the title of a curious book in English by Amabel Williams-Ellis (John Lane, Bodley Head 1935) which describes the builders as joyous and enthusiastic teams, singing as they worked and finally cheering kindly old Uncle Joe as he smoked his pipe on the sundeck of the first steamer to pass. Through the fog of much that can now be discerned as misconception and propaganda, it records plenty of interesting details.

LAKE ONEGA

And so in later afternoon, happy to be free of the mosquitoes and the claustrophobia of the sad canal, the crew made sail on the dark green waters of Europe's second-largest lake, amply large enough for you to lose sight of land in the middle and to feel as if at sea. 'A wonderful middle watch', notes Miles, sailing through the night, past an extraordinary string of water-thin islands which straggle down the chart. 'At last light, passed small inflatable catamaran with unstayed mast and small blue sail, going rather well to weather'.

A clear sun at dawn flashed off the golden domes of Kizhi island. The Transfiguration Church in beauty and design is compared with St Basil's Cathedral in Moscow. All timber and 120ft high it has three tiers and 22 cupolas. Nestor, who built it in 1714, threw his axe into the lake on its completion, saying that there would never be another one like it. There never was. The low grassy islet, smiling green in the sun as Wild Goose sailed in, was in the past a pogost or trading station for the considerable population of the archipelago which surrounds it; also at times an entrepot where people from the Finnish and Russian shores could meet for business. It is now an Open Air Museum. On it have been gathered old wooden churches, dwellings and farm houses from all over Karelia. The sight of such virtuosity of craftsmanship and marvels of ingenious fancy can leave no visitor unmoved.

The superb photograph taken by Jim Blair of Wild Goose alongside the church shows the complex and striking effect. This can look like a jumble at first glance but an understanding of the simplicity of the plan helps one to appreciate the skill of design and structure. Nestor, who incredibly combining the functions of designer and master builder, worked with traditional forms; the octagon based cruciform plan, the bochka or vertical surface shaped like an inverted playing card spade, and the bulbous dome. The octagon centre of the plan is converted into a crucifix by rectangular arms projecting from alternate faces. Each of these projections rise in four stages with a dome framed by a bochka set at each stage.

The silvery grey shingle cladding gives a unique lightness and sheen to the multi-facetted structure. Why have the Russians made such glamour from a shape that is essentially an inverted turnip? Such cupolas, one is told, have been adopted in Russia for a practical reason; snow does not cling to them in destructive weights.

Inside is a breathtaking iconostasis. Four tiers of gold framed and lustrous portrayals of saints and biblical scenes. This was to Miles a first introduction to the immense value justifiably set by the

Russian Orthodox Church on this form of pictorial art. He was to see many more icons further south but no example of vernacular art so striking as the Church of the Transfiguration at Kizhi.

Many tourist ships visit in the summer and there is radio station, souvenir shops and a small café.

Vitali recalls: *There were all sorts of human interests in Kizhi, in the shape of the crew of a big white cruise ship who were glad of our company, because they did not have many tourists that year. A short dark haired guide with a broad winning smile called Rita visited Wild Goose, then invited us for a drink in the bar which gave a splendid view over the narrow channels between the islets that surrounded Kizhi. She told us that she was from Yoshkar-Ola, a town in the Mari-El Republic, much further down the Russian waterway. It is a place apart that has a reputation for magic or sorcery and the church there has a hard time stamping out paganism.*

Anyway she seemed charmed to meet us all, particularly Miles who was very polite to her but made it quite plain to her in his own subtle way that he was a happily and faithfully married man. However far afield he roamed I could see that he gave his first loyalty to his wife, his parents, his son and his brother. That was one of the many things I liked and respected about Miles. But later Nikolai pulled his leg about Rita who was to meet Wild Goose again near her home.

More islands threaded past in the sunlight. There was time for an afternoon anchorage in a baylet for photographs before an evening landfall as they lifted the shabby docks of the industrial city of Petrozavodsk – the 'Workshop of Peter', where the Tsar had ships built and guns cast.

Miles, tired, wrote, '*A strange day, an off-day. At five mile range could smell baking bread, wood smoke. Docks spread along 5-6 miles of lake shore, a forbidding and miserable sight. South side is forest blocks, smokestacks and clouds of smoke. Up on the hill in the forests, flames flicker, burning off gas. Told to move by officious policeman – 570 roubles for anchoring under the cathedral. 2350: anchored off ferry port. Drank vodka and tonic with ice. Vitali getting all matey. Rosy sunset, but cold, sun behind a cloud. Freighters lying offshore, one violent green*'.

Reading the logs now, the fatigue of the journey begins to come through. Long, northern summer days, with enough light to anchor by at eleven p.m, take a hard toll on voyagers: if there is light, you must be under way, or cooking, or working, or writing. The comforting darkness does not come down, enforcing rest, for long enough. Every run ashore, on this journey, was a scavenge for food and fuel and information. Back on board, Wild Goose was becoming a shambles, with too many people aboard, too much gear, and – for reasons of provisioning caution – all the cooking left to the young, exhausted owner.

'He knew his own galley best', said Nikolai. 'He cooked really artistically; he would stand on the steps and start chopping bits of carrot, all those vegetables one after the other. He liked it when people ate up their food'. Vitali, however, fiddled with his, putting carrots to one side. One night Miles looked at him and said, 'If I killed somebody, the most terrible punishment would be to cook for you all my life'. Nikolai was much struck, 'That was my first taste of English humour'. Political discussions arose, inevitably, with Nikolai being all for 'a bit of discipline at last', and Jim saying 'Oh, that's your red communist past', and Nikolai remonstrating, 'Are you free not to fulfil the orders of Mrs Thatcher or the Queen, then?' Miles would continue the debate, good-humouredly; Jim at times less so. It would conclude with Nikolai – fifteen years a party member – loftily quoting, 'There are no heights too high for a Bolshevik to scale'. Physically, emotionally, intellectually, the voyage was constant work.

The two Russians slept in the forepeak, firearms by their side; Miles and Jim aft. The narrow saloon floor was piled with photographic boxes, leaving hardly room to walk fore and aft, let alone set up a table. Freed from the disciplines of stowing for rough seas, the boat came to seem not the purposeful entity she was built to be, but a too-small, too-awkward, unfit canal-boat. At Petrozavodsk, Jim rented a room ashore, rather to everyone's relief.

As provincial towns go Petrozavodsk is certainly not the worst. At least to Russian eyes the streets look well swept and there is a quiet shabby dignity about the place, perhaps the influence of the Finnish community. Half the sign boards are in that language but its charms aren't obvious to visitors. 'Reminds me of an Irish market town after ten years of falling cattle prices', said Miles. Jim muttered something about a one horse town and the Appalachian Boondooks and scolded Vitali when he could not immediately translate.

Nikolai recalled: *As the four of us huddled together in the cabin with the heater on and the rain hammering down outside I longed to convince Miles that Peters Foundry, that's what the towns name means, had something to offer. Now I had been on Wild Goose for just over a week, enough to realise that Miles and I had a good deal in common, that we were as near being soul mates as two people can be when they come from different countries, different sides of the looking glass.*

It was a grey wet morning, with driving rain. They observed, before plunging into the practicalities of provisioning, the strong

Finnish influence of that northern city. Old stately boulevards from the days of Peter the Great contrasted with brutal new accommodation blocks for workers, radio antennae towered over church domes. Then the treadmill of duties and attempted rest: 'Shopping, lunch, taxis, sleep, radio telephone, Sarah, Wimbledon'. And the nightmarish bureaucracy of trying to re-organize the radio licences; and a visit to a wooden-boat yard for vodka and mutual compliments, and an encounter with Project Harmony, a student exchange scheme from Vermont, appearing alongside Wild Goose at her berth. 'Staring eyes, earnestly nodding hear, speaking slowly. We're having a really wonderful visit with Tamara and Art. Hi guys. Your book I will buy'.

The next day it rained, again foiling attempts at photography. The cabin heater had to be put on, and Miles ventured out to buy a chicken, with head intact and cold, sightless eyes. Off for a lone walk, Miles met Sasha from Tallin, small time businessman and exchange broker, losing money hand over fist, living with Katrina on a boat festooned with eels, cans beneath them to catch the drips, wearing a flowery shirt. 'Brought him back to the boat much to the disgust of Nikolai and Vitali'. Another encounter was a Russian oarsman, Eugeny Smurgis,* planning to row to England on a diet of dried bread, all he could afford. 'My wife,' he said proudly, 'is an independent person. We don't live together, so I have only my son to do our journeys together. I am a journalist. I am correspondent of Russian magazine Katyra y Yachtie, motorboat and yacht. I write an article and let people know my experience of the interesting things I saw and did. If not enough money from writing I always find a different job.'

A mirror image of Miles himself, an uneasy view of the lonely, determined, traveller and communicator. 'Man who starts going on the way road to somewhere, he is considered to be respected. But the man who gets his aim is twice respected. My aim is to do my own way, my own project, to have my own opinion ...'. Much the worse for vodka, the men talked into the night, the notes incoherent by the end. Just before dawn Wild Goose sailed for Vytegra on the far side of the lake, with a forecast of strong north winds.

---

*Smurgis and his son reached London by canoe the following September and were well looked after by Milo's friend Simon Pelly. The son decided he'd had enough. Smurgis against advice set off late in the season for Spain and disappeared in a Biscay gale.

CHAPTER FOUR
Over the Hump

By WALLACE, *MILES* and NIKOLAI

*'I love to sail forbidden seas
and land on barbarous shores.'*
Melville, Moby Dick.

Leaving the lights of Petrozavodsk astern Wild Goose reached south through the night. Lake water lapped in a light offshore wind. Nikolai out for the count, unable even to eat supper, Vitali in the cockpit, objecting to 'green stuff which goes into curry'. This was identified, by a rather hazy Miles, as curry powder. With the crew in their bunks Miles steered and kept a lookout. Neither Jim or Vitali had enough experience to keep a solo night watch.

Wild Goose unlike most modern boats has a long keel and can keep herself on course for quite long spells if the sails are well trimmed. So he was able to make calls home on a good radiotelephone circuit, and listen to an interview, on BBC World Service, with John Fowles. The surreal qualities of the voyage, of taking in familiar sails in strange, strange places alone in the small hours, thinking of home and of a world full of other dreaming voyagers like himself, began to tell. It needed all his gusto, and he had plenty, to fight off spiritual exhaustion. There was never the chance as one gets when offshore on an oceanic voyage to relax and let the boat look after herself. Instead endless minute by minute vigilance was the price of success, plus a determination to avoid unnecessary risks, particularly in squally weather like this. The consequences of a damaged rig would have been very severe.

'0400: blackness gone out of sky, Wind still fresh and gusting up to Force 7. Decision needed to set the storm trysail and go on or seek shelter in an unpronounceable port. Brown water volleying downwind, landscape a study in shades of grey.'

He stood on south for a while, still solo, until abreast the mile-wide tree ringed bay of Rog Rushay. It was on the same western shore of the big lake as the port they had left and looked temptingly placid. As Miles put the tiller hard aport to make for shelter in the cold morning light Nikolai popped his head up the hatch to 'pretty himself' with a matchstick toothpick, yawn and sniff the wind.

Fierce gusts came off the trees but moments later Wild Goose lay in their blessed lee, comfortably tugging at her chain. Only long after dawn did the wind drop.

Nikolai relates what happened next.

'Sailing out at midday we suddenly struck something very solid. It was our second grounding and clearly a serious one.Our bow had risen nearly a foot out of the water. There was nothing visible on the surface and a check showed no warning on the chart. Sounding we found 25 feet on one side, five on the other. We had run onto the outermost tip of a lengthy forestry pier, sunken and abandoned. Half a metre south and we would never have known it existed. Hours passed trying to haul her off by laying anchors out on long lines. Time and again they dragged in the soft mud. We lightened ship by taking out the chain and four hundred weight of rusty pigs of inside ballast. We made up more than 300 yards of heavy rope by putting everything on the ship together but it was not enough to reach a strong point on the shore. Things looked bad. As we paused for coffee, exhausted and frozen, a fishing boat offered help. With his ropes added to ours, perhaps we could pull her off astern by rigging a line to a tree.

Miles knew just what to do. He told me that he had grounded Wild Goose so often when exploring remote Irish creeks that friends used to say he should have wheels fitted to her keel. A small crowd had gathered and he realised the line was secured ashore when he saw the world wide sailor's signal – arms fully raised and crossed above the head. That means 'All Fast!'

Then the fisherman took a line from the Goose's masthead and pulled sideways to reduce her draft by heeling. A pull on the electric winch and her head swung a little …, then it came round in line with the rope. Imagine our relief! A big tug o'war style heave from the gathering group ashore then made her slowly slide forward. We all shouted "Harroch"!'

Everything was a curiosity to Miles and he learned another lesson from this delay – mainly nautical expletives!

In a moment Wild Goose was back afloat and her deck level once more.

The long iron keel had prevented damage. The rescuers would accept nothing but a dram. But it took hours to get the mud cleaned off the decks.

Beyond the arms of the bay dun horses drove past on top of steep short waves. The masts of slow-moving fishing boats appeared above them and the low hulls of tankers bound south. Beyond sky and sea melded almost imperceptibly. A haze rested on the low wooded north point which ran out towards the lake. Wild Goose was ready to sail again by 1700. But impatient as Miles felt, it was no use sailing late in the day to arrive before dawn at the tricky entrance to the Vytegra River. They sailed at midnight in pale daylight.

It was a cold and Milo at the helm, wrapped in oilskins with furred collars up to the eyes, almost envied the passengers on a big liner speeding in a blaze of light towards the River Neva for St Petersburg.

A squall came shrieking at them across the lake at about 0200 without warning, a 'Barney's Bull' of blasts with face-lashing sleet and hail hissing on the water. Luckily Miles was on the tiller and eased her head north so as to spill the wind out of the mainsail and yet not let it shake too violently. The lake water alongside writhed in brown coils as though a huge snake was pinned under the surface. By the time Nikolai was forward to shorten sail, the blow was over.

It is of such moments that Hal Nossiter wrote in his classic book *Southward Ho*. Caught in a pampero off the River Plate he felt a mortal strain as though he was actually working with the yacht as she fought the wind.

A Finnish skipper put it differently off Cape Horn describing how his ship laboured in Force 9 nine gale. 'I feel like de heart of de ship. I urge her through every wave'.

In a squall like this understanding was vital. Nikolai recollected further: 'Between Miles and myself there was a pleasant, calm, good hearted relationship. We could communicate with a single work for we were both sailors. I had little English but in anything to do with the boat a single word was enough to make the other person understand'.

At 0325 grey hills appeared ahead under a sky the colour of smoke with a pink band to the south east. Then they picked up lines of red and black buoys off an entrance. At 0500 in full daylight they entered the Vytegra, sand banks on either hand. It was morning rush hour – three steamers ahead and the Volga Don 5004 honking astern.

Miles' log reads: *'As we got into the river I felt relief at having avoided an order from officialdom to turn back east to the Baltic. There was an exciting sense of leaving the Atlantic for good and being committed to the big crossing.'*

The northern shore of the river was marshy, with cows grazing, gulls screaming and an osprey quartering the rushes for a surfaced fish. Let us leave Wild Goose here in the security of the rushy channel and have a look at the Canal system which lay ahead.

THE MARIINSKY or VOLGA-BALT CANAL
(Earlier known as the Empress Canal)

Peter the Great conceived the idea before 1600 of this second
waterway connecting the Volga to St Petersburg via the River
Neva, and hired an Englishman John Perry to carry out a survey but
it was almost a hundred years after Peter's death that construction
was started. Then it was financed by the wife of Emperor Paul I.
She ordered the loan of 400,000 roubles from the St. Petersburg
Orphanage Funds. The deed sounds rather like a Fleet Street firm
raiding the Pension Fund to keep of the hands of its creditors but
whether the money was ill-found or not the Empress had her name
given to the canal in gratitude. Construction was completed in
1810. In subsequent years many small vessels sank, heavily laden
in storms while crossing the big lakes, Byalo and Onega. So at a
later stage canals passing along the south and west side of these
were undertaken to eliminate the dangerous passage and make the
Marinsky system a safe water way for shipping. The new route was
deeper and shorter than the Vyshny Volochekey system as it elimin-
ated a number of rapids and bypassed the difficult section of the
Volga between Rybinsk and Tver. But it was still appallingly slow.
The locks although relatively small and shallow took several hours
to fill or empty. Thirty eight of them were required against the
current seven. The completion of the Empress' system of improvements in 1852 gave the canal an importance which it later maintained in spite of the development of railroads. At first the towing
was done by horses but there were problems when large numbers
of these fell victims to anthrax. With the invention of steam power
a new device was installed by which tugs negotiated the rapids of
the Sheksna and the Svir. The tug picked up a chain laid along the
bottom of the bed of the river and wound it onto a drum thus pulling
itself upstream towing from four to six barges.

In 1890 and 1895 another series of improvements was taken by
which a canal called the Likovets of 10 miles long was built on the
Sheksna and another of 16 miles on the river Vytegra. This system
permitted the passage of boats up to 200 feet in length with a beam
of 30 feet and drawing up to 6 feet. The Marinsky System at this
stage covered a total length of 700 miles it included the Sheksna
river from its source to its confluence with the Volga, lake Byalo,
the Kovzha River, the Mariinsky Canal, the Vytegra river, lake
Onega, the Svir river, lake Ladoga and the Neva River.

Russia's very existence depends on her rivers. This is hardly
surprising when the list of 35 Great Rivers of the World is examined;
almost a third are in Russia – South America has four, North America
eight, the old Soviet Union thirteen and Russia itself ten.

Canal development slowed in late 19th Century with the arrival of Railways could be used all the year round against the few months that the rivers could stay open.

THE GREAT RIDGE

The ridge Wild Goose was about to cross is the biggest physical obstacle in the whole 3000 mile traverse north and west of Russia. It is no less than the barrier between the Baltic and Black Sea basins, extending over 800 miles north and south, on a line 300 miles east of Riga. Although less than a thousand feet high it is one of the most important watersheds in Europe.

It has of course always been a considerable barrier to boat traffic.Portages were numerous but rarely meant a lift of more than 30 feet.

On the long ridge, among the woods of Valdai, about 200 miles south of Wild Goose, are the sources of the Volga, Dnieper, Don and Lovat. They lie within a few miles of each other. To there a man with a stout heart could in a light boat arrive from the Baltic, and proceed by water and portage 6000 miles east to the Sea of Othotsk in the Pacific – a challenge that Milo tucked into the back of his mind for a future venture.

To this juxta-position of streams, and the spider's web of water-ways that extends from it, olden Russia owed its coherence, indeed existence, as a kingdom. It relied on rivers, lakes and canals for its defence, government and trade.

During World War Two, for example, submarines built at Novgorod were shipped up on the deck of barges to Murmansk.

PRINCIPAL ROUTES OVER THE RIDGE

Four principal routes by river developed across the ridge. Along them about the year 800 Vikings started to trade and fight their way eastwards. On each route there were up to half a dozen portages. Each main one was guarded by an ostrog or fort. Passage through these had to be taken by force or paid for in kind. Either way, getting across meant enormous sweat. A forty foot boat might weigh two tons unladen and have to be hauled up slopes of 30 feet or more.

Cargoes would consist mainly of furs. Sable and black fox were the most prized, but skins of polar and black bear, antelope and reindeer had an unlimited market. Walrus tusks, amber and of course slaves would fetch a good price in Kief and Kazan, or if of exceptional quality might be worth carrying on as far as Constantinople.

Repayment was in Greek money or silk. Silk exports were strictly controlled but several yards could be obtained for a young slave. Teams of grunting, smelly, hairy men, sometimes aided by horses, moved the ships. Few portages were more than two or three metres high and boats were lightly built for river work but the haulage was still cruelly heavy.

I speak from painful experience, having taken part in the portage of a 16 oar Highland galley weighing about two tons from West Loch to East Loch Tarbert in 1993. Forty men including twenty Scots Guardsmen failed to move her up hill. We had to send for a tractor.

Mediaeval illustrations of the main portages show a carpet of logs or 'corduroy' road to lessen friction and provide a foothold for the handlers. Posts on either side were for securing pulley blocks or check ropes. The ostrogs and wooden storage sheds for goods were often sited on a point where two river joined so that a stockade for protection could run across the base of the triangle. At more remote portages slave crews would fell and lay down their own logs ahead of the hull while warriors scouted and protected the ship from attack. A vivid scene it must have been, repeated day after day, as up to 5000 ships a year made the crossing for the rich rewards which lay at the far end.

THE HIGHEST POINT OF THE JOURNEY

The Wild Goose crew found it cold on the river, below 11 degrees, with an added chill factor. Under an overcast sky rotting boat-houses and dying trees, the smell of eucalyptus, huge timber yards and a brick factory marked the landscape a round the sprawling town of Vytegra.

After ten miles of river Lock One was heralded by the pylons and dark masonry of a hydro-electric barrage, the first of four in the series. The stones in the dam wall lock seemed huge compared to those on the White Sea Canal. Foam streamed out of the entrance four inches high as Wild Goose motored in at full revolutions to beat the propeller wash of rusty old ship Volga Don 504.

So the Wild Goose crew could readily understand how the Volga-Balt has remained the most important route because of its ability to handle ships up to 5,000 tons, and of the speed of transit.

'We tied up tight to cylindrical floats sliding up and down captive in vertical recesses in the wall. Gates clanged shut astern. Four square control boxes, one each side at each end of the lock, towered into the heavens – nothing human in sight. A loud speaker shouted instructions as from God. Then without overt warning the waters started to bubble and erupt in this vast concrete chamber, 300 yards

long by 20 wide. It felt and smelt like an enormous slurry tank. As waters roared we swiftly rose 40 feet until the mast came up into sunlight and then our deck, level with gulls trotting along the lock edge. Wild Goose, 504 and a tanker called Happy Navigation 214 had all risen at the same speed, a miracle of physics, slightly numbing to the mind. Looking over the lock gates astern we felt on the edge of the world, sitting on a shelf of water suspended above the landscape. Had we really been down there?'

Now they were into the Vytegra Reservoir. An elderly artist, Nikolai Tramzin, watching them from behind his easel emerge from the lock, told how his birthplace had been flooded by the rising waters, and of the agony of resettlement – pitiless evictions and inadequate recompense, doubly painful here as the area was some of Russia's richest pastureland. One more example of how the story of Russia is of man's inhumanity to man.

At 0845, 13 miles on at Belousky Lock, Nikolai went ashore to ask 504 to keep the revs down as his propeller wash was so dangerous. The captain agreed and quoted 49 feet as the clearance under the bridge, in theory enough to let Wild Goose's hollow wooden mast through with two feet to spare. It did so by six inches. Miles blessed the foresight that had made him shorten the stick before leaving Ireland.

A Volgo Neft grain carrier registered in Astrakhan in the ensuing channel encouraged a feeling that they were bound like her for eastern lands afar, *'where there ain't no ten commandments and a man can raise a thirst'*.

They had emerged into a pleasant world of hills and meadows, more cultivated than anything seen.since leaving Ireland. Beyond the rushes on the bank Douglas fir blowing in the wind, reared tall amid well kept meadows.

Milo's imagination was hard at work.

'In the narrow reaches of canal between the locks the sight seems extraordinary, leviathan ships amidst a rural setting – as if a 5000 ton Cross Channel Ferry should suddenly appear on the upper Thames. From the air the system must look like a brown thread winding through a wilderness... and yet it is the lifeline of a great nation. In every mile thousands of waders and gulls are building their nests, ten thousand frogs are croaking, all in total isolation and none of them making so much as a fleeting appearance on a David Attenborough documentary. The whole cycle of life is going on, being born, breathing, feeling, growing old, while we glide silently by under sail so close to the shore that you could toss a pebble into the willows.

'Full many a frog is born to blush unseen and waste its croaking on the desert air.'

At ten o'clock came Novinsky Lock, the beginning of a ladder of three with a combined rise of 130 feet. Here the Regulations lay down that captain must be on the tiller of his ship, big or small. Nikolai reassured the lock keeper on the point.

We were sailing over the top of the small wooden locks of the 18th century system – one is preserved ashore nearby.

But there were compensations. A single lock could take hours to fill, so that passengers went off for an afternoon in town.

The high wire and guard towers of a Labour Camp were a chilling reminder of the cost of the more recent works.

Ashore now there were brightly painted farmhouses with neat fences. A joy to see some whaleback hills like Salisbury Plain. Thickets of tall birch, spruce, and alder all round us. Meadows looking unsettlingly English at times especially those with the red Devonian soil.'

A ship's location can be checked anywhere on the canal system from numbered buoys, also boards marked with the kilometres from Moscow. Miles logged Km 838 as the village of Rubezh, named from its proximity to the top of the great divide, just west of the actual split between the two vast catchment areas. So next they climbed to the top level, not just of the day but of the whole voyage, by ascending Lock Six Pakhomovskiy. They floated out 370 feet above Baltic Sea level. Over a hundred and seventy feet of climb had been achieved already that exhausting day.

But there was little alternative to keeping going--no quay to tie up to or bank to approach without risking another grounding; not enough room to anchor.

Miles continued his notes.

'The water in the canal and rivers remains very muddy. The river and banks are constantly changing but everywhere there is timber. How could the world ever be short of wood with a country like this to supply it?

'Life has become imperceptibly more primitive. Things I missed earlier like mail and telephone, someone else to cook meals, a table to eat at, English conversation, a loo you can empty with a touch instead of a hand pump; all seem unimportant now. Our sole object is to get safely down the canal and into the Volga. Our visibility is cut off at thirty yards except for up and down the channel. We long for a view but the sky is the only contact with the outside world. Much of the day seems to have been spent looking at it and nothing else from the bottom of a lock. Cruise ship passengers on promenade decks must see the landscape so much better. ... But I wouldn't swap.'

At 1740 passed Annenskiy hamlet in a clearing in the woods. Greeted with much tooting of cars. At 2100 we were still motoring to the accompaniment of Wimbledon Ladies Final – Seles against Stephie Graff. Passed, almost squashed, by a procession of four ships at 2045, a speed boat, a dredger at full volume and a Volga Balt followed by a tiered white cruise liner with passengers lining the rail and American flags out for the 4th of July. Darkness begins to gather round us but still nowhere to stop until we get to Byalo (alias White Lake). How long must a 100 mile stretch like this have taken in pre-WW11 days? Engine running beautifully; I take a look at it once in a while to see why it's going so well. European football results come through. Vitali spits. The area we are passing was once Constantine's Rapids (in Russian Porogi) where the canal joins the Kovzha river bed. Site of a portage that must have seen an infinity of laborious hauling of boats and backpacking of cargo. Fighting too. A man living here had to keep his sword pretty sharp. The endless dramas have increased the vibratory frequency of the shoreline. There's a palpable atmosphere.

At km 765 a soiled sign on a white obelisk protruding out of the rushes marks the entrance to the old White Lake Canal which allowed small boats to bypass the lake and avoid the risk of foundering in bad weather.

It's now a of matter for us of getting into Byalo, a natural lake raised thirty feet by the Soviets. Thankfully at midnight we sight in the dusk a 200 year old navigation mark, the stone tower of the Purification Church on a rushy islet. It is all that is left of the homesteads of Kovska village on the edge of the lake.

Now it's another day, Sunday, 5th July, as at 0130 we nosey cautiously into an anchorage in the lee of an ostrov by echo sounder and a glint of starlight. There we'll be sheltered from the northwester now blowing. We lay out the bower anchor on its chain, then the 56 pound sheet anchor on a big warp, and go astern to make sure they were both well dug in. The glass has been falling all day. Hang out a paraffin riding light, We've put a hundred miles astern in 26 hours. A dram and into our bunks.

LAKE BYALO

While the Wild Geese sleep let us take a broad look at their surroundings. As well being as on the north south ridge just described they were on one of the great east west divisions between bands of vegetation which run across European Russia. Geographers of Russia identify four zones of trees and grass, geology and climate.

The Tundra is northernmost where summers are too short for trees to grow. Wild Goose had passed through this briefly in the entrance to the White Sea.

The Taiga, literally trackless forest, a coniferous tree belt comes next south. Over 700 miles wide, it is one of our globe's mightiest features; inhabited only in sparse settlements along the rivers. at isolated forts, monasteries and island trading posts, supported by hunters and gatherers. A little cultivation is possible but in most places the soil is poor, the growing season short. The principal export from the region for millenniums has been furs.

For Wild Goose the Taiga had begun at Belomorsk.

In the Taiga the Admiralty Pilot mentions that 'gluttons' are numerous. Some Wild Goose crew members might have qualified but Miles found the word in the dictionary as an alternate name for the wolverine. None had so far appeared, but they'd seen lots of game. If it hadn't been the close season Miles' 12 bore shot gun, the old family bramble poker could have bagged pheasant and partridge for the pot. Lake Onega now astern and the Rybinsk Reservoir, alias Mologa Triangle, just ahead of Wild Goose, are by definition in the Taiga.

Sailing down the Volga for the 500 miles east of Mologda Wild Goose would be on the southern edge of the Taiga tracking the division between it and **The Wooded Steppe** whose name is self explanatory.

The True Steppe the next band south – horseman's country of vast prairie and black earth – would be entered after reaching Kazan and the 20 mile wide confluence between the Volga and the Kama.

Here on Byalo where they lay they were still north of the Wooded Steppe but due to rivers benign influence on the soil, trees of more southerly type had already appeared.

To resume the narrative: The gale that blew next day 5th July was not that unwelcome.

> *'More rain, more rest*
> *Fine weather is not always best.'*

It was a fair gale and Nikolai was for sailing but Milo ruled against leaving their snug berth.

An enforced day at anchor was a blessing. It gave everyone a rest and Miles time to reflect on how the venture stood, examine his surroundings and plan ahead.

Uppermost in his mind was cautious satisfaction at having got so far, 2,000 miles, almost a third of the way to the Black Sea, on schedule – and, dare he say it? – all going well. Five crew changes, Stornoway, Lerwick, Harstad, Archangel, Belomorsk effected without delay: North Cape and Barents Sea negotiated safely; papers proved OK for entry into Russia, and later into Volga – Balt. Big one that – A Russian in doubt will always say no. A nyet from a lock keeper could have taken a couple of weeks to get reversed and upset the whole delicate timing. Boat a-taunto and rigging in good order, Radio connections with UK working, Paraffin cooker moody and maddening but at least one burner OK.

Above all the Russians were proving such stout and resourceful crewmen. He thought back to the days when he was a soldier, proud of a commission in the Royal Greenjackets, and sailing friends teased him with the 18th Century matelot's mantra:

> *'A messmate before a shipmate,*
> *a shipmate before a stranger,*
> *a stranger before a dog,*
> *and a dog before a soldier.'*

Top of the list were messmates and shipmates. He'd picked good'uns.

Then there was the unveiling of the history he had dreamed about since boyhood. He was traversing, in his own boat,one of the greatest ancient routes east from the Baltic. Seeing this one was enough to appreciate the significance of others further south.

'A voyage to a far land with adventure on the way is a sure cure for old age and sorrow', was a quote he had enjoyed from a Norse Saga – and now he was in the midst of one, by God!

Atavistically he imagined that a direct ancestor, maybe a stout-hearted grandfather of Somerled, First Lord of the Isles, had travelled this way a thousand years ago.

Miles had Viking blood in his veins from Stuart and Bruce ancestors. As of course do half the population of Scotland but few can prove it. Miles' share must have contributed to his precocious competence as a sailor. Aged fourteen he had kept night watches solo on Wild Goose. Aged seventeen he had skippered her, with a crew of girls, safely on a cruise among the wild and rocky Outer Hebrides.

So, he mused, many perils lay ahead but there was cause for quiet satisfaction for so far the voyage had gone exactly as planned. The feeling of urgency had not slackened; a hurried jouirney still lay ahead to make the Black Sea on time.

Nikolai later reminisced sympathetically:

> Only now looking back do I realise how tiring it was for Miles to hold us together as a crew, make notes on everything he saw and keep Wild Goose ploughing through the water virtually round the clock. The white nights of summer in the Russian north are a wonderful thing to behold but they are also a cruel taskmaster. There is hardly a moment of comforting blackness when you can take a rest without feeling guilty. I was thoroughly enjoying myself and I saw no reason to worry that Wild Goose would not reach the Black

Sea as planned. Perhaps that is because we Russian, (even Russians of German origin!) have a different sense of time. However practical we are there will certainly always be certain things beyond our control, you simply do as much as you sensibly can and leave the rest to fate. But Miles, I can only realise now was watching the calendar the whole time wondering whether we would reach Turkey before the storms of autumn as he saw things. The prospect for success or failure were resting on a knife edge and it was up to him to make the judgements that would maximise the chances of completing the journey. So it had been a relief to him when we entered the Vytegra river and began the steep climb through another lock system.

Listening to the odd clunk as Wild Goose snubbed on at her chain and feeling her heel to the gusts, the rest of the day passed in writing sleeping with a sortie now and then to look at the sky check the rigging for a rough sail across the lake.

An Ostrog (blockhouse) and Portage in Siberia.

77

CHAPTER FIVE

The Mologa Triangle

By WALLACE, *MILES*, NIKOLAI and VITALI

> '*Their chaumer was the mune-bright sky*
> *The siller stream their lullaby*'
> John Buchan

Miles was up several times through the night to see that all was well. At dawn on 6th July he checked once more by the alignment of two trees ashore that the anchors were holding, made his usual run in dinghy and explored the island that was providing shelter. Returning he cooked breakfast a big Ulster Fry, 'to keep the Russian bear from the door' and handed plates forward to the crew in their bunks. When Vitali came hunkering aft under the low fore-peak deckhead to wash up, Milo lay back in his bunk and looked up meditatively at the coachroof, where it was clear of nets holding fruit and clothing. He could see the harmonic curves of the oaken beams flickering as dapples of light reflected up through the scuttles from the wavelets alongside. On the bulkhead below them he watched the clock, and the barometer which he read and recorded daily.

His intense preparations were paying off.

It was a Russian World War Two soldier Vladimir Peniakoff, who summed up better than anyone else the essential link between preparations and voyaging.

Peniakoff who trained and led a unit known as Popski's Private Army to raid behind the German lines in the desert and Italy wrote:

> 'Successful adventures ... depend on rigorous attention to detail as seamen know well but soldiers do not readily admit. I wanted my adventurers to be tidy and thrifty, misers chained to a perpetual repetition of piddling cares. They had to have minds like ants, stamp collectors, watch makers and accountants, orderly, precise and unhurried. At the same time I expected them to risk cheerfully the sudden loss of everything they had, to take chances, to make quick

decisions, to keep their heart when fortune changed and to carry out unexpected orders vigorously. I required of them to be both cautious and extravagant, matter of fact and imaginative to plan carefully their enterprises and also act on sudden inspiration. Conflicting qualities seldom found in the same man.'

Miles had been through the meticulous assembly of stores and spares, the checking of every wire and fastening, the attempt to foresee each peril ahead.

Once this was over he had to push on and be ready to improvise. – 'If the mast busts, we'll motor. If the Sea Panther Diesel fails we'll use the outboard. If it packs up we'll make oars and row!'

That's the attitude which gets places and is the essence of ship driving, a higher art in many ways than helmsmanship or navigation.

At dawn on the second day the wind had eased to Force 5, still northerly. They sailed away with a reefed main, full jib and staysail. Wild Goose was soon was roaring across the 30 mile stretch of Lake Byalo towards the Sheksna river. They 'took it a burster nor eased her nor nursed her', so that she and her crew enjoyed to the full the zest and contrast of sailing across a stretch of clear water. Shallow it was, never more than five fathoms, with short steep following waves but clear of obstructions – Wild Goose going near her top speed between the buoys of the channel with a bone of brown water in her teeth. Her stern was well down, her bow up, water streaming past the hull, sails full with just an occasional flutter and jerk on the sheets. The low distant shoreline was fretted with trees except to the south east where the towers of the town erupted in curious combination of square blocks and onion spires

At 6 pm they were into the rushy mouth of the Sheksna River, meandering through reed beds once more but in a channel wider and easier to steer along than the Kyzhoy they had left. There were rain squalls and it was still very cold. The river gradually led into a land of broad meadows, plantations set back from the shore, carpets of fireweed and isolated trees.

This was a fast river before dams lower down killed the flow.

Wild Goose was creeping into civilisation. It seemed quite populous when the anchor went down for the night at 2100 in sight of three villages.

SHEKSNA DAWN

It dawned a fresh sunny morning, reminiscent of spring on the Shannon. Wild Goose lay in a half-moon cove with trees to the water's edge. Milo was up first as usual and rowed ashore. Initially this had been to fulfil his private vow not to add one stool to the pollution of the waterways, but he soon found that the sortie gave him a precious few moments of privacy. Some mornings it was so quiet that all he could hear was the blood singing in his ears but that day a crow perched above him repeating its single note; there was the familiar chuckle of a magpie and the chink of two wagtails trotting along the water's edge. Gulls on the water looked as big as swans in the mirage effect of low morning light.

First traffic was a Meteor hydrofoil, the steam underneath it in the chill of dawn cool filling the whole underbelly space before swirling astern.

Back alongside Wild Goose Miles tied up the dinghy with the twin painters which were used all the time for security. In the cockpit he heard the boat noises again, a babble of Russian from below, the tiller creaking as it moved in the wash of passing traffic. the flutter of the burgee, a low hum of wind in the backstays, the tap of rope halliards against the mast.

This passage crew, the fifth, were 'Wild Goosed' by now. They'd stopped asking, 'How many horsejobs is your engine? or 'Where's the bosun's locker?', every time they wanted a shackle or some whipping twine. They knew the colour of the outboard fuel tank or where to find a biscuit. They'd got over making the usual new chum mistakes of trying to pump out the loo with both seacocks shut, resulting in Miles having to spend a morning as Dan, Dan, the lavatory man to put things right, or throwing the washing up water over without checking for hardware in the bottom of the bowl.

No more cracks like:
'Tinkle, tinkle little spoon,
Knife and fork will follow soon!'

And they could launch the dinghy square over the side, so that it didn't dip its stern and get half full of water

Jim had abandoned early efforts to wash up by this time and took station each morning with a load of camera gear on the coachroof, eagle-eyed for a shot, particularly one showing pollution. He did a little deck scrubbing and expected continual explanations and comments from Vitali as part of his fixation that the whole trip was being run for the sole benefit of the National Geographic.

Miles got the main brunt. 'Yea, I can just see old Pushkin wandering through those woods'.

'Amigo, old buddy, my friend, ... glad to see the Russians are getting along ... and if you don't mind me saying I think we get along too.'

A remark to Vitali. 'You have a wonderful country. People with so much energy. I mean, I sure wish I had a dacha like this close to my city. I have two friends, a lawyer and a doctor and, believe me, they make a lot of money. But they can only afford a little itty bitty dacha 70 miles from Washington …

'How about the toilets?, what happens to the shit? – do the people all get together with the town council and dig sewers?'

'No Jim, they find earth closets much better.'

Jim: 'That is the most fatuous comparison I think I have ever heard …'.

The previous night he had said to Vitali 'You have a knowledge far beyond your years', and then, enunciating very slowly as though to a subnormal idiot 'That is … very … good'.

Nikolai was fortunate in not having enough English to understand more than a fraction of what Jim said. He took turns with Vitali and Miles at steering, keeping lookout, sail trimming and tidying the deck.

They never left Wild Goose unattended, not once. Today Nikolai stayed on board while the rest outboarded ashore for a 'meet the people' morning.

THE GOOD LIFE IN TAMARA

A plump woman with a piece of white linen tied round her waist was bashing laundry on a stone by the pier, as we landed; her husband loading metal panels onto a green motorboat.

After nodding to them we were greeted by Dmitry Fyodorov age 52, 'Eighty percent of people in this village are retired, come from the city on account of relatives here. I'm here for three days from Cherepovets to prepare equipment for forestry and organise the work. Then I go off to Bradsk near Lake Baikal, a couple of thousand miles away, to set up new equipment there.'

Do many people own their own land?

'People rent some spots of land near their cottages.'

'Is it possible for them to buy it?'

'Yes, you can, but its so expensive that very few people do.'

'The only means of transport here for the elderly and retired people is a Meteor Boat in summer. There are piers everywhere. It is about 60 miles from Cherepovets and they do it in two hours in the Meteor.

Antonida Gitina, 61, took up the theme. Her figure ran in a single bulge from chest to waist, her hair straight and black, a large mole on the side of her face.' Its the wind that controls our lives. If we have the wind from the south everything is okay but when it blows from the Arctic life become very difficult. The river freezes seven feet deep in the winter; only open for navigation from April until October. All the villages between here and Kovzha on the other side of Lake Byalo were destroyed after 1960 when the the river was changed. Only three houses are occupied here in the winter, so it is very difficult for old people because there is no road. No doctors, no medicines.

What happens if you become ill?

We can do nothing. People call this a Lost Place. No shop, no store, no cure. We have to do everything for ourselves.

Once we were told to leave because there was a plan to build a big lock not far from here. When the War began they decided not to build the lock so people came back and built their own houses. We grow potatoes, some vegetables and have our own milk and meat because we have a cow. We buy sweets and tea, nothing else. Of course there is hunting, one man in our village has a rifle, a dog and a licence. He brings in elk and bear. It is much better to feed ourselves. And we're lucky because we have six sons living in Cherepovets.

'How important is the river in your life?'

'Not important at all because this river only brings us trouble. Earlier people lived well here; they had places to cut grass for their animals and they could cut trees when they needed. Now all the forests and good meadows are under water, that's the trouble.

And many people get drowned here. Some of them rammed by the big ships, and some of them are not cautious when they drink alcohol. Now it is difficult to get petrol so we can only use oars to cross the river; the ships are very fast so we have to be very careful not to be cut down and sunk.

Of course we all look forward to summer, this time of year; it is so beautiful here after a concrete flat in the city. Something pulls me here, maybe because I feel spiritual roots in the soil.

'I wait all the year for this moment, and when I get here it seems that nothing has changed.'

Gifts were offered of bread, butter, olives and vodka. They would have killed a goose for us and fetched strawberries from the woods, if we'd been able to wait.

The village gardens were beautifully tended full of with lettuces and, cabbage. Chickens wandered round. Antonida pressed on me a string of onions, saying, 'If you try to pay me I will not give you them.'

Her husband Nikolai picked up the spade, saying, 'When I was born this was the instrument for the collective farmers. Now it is still the instrument. People want to work the land but when they try to manage two hectares with only shovels of course it is exhausting. The Administration say they will produce a great number of small tractors but now the price of a small tractor is the price of a Lada car, so where is the sense?

Inside their wooden house, held together with electric wire

around the outside, cooking was on gas. I noted nice curtains and coir mats, lace curtains, painted brown floor and that most Russian of chattels a couple of passable icons.

I had to stop myself from hugging the babushka, and then when she welcomed me warmly I did. Vladimir showed them how he had built a stove because his mother was going to stay on the next winter. We were offered a meal of pickled salad, spring onions, potatoes, bread and rich butter.

It looked like a practical example of the good life, but hard work to imagine these green meadows under many feet of snow for six months a year.

At 1740 got anchor from very silty bottom and motored south to get to Lock 7 and be sure of Cherepovets tomorrow.

The river scene is largely of passing ships, almost all of class called Volga/Balt; some have cars on deck and families on board. Terns fish in their wake, mops hang over the stern. From our river level viewpoint, all else there is to look at is a thin line of trees or sometimes rough grass between the water and the sky. It is cold again – 16 degrees.

The numbers of jetties and boathouses is increasing all the time. Power pylons more numerous as we get towards the city, cranes and scrub. Disorder rules as pride begins to ebb and the water becomes brown and dirty. In outline the buildings of Cherepovets look like solid hunks of concrete. Functional blocks of humanity with no softness – a world without comfort.

THE LADY OF THE THE LOCK

Hailed Baltika, a 5,000 ton ship bringing huge deck cargo of timber from St Petersburg. Nikolai was allowed by fat lady to call Lock on her radio. Tried get permission to pass through in dark. Answer from a female voice was equivocal but as we drew alongside in the approach a figure appeared from the Control Tower.

Under the harsh sodium lights of Pochinok lock I watched Nicholai look into the eyes of the lady in charge for her it was who had deigned to emerge. Her charms might have been enthralling if they hadn't been hidden under layers of shapeless clothing. He guessed at how Nik was explaining the voyage and persuading her to let Wild Goose into the lock behind Baltika and two other iron monsters.

It was an important moment – and we were at the cusp of the crossing, leaving the highest point and descending to traverse the northern edge of the State of Russia between the Taiga and the Wooded Steppe.

Nik gave the thumbs up and we moved. The bowels of the huge lock began to appear as we fell between black wet walls that smelled of oil, peat and dampness. I blew a kiss to the lock lady. She disappeared. 'My God, I've done the wrong thing now,' I thought. Then she leaned over to drop chrysanthemums into my arms, pale red under the sodium lights and icy cold to the touch. The sound of the ship's engines increased as the water fell and revealed the upper gate, a lattice of steel joists, concrete slabs and wooden beams two metres thick that might have been the blade of a Brobdinagian fly swatter – not the kind of thing you expect to see appear just under your stern in a lock. We dropped a hundred feet in this one. The whole surface was marbled swirling brown water, reflecting the lights along the 300 yards of its length. That's two and a half times the length of a football pitch and as broad as a motorway. The evacuation was the rough equivalent of emptying the Serpentine in ten minutes.

The gates worked by vertical movement, not on hinges as expected. I wondered what would happen if the control lady pressed the wrong button and drained all the water out instead of just some ...!

But all was well – the lower sill gurgled below the surface to leave us level with buoys winking out of Stygean waterway ahead. We got out last behind a pusher tug fussing astern of its log raft, and a nameless freighter. Baltika boomed garbled Russian out of darkness with a bow-mounted speaker, dazzling us with his searchlight the while. As soon as possible we turned out of the channel and into a basin whose limits were lost in shadow. The anchor went down at midnight in a welcome rattle, tied to a recovery line in case the bottom was foul with wreckage. Very tired.'

APPROACHING CHEREPOVETS

Wednesday, 8th April.
Another unseasonably cold, grey morning. Up 0545: No expedition ashore as daylight showed black greasy walls and tumble-down warehouses. Motored away at 0600 through anchored ships. Baltika, our chummy ship, had been unloading all night and some of her logs which had slipped away from the grabs obstructing our path. 0640 – passed with minimum clearance under two bridges. Porridge and tea for a sleepy crew. 1020 – motored through grey drizzle, later heavy rain. The sound of trains came booming through the forest and then the trains themselves half screened by trees. Fishermen sitting disconsolate in the rain. The sun struggled to get through as we progressed over steely water with the dirty white squares of Cherepovets appearing to the south west.

At about eleven I felt the touch of a grian, that splendid Gaelic conveying in one word 'the first feel of sun on your back after a shower of rain'. Watery that sun may have been but it was over the yardarm justifying a dram of Bushmills whiskey as a noon balloon to mark our nearness to the Volga.

Cherepovets, our first big city, was in the pattern of the deadingly similar Soviet ones I had seen the previous winter. Forty smokestacks threaded together with a King Kong tracery of power cables; red and white pylons, three where one would have done, supported twenty wires drooping over the rooftops and across 200 metres of river – a scene from an engineer's nightmare. Cherepovets, as the canal guidebook Russia by River tells you has 300,000 inmates. From a boatbuilding village 70 years ago, it became a sprawling industrial city producing steel and chemicals after World War Two, showering grey soot over every tree and building.

A huge pall of smoke hung to leeward of the rooftops and one vast but smokeless chimney climbed through as if probing the heavens above for fresh air

A Meteor overtook from astern with a Wham! And a stagger, as the first sound waves of his engines and then his frothy wake hit us. There were small green bulbous inflatables known as Jon boats all over the river. Over them screamed a nimbus of chaika, as Nikolai appropriately calls the seagulls. Each little rubber bathtub was marked with six digits and propelled by an outboard. Each carried one man. Some lay flat-a-back, legs trailing over the side, apparently dead, others busy with rod or belled handlines. 'Jon boats,' said Nikolai, 'are food for the family, and escape for survivors', the name we have for their owners. He was, I think, a little envious. We were travelling too fast to fish.

As if to match the drab surroundings the sky turned darker still and the wind chill from the north east, heeling Wild Goose under bare poles in the gusts. The Lock Lady's flowers whirled overboard. An interlude of Scotch mist, then heavy rain once more.

A last glimpse of countryside where a man on horseback was rounding up herds of cattle in deep scrub. Houses with double pitched roofs in the Canadian style, made from locally produced alloy sheet, open meadows between them and new bright dachas and izbas give the suburbs a brief air of prosperity. Then a huge power plant, followed and allotment huts with their owners tilling plots on ground sloping down to the river. A class of students, learning how to survey, studied us through a theodolite. Jon boats pulled up under covers, yellow parasols stuck absurdly in dirty sand by rusty railings and a couple hugging under one. Felt like prying to be using binoculars; but why court just there? Perhaps because a notice declared 'This is a Zone of Strict Sanitary Regime'.

The Pumping Station which had once taken water out of the river and filtered it for the city seemed to be derelict. Sewage, or least brown water, pouring out through large cement pipes, cold, foamy, and depressing. One flat in a block of three hundred had a window box with flowers. None had balconies.

Nicholai is clad in oilskins like they used to make 'em, of cotton cloth, pale yellow from many applications of linseed oil, odorous and sticky in patches. Vitali is a figure in blue, padded jacket, blue trousers and trainers, navy peaked cap marked Canadian Airlines. He has on his glacier glasses and affected constant tuneless singing under his breath. When I handed up a sandwich he explained in detail about the lord who liked to play cards all night.

There were dozens of cranes, none apparently working, piles of sawdust, rusty tugs packed so close together it was impossible to see between them, a small yacht which looked like a Flying Dutchman, smells of gas, wood and sulphur. I had been feeling in the need of a city but not one like this. Then a couple of 50 foot patrol boats, guns shrouded in canvas and tired sailors smoking. 'Run aground on their own beef bones', said Nikolai, or the Russian equivalent. Big barges beside them for bringing submarines built in Novgorod up to the Baltic fleet.

Then concrete cliffs; slab-sided tasteless blocks of flats. Cruelly I asked Vitali, 'do you live in one of those big grey apartment blocks'. 'Yes, it is just the same at home'. 'Is it nice?' 'I don't think so'. Then after a pause, 'The house is big and no one knows each other'.

At noon tied up to a black barge to take the chance of shopping. We were guided in by the crew of a graceful varnished Folkboat, two friendly couples from Moscow en route to Petrodavodsk for the Regatta, The barge was disreputable and the owner Sasha, a curious figure with a boxer's nose, bulging eyes, brown plastic sandals and a black track suit with white lines down the shoulders. He smoked crumpled cigarettes and whistled through a gap in this teeth. His eyes had small flat pupils like those of an eagle and seemed to guard his face but he acted friendly. Sasha took our bags of rubbish and threw them on a heap on the shore, said he would pay a man with a digger to come and bury them. A passer-by retrieved a couple, looked inside and then threw them down. Sasha works his steamer up and down the river picking up cargoes of timber, hay or steel from the towns or factories as opportunity comes. 'How is work?'

'Not bad', he replied. 'Pavlov (the local boss) cuts all co-ops with a big knife. Moscow raises the taxes slowly', adding unnecessarily, 'My work is done in cash. Yeltsin lived here for a year or two when he was younger. All these houses were built by German

86

prisoners during the Great Patriotic War, that was after they had finished building the barrage to create the Mologa triangle.'

Sasha himself had worked in co-operatives as a mason and when they packed up, took to river work.

We moved on to a cleaner barge called Ulitsa Lenin and yarned to her skipper, helpful with tips about the river ahead. He showed us where to get a truck to market. On a crowded cobble square was a single-storied building containing an extraordinary assortment of humanity and goods for sale. Engine spares beside pig's heads with a purple stamp between the eyes, cherries, bananas, and coarse bread. A boy was selling a game called Stock Exchange. Beside him was another with a heavily thumbed copy of Kama Sutra, illustrated with retouched photographs – Bibles on the same stand. A woman with a large moustache was selling sausages beside an Azerbizanyi with gambling machines. Seemed to be no centre to the city, just a series of shabby buildings and nondescript shops.

Ulitsa Lenin offered us diesel at thirty roubles a litre. We knew the state price was seventeen. I really did say, 'I could buy two eunuchs for that price in Smyrna', which Vitali may have re-arranged in translation. At least he settled for ten which turned out like free love and duty free booze to be very expensive indeed. At 1830 we retrieved our oil-smeared lines and sailed away.

No one but a besotted admirer could call Cherepovets a pleasing city but we were to remember kindly attitudes there against what emerged later as one bad turn.

On towards more concrete jungle, under the October Bridge, soaring 250 feet above the water. A motor boat sits high and dry on a pile as if the water had suddenly dropped and left her perched. Could it happen to us? Overhead was a bi-plane with sky divers. At 2100 a breeze came up; we set the staysail and jib and took turns at the tiller to glide on during a table d'hote lunch – a major beef stew improved by a lacing of undrinkable local vino corroso. We had to start the motor again an hour later.

FLOATING SABOR (Cathedral)

Came to a tall 'floating sabor'. Floating is the local adjective for a building half submerged during the creation of a reservoir. Sounds pleasantly Irish as it is neither floating or at present a sabor. It stuck out of the still water like a finger wrapped in a bandage. Anchored early in hope of better light in the morning. A half moon rose as river traffic throbbed past unabated. The sunset in the east was banded orange and grey with tendrils of smoke drifting along the horizon.

Next day, Thursday 9th July, dawns moist and grey with a cold north west breeze. We sailed back to the floating *sabor* for Jim to photograph but the light was again poor. Inside we could hear little wavelets echoing against the walls of the empty nave and the murmur of starlings until we turned south again, leaving the doomed tower limned clear against the north horizon. There was good sailing all that day. Vitali singing,

> 'I am crazy like a fool,
> Da, da, da, daddy cool,
> Ra, ra, Rasputin
> Lover of the Russian Queen'.

He was discussing melody and kareoke with Nikolai. Wearing headphones he couldn't hear his own grunts and groans sounding as if he was about to die.

Suddenly we were in open water, crossing the Mologa triangle – called after the river which flows into it.

It sparkled in fitful sunlight. Wild Goose gave a little rollick of joy as she slapped the wavelets off her shapely bows, and pointed the barnacle goose figurehead skyward.

It would be a fool who would deny that a ship has a spirit of her own, certainly one as old and experienced as Wild Goose. You may know, in your reason, that she is just a piece of machinery but the mere feel of her as she moves through the water is poetry. Wild Goose was repeating the frison of excitement I'd felt in her shed at home just before the voyage started.

Now as our wake broadened like a bridal train as she gathered way she must have made a sight to inspire admiration.

Gradually the city skyline sank astern; everywhere else you looked the shores were low and tree-fretted We saw distant tips of more floating buildings. The easy progress, drowned landscape and floating sabors made for a day of meditation. Radio news came that Yeltsin had been granted a loan of $1000,000,000 and delayed payments of his debts to try and save the Russian economy.

We exchanged cheers with a yacht going north, only the second seen underway since we'd entered Russia. By midnight Nikolai reckoned by divination, or taste, that we were in the waters of the Volga which mingles here with those of the Sheksna Molova and half a dozen other rivers. And so decreed a second celebration. We 'hit the Bush' again. That blessed case of whiskey had been kindly given to us by the 300 year old distillery which lies only five miles from where Wild Goose started the trip. It was lasting like the widow's curse.

Nikolai, relaxed by Bush, began to talk about his feelings for the Volga. This was his fourth voyage on it. 'I followed the first part from its source as a small spring in the Valdai Hills, a very picturesque place, on foot for four miles, then my wife and I crossed

Vishni Volskiy lakes in a kayak, and after that down the Volga to Dubna in two summer voyages. Then I was mate of a 50 foot yacht and a crew of ten which sailed from Dubna to Rybinsk and down to the Black Sea and Athens in 1990.'

'Was that unusual?' Miles asked.

'It certainly was in 1990; it was very difficult to arrange for reasons not connected with the Communist regime. We had to get Visas and sponsors and solve other problems of organisation but we had very good invitations from yacht clubs in Turkey and Greece. Officially there was no great problem. It was the leader of the Moscow Club who organised the voyage and lead the four yachts. That year some Soviet yachts did long passages; some guys from Nikolayevsky went round the world so there were yachts in Istanbul from Odessa.'

'What does the Volga mean to you?', asked Miles.

'I know in my mind that it is the longest river in the European part of Russia and vital to the whole country. So I respect the name of Volga but my heart does not feel anything more than that of any middle Russian because I was born in Kazakstan and spent all my childhood there.

(He was of German parentage; his family were deported by Stalin with half a million others during World War Two.)

Vitali agreed saying that he had his own river, the Kama. 'It flows near my home town of Omsk. Its name tells me more than the name Volga, but many people consider that those living along Volga are the only native Russians. So it is better for us to come and see what life is like along it and what they themselves feel about it'

They got the pick down at 0130 the next morning, Friday 10th July, off a scrubby islet near Rybinsk lock. Dawn came grey with a band of bright gold light to the south east giving little promise of the day that was to come. One clue was that Wild Goose was, amazingly, snubbing her anchor to a north easter, the first wind from that airt for weeks. The water surface was green with algae as they chugged down the last few miles to Rybinsk and Lock 11 which would take them into the Volga itself ... Miles had come by now to refer to it in more euphonic Russian style as Wolga. Readers should mentally do the same. But still, 'Terrible name for a river', he noted privately.

The lock they entered was the widest yet 300 yards long by 70 wide. Curious green plants grew out of its sides, able to endure desiccation between frequent jacuzzis. Familiarity with such vast locks did not breed contempt, just continued awe. The rate of emptying was alarming. Wild Goose fell a yard every fifteen seconds, or four a minute.

And so, unceremoniously, Wild Goose dropped in on the Volga.

The crew's first glimpse of their water world for the next 1200 miles was a tree-lined blue shimmer 200 yards wide, dotted with jolly little conical buoys -a sharp transformation from the steel and concrete of the barrage they had just left.

Ahead first lay 500 miles to be made eastwards in quiet waters, five barrages to be passed through but no rapids to reach Kazan. There the Volga turns south for Astrakhan. The river scenery would change but not the welcomes from its people or the now familiar Volga-Don boats sliding past with mops over the stern.

The spirits of Wild Goose's crew effervesced, like the waters of the lock that had delivered them into the Volga.

Survivor in Jon Boat.

CHAPTER SIX

The Golden Ring

By WALLACE and MILES

'The Central Water System of Russia is that of the Volga.'
From THE URGE TO THE SEA

THE VOLGA AT LAST

Blinking from the shadows of a lock that felt like a canyon, Miles
saw ahead a broad shimmer of pale blue water ... tree-lined, twinkling, tranquil, tempting ... Mother Volga – his highway, challenge,
friend and potential deadly enemy for twelve hundred miles ahead.

Wild Goose was at first speeded on her way by the two knot current, usually found below the barrages. It caused Vitali at the tiller
to say, 'I am feeling someone tugging at the rudder.' The tugs were
nothing of course to those in fierce whirlpools met earlier in
Norwegian tide rips but the helmsman had to concentrate to keep
her on a straight course. More dramatic was the change in the
weather – It was the first day of summer!

The temperature had shot to 23 degrees. The crew found themselves in baking hot air on a broad continental river with freedom
to steer this way or that, and not pursue a narrow course between
buoys. Possibilities for comparison were almost endless, the
Missouri, the Yangtse, St. Lawrence all contain stretches such as
they were traversing now, with nature very much in control. But the
freight trade has left the American rivers and gone to the railroads.
On the Volga, at least for the seven unfrozen months, freighters survive, and tens of millions of tons are transported annually.

The Volga, anciently known as the Ra and in the Middle Ages the
Itil, is Europe's longest river. Her 2,200 miles were a long pull for
the Vikings but that is only two thirds of the length of the Nile and
about half that of the or Amazon. The Volga's source is 728 feet
above sea level in the Valdai Hills. It finishes 92 feet below sea
level in a seventy mouth Caspian delta. Her basin of half a million
square miles includes 1080 rivers, rivulets, streams and lakes.

91

The Volga comes nearest of any western river to linking the European with the Siberian water systems. Had it not been for the introduction of railways an artificial water link would almost certainly have been created a hundred years ago.

The Volga is two thirds fed by snow, almost another third by underground water, and only one tenth by rain. That means an enormous increase in flow in spring. The thaw used to bring vast floods when the level rose up to fifty feet in places and inundations in places extended a hundred miles in width.

For all that Mother Volga is gentle as rivers go. She drops only six inches per mile against a foot per mile for the Nile. Unlike the Dnieper she has no rapids with awe inspiring names like Watch Out, White Water, Mankiller and Breaker of Ships.

She has no gorges with twenty knot currents or habits of drowning her people in myriads like the Yangtse, no man-eating alligators or piranhas like the Amazon.

Such floods as she once had are now tamed by five barrages. To produce 11,000,000 Kilowatts of electricity, the Communists have created five elongated reservoirs – by name Gorodets, Cheboksary, Kubyshevskoy, Balakov and Volgograd. This has been at the price of virtually destroying the life-giving flow which used to take a chip of wood from Yaroslavl to the Caspian in under two months.

The bonus comes for navigators as the increased water level means floating over the top of most of the shifting sandbanks which made the Volga pilotage famed for its difficulty.

The Volga somehow survives all and is perhaps a symbol of the evanescence of human effort.

Miles remarked in the log that he could see why the Soviets felt there was no harm in putting factory or two on the banks. There is so much room.

At 1030 came the first Volga sobor. Suddenly a bow shot from the river edge appeared Kazansky. It was a riot of colours brilliant enough to raise a gasp. A bedizened pepperpot in red and white, topped by five onion cupolas in green, each crowned by a golden cross.

Landing, the crew walked across the rough grass to be greeted not by nuns but a serious lady in thick brown tinted spectacles and a fine moustache, clad in a purple jumper dress and grey jacket. Elena had worked here for 15 years as an archivist.

She told of the shock of the ultimatum of the Mologa Reservoir Barrage which was to flood land where her husband had lived for 40 years. At first they could see his house and the streets clearly underwater but over the years it had become covered with silt and sand.

Then she took them to a Versailles style building of late 18th century construction which had been in use as a Labour Exchange, somewhat exceptionally, during the Soviet period. Later it became the Peragov Hospital. Now it is a Museum and Elena was arranging an exhibition of documents selected from 150,000 Soviet and Tsarist papers. 'My first care', she said, 'was all the Soviet papers. Recently a special project has been created so that I can spend time examining documents about earlier history.'

Among the most fascinating of these was a decree signed by Svyatoslav, Prince of Novgorod in 1137 referring to a village called Rybansk. And another signed by His Imperial Majesty the Tsar Fyodor of Russia in 1746, addressed to the people of Rybinsk authorising them to sell grain, wheat and fish to his own kitchens in Moscow. The Imperial Eagle seal was in place, faded and cracked but whole. For most of the last few centuries, she explained, the Rybinsk region and its rich harvest of fish and farm produce had been under the Tsar's direct control, with no boyars or noblemen in between. There were security reports from the 1770 period showing how nervous Catherine The Great was about Pugachev's peasant uprising.

There were references to the creation of the 55,000 KW station to supply to the War industries in 1943 and the initial delight of the local communists that their area had been selected for it. This was before they realised the appalling ecological effects

Elena was working at a giant manual typewriter surrounded by endless bundles of yellowing paper. There was a letter from the workers of Rybinsk in 1922 conveying greetings to the world proletariat leader, Comrade Lenin. That was about the time of the last service in the Kazansky Sabor. Elena led us to its entrance where a 15 foot wheel raised a drawbridge by ropes emerging from two red circular columns.

All too soon it was up anchor and off once more. They were now entering part of the Golden Ring of churches which surround Moscow, as in smaller scale in Ireland the castles of the Pale surround Dublin. One sight which gave Miles a shudder was the Cathedral of St. Elias, with its wooden domes split and covered in rampant creepers. Tall weeds grew out of roof and walls. Miles' log entry was revealing –

'After Anser Island I didn't want to stop'.

That evil hyperboreal island, their first call after Archangel, had made on him a deep and horrific impression.

Wild Goose was now in a world of more vigorous nature but the consumption of churches was the same as in the North.

The high banks to the right showed exposed red soil and a tree line broken occasionally by sandy beaches. There were smoke stacks in the background beyond herds of cattle as big as plains bison.

The buoys bobbing in the current and reflected in brownish water had changed colour from black and white to green with yellow stripes. A small Volga yacht came by with friendly gestures and Nikolai shook his clenched fist towards it as an expression of solidarity.

The last couple of hours, once the depression of derelict churches was over, became *one of the loveliest evenings afloat I ever remember.*

The warmth, the feeling of having arrived ahead of schedule with a day or two in hand, easy navigation on the broad bosom of the placid Volga all played a part in the euphoria.

Seven Orthodox churches all in good order appeared in a space of three miles. Wild Goose anchored off Tutyaev, a town named after an 18th century soldier.

'Sense of relief at the softness, comfort and ease of the land-scape, heightened by contrast of our long approach from the Arctic. Riversiders can be seen relaxing in the sunshine, the rare cessation of work being fully enjoyed as perhaps the only luxury they have.'

The church itself was known as Tulyma. and the sabor as Voskrenenskiy, built between 1652 and 1678, one of the best examples of creative work in the Yaroslavl region.

High in the air gleamed ten gold crosses, supported by gilded chain backstays on top of green cupolas. Above their heads was the squeal of sand martins twisting through the air and dipping their bills in a weedy well. Pigeons, sunning themselves under the eaves, rattled wings as they preened and nibbled. The grass was alive with crickets and flickering with moths.

As the crew walked back to the main church stepping carefully among knee-high nettles a man of slow speech smoking through a cigarette holder pointed something out. It was a wooden two storey house flat roofed in Mediterranean style where he lived. There he showed them pictures as he spoke of the 23 churches once in this cluster and the ancient fortifications on the river bank.

Twin towns here were previously known as Boris Oglebskiy on the south bank and Romanov on the north. Then came the story of …

The Great Icon

A sacred stone had been removed from the open air altar near Voskrenenskiy by the Soviets – also a famous icon, weighing a ton and credited with many miracles. Both were 'lost'. Then someone found the icon beside the spring which had grown up where it lay. The finder tried to bring it to Romanov but his boat stuck fast in mid river. Luckily there was a monk on board who sensed that the icon did not want to go to north bank. The boat moved easily south and the icon back to where it belonged. Now only the relief Golden Halo remains there of this huge Icon known as 'Salvator' (The Saviour) which once measured 12 feet by 9 feet.

To it many miracles including the preservation of the local sabors are attributed.

The events in its return were similar to those told to a Wild Goose crew of a Holy Stone from St Patrick's Church on Caher island off the wild west of Ireland. There had been total belief on Caher as there was now in the wonderful powers of this huge gold framed painting.

THE GENTLE NUNS OF TOLGA

Anchored for the night off Tolga monastery Vitali landed to talk to a nun with the unlined face of a madonna. She wore a black kaftan-like dress (Ryasa) with a round pillbox hat (Kamilavka), her face framed in the upper part of a smock (Opostolnik), prayer beads in her right hand.

'God created these churches', she said, 'to save people. Stay until tomorrow.' They did as bidden.

It was a wonderful luxury to be at anchor early in the evening and have a slow meal in the cockpit – followed by the voluptuous prospect of a full night's sleep. Total relaxation in a bunk that didn't roll about, under a deckhead through which no raindrops would come.

Waking briefly at midnight Miles heard but couldn't see the fishes nocturnal ditty *Fisches Nachtgesang of Christian Morgenstern.*

In the morning, Saturday 11th July, they awoke to a couple of days different to anything that had happened since the boat left Ireland. Brother Bruce was expected at Yaroslavl sometime on Sunday, so Miles had a day to absorb as much as possible of this monastery and some of the other classic buildings in the surroundings of the city named after Yaroslav, Grand Prince of Kiev. Tolga looks like an army barrack, enclosed in four whitewashed castellated walls capped in blue, with a fortified land entrance and a water gate facing the river.

Inside the square are roughly cut lawns, flower beds and a church with its accompanying campanile. Bells were often housed separately because of mechanical difficulty of hanging them under a dome. A shop sold small religious tokens, postcards and prominent among them pictures of Tsar Nicholas and his family.

The crew were received gracefully by the Abbess, a friend of Lady Braithwaite, the British Ambassador's wife, who had helped her with fundraising for restoration. They attended a service, at least part of one, for Orthodox services run three hours or more with seats for only a few. The liturgy with a musical tradition unbroken for hundred of years was of exceptional beauty.

After the bliss of a day in the sun amid the near perfect peace of the convent they sailed slowly down the river to Yaroslavl itself.

Yaroslavl is an old old city, founded in 1010 AD by Yaroslav The Wise; wiser perhaps than he ever knew for his name remains a celebrated one after a thousand years. His city was destroyed in 1238 by the Tatars but recovered to be sacked by the Russian Ivan 1 in 1332. After another quick rebuild it was captured and colonised by Novgorod. Its key position where the Moscow-Archangel trade route crosses the Volga gave renewed prosperity in the 16th century with the opening of trade with the West. The English were in early, having built a naval shipyard there in the 14th century. Dutch, French and Germans had trading bases in the 1600's. In spite of this there is little foreign influence in its magnificent churches.

This is a vital link in part of the 'golden ring' of churches. It is the nearest point on the Volga to Moscow.

A striking sight as the yacht arrived at this gem in the Golden Ring of Churches was a huge statue of a yellow bear with an axe over its shoulder against a red hoarding. To see that and the gleaming onion spires and industrial chimneys of Yaroslavl itself through the portholes of your own seagoing ship was a good illustration of what this voyage was about.

STERLET

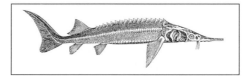

Here for the first time Wild Goose saw sterlet (the name for the Volga sturgeon) being taken in nets. They were lean shark-like fellows, a yard or so long with a mouth set low for bottom feeding and whiskers to help find the small fish they eat. Their skin is raspy, their heads as hard as steel and they have lines of white star-shaped

Lighthouse marking exit from Lake Onega to Volga-Balt Canal by way of Vytegra River.

Navigation buoys are often laid in pairs in case one is swept away by ice.

In Volga-Balt Canal lines are secured to a ring, as on the red float in centre of picture, which conveniently moves up and down in grooves.

Myriad tussocky islands on either side of the Sheksna River melt into the blue distance. Hundreds of miles were submerged to form the Rybinsk Reservoir, also known as the Mologa Triangle.

After a day of sail changing and working through locks, Jim finds a little space on the cluttered deck. [Vitali Chankseliani]

Floating Sabor left behind when hundreds of square miles were flooded.

Control towers like sangars stand at each end of each lock in Volga-Balt Canal.

Miles, Vitali and Nikolai celebrate arrival in the Volga with Black Bushmills whiskey.

A monastery of the Golden Ring above a row of dachas, seen over the dinghy.

Kazansky.

Voskresenskiy Cathedral near Yaroslavl. [Jim Blair, National Geographic Society]

Barrage at Gorodets. Bridges were often only inches above our masthead.

Holidaymakers re-embark on a meteor after a day of privacy in the woods.

Waiting for Arkady to join at the yacht club at Gorky. Crew change delays can be a nightmare in a land of minimum communications.

The Kremlin at Gorky seen above the Admiralty style waterfront.

Ferry stations like this became a familiar sight.

Meeting Betelgeuse, the schooner belonging to Vadim Romanov.

Makarief with ferry pontoon so like a Noah's Ark that it would not have been surprising to see a giraffe's head sticking out of an upper window.

The monastery at Makarief which six nuns were struggling to restore. A round tower stood at each angle of the defensive walls.

The singing of Matins could be heard softly over the the river at dawn.

Cockpit scene – Nikolai and Jim. [Vitali Chankseliani]

Twin locks and elaborate control systems of sliding gantries at Cheboksary.

Below the Cheboksary Barrage the channels re-unite.

Miles Clark, aged 32. The fine beard, grown for the voyage, was shaved off not without regrets by a barber in Karima, Turkey.

Galina,
the witty Russian yachtswoman.

Arkady takes down the riding light at dawn.

Algae in Kubyshiev Reservoir made the navigator wonder if this was the Volga or the 'green greasy Limpopo River' of Kipling.

hard scales along the back, down each side and positioned like bilge keels on each side of the tummy – the iron clads of the fishy world. The big sterlets, up to twenty feet, are rare now and the catch only a fraction of what it used to be. Most of the roe for caviare is produced in fish farms beside the banks.

Milo wrote: *The first impression of Yaroslavl is that it is fashionable.*

There were Black Jack girls wearing T-shirts with the Perfect Swing logo and black leggings. Many had dark wide eyes, silky black hair and tall, slender figures. You could see at once why the Vikings travelled a thousand miles and made six portages to come here. The beach, crowded with sunbathers, was like that of any other country. To a glance it would be almost impossible to tell which Continent you were in except perhaps for the lack of inhibition.

We turned into a smaller river which leads into the Volga from the north named the Kotorsila, passed under a girder railway bridge and anchored in a pool. Then it was a question of waiting in subdued excitement for a rendezvous with Bruce and Nadia. Wild Goose lay opposite the hideous hotel where they were to arrive, a solid mass of concrete with rows of small severe windows. At last in the moonlight two figures appeared on the bank. Even at a distance it was obvious that they were well laden!.

Swiftly ferried out by dinghy, they relaxed on deck cushions and handed round Muscovite food and wines.

To understand the drama and joy of that rendez-vous you must think what it was like to be isolated very far from home in a country where English speakers are almost non-existent and most signs incomprehensible. To meet a well-loved brother was thrill enough – to meet one speaking fluent Russian, with bulging bags of delicatessen and ship's stores, and possessing high level contacts in most areas, was just the sort of tonic needed in mid voyage.

Later in the cabin the talk, under the packed deckhead nets and across the crowded cabin sole, went on until dawn began to streak the sky. Nikolai and Jim were ashore so Bruce slept in Miles' bunk and Nadia in Jim's, Miles on deck under the trysail.

In the morning it was decided to use the next precious day, all that Bruce and Nadia could spare from international journalism, by going ten miles upstream again to Tolga, It was a holiday Monday, a trapeza or feast in honour of St Peter and St Paul so the world was afloat. Wild Goose dodged craft of endless variety – pedalos, canoes, windsurfers, sailing dinghies, large and small motor boats, eight oared racing skiffs and single sculls. Curiously shaped gazebos on the bank each had a family picnic in full swing in the shade of lime trees; Party bosses' dachas peeped more discretely from fir plantations.

A small crowd was fishing off the outflow from a filtration plant because the water there was slightly warmer. At Tolga some of the nuns were bathing in the river, others seated reading. 'Today we give our nuns an opportunity to rest', Mother Barbara told them, but still there are twenty cows to look after and the surplus milk given to families with small children. We try to keep some fields tilled and grow our own vegetables and more and more people come and ask us for help. One problem is to try and find a system of air circulation in the monastery. It is very difficult because it is easy for the icons to become mouldy'

Bruce with his specialised knowledge was able to point out many features of monastic life and icon significance. After a day of basking in home news and gossip Miles steered downstream again and entered the same creek. A horrible shudder forced Wild Goose inches out of the water as they passed under the railway bridge. She came to an abrupt halt. Soundings with a boat hook showed deep water all the way round the hull so it appeared that they had struck some isolated obstruction and damage was unlikely. However, it was not possible to get Wild Goose off there and then. Bruce and Nadia were leaving that night by taxi for Moscow so the crew left Nikolai on board and went up to the hotel to have dinner.

The visit had been totally enjoyable but the aftermath made Miles feel homesick and, *'wishing I could do anything rather than travel down the Volga for a few days'*.

That night he had the privacy of a hotel room but it stank of rubbish and dirty socks. He fell asleep in his room while Vitali was making his call home to Omsk.

Tuesday, 14th July: It was curious to wake up in a wide soft bed and have breakfast in a dining room of sweet bread rolls and semolina. The hands of the person serving was so begrimed that he recalled the old Navy couplet:

'What 'll you 'ave,' said the waiter, pensively picking his nose.

'A pair of boiled eggs, you old bastard. You can't get your fingers in those.'

But there was not much time to dwell over the meal. Fresh food had to be bought and Miles with Vit made for the market.

If the Russians went alone, he had found that their long enforced parsimony meant they came back with miniscule quantities. A wonderful selection of fruits and vegetables, strawberries, cherries, iron berries and ice cream lay spread on rough stalls. The Bank as usual refused to change money but Vitali got western notes for roubles in a restaurant kitchen for some of the dollars delivered by Bruce, brought by neighbour Rory Peck from Ireland. This cash as well as a mammoth re-supply of wines and food from Moscow made meals much more interesting for the next few weeks.

Now Bruce had gone there was that sense fracture that used to come after a day out with relations from boarding school.

At 1340 Wild Goose, afloat once more by Nikolai's efforts, was off east with a sense of leaving civilisation and heading once more into the wilds. East of Yaroslavl distances have a much bigger magnitude.

It was windless and scorching hot. Gradually the holiday atmosphere thinned out but the Meteor boats kept roaring by, making sudden stops at little piers, then giving a Sci-fi impression of a huge insect rising out of the water on legs and taking off like a wingless dragon. The banks showed sand beaches and trees well back from the river edge. There were tractors pulling trailers full of grass for hay. It seemed to be within the space of an hour we had crossed the double spread of an atlas, so different was the scene to what it had been a few days ago. Then came a large army barrack behind earth berms, with sangars and sentry boxes, red and white ball-top towers, guarded by patrolling soldiers.

From the river the sky always seemed enormous. From our viewpoint six feet above the surface the terrestrial view comprised a hundred yards of water and on either side, maybe a meadow some dachas and a row of trees. The rest was sky – often filled with towering cumulus clouds of wonderful shapes and constantly changing heights.

Miles had a curious sense of travelling for ever in space. They had come so far and yet had still 2000 miles to go before they could relax and reach friends again. His note read: *'No one likes to travel all the time; the ideal perhaps is to travel about ten days a month or the equivalent in a longer cycle.'*

Dinner that night was splendid, although the meat they had bought looked and felt as though it had been dissected with a sledge hammer. With Chablis to wash it down, the ragout and rice tasted good.

At eight o'clock they anchored just out of the channel 15 miles short of Kostroma. Milo slept on deck to the whine of mosquitos, an orchestra of croaking frogs and the yeasty smell of bread from a bakery. Sandmartins fluttered in to roost in their holes in the banks as the sun set red and small through gossamer cloud.

The full moon shone on his face for much of the night, something which I was warned about as a young cadet. Old fashioned sailors looked on this as unlucky to the point of being lethal. As he stirred in his blankets at dawn a heron came gliding in to extend his wings before settling to fish in the shallows. There was the pleasant prospect of a short three hour sail downstream the next day to see the famed Romanov stronghold of Kostroma.

99

CHAPTER SEVEN

Four Towns and a Romanov

Part One by WALLACE CLARK
Part Two by MILES CLARK

'Time and tide nae man can tether.'
Robbie Burns

15th July

PART ONE

The relaxed feeling of the last three days turned to acute concern soon after getting under way from the first anchorage after Yaroslavl. The engine made a series of expensive noises, settled down a little, then stopped. Perhaps they were only backfires; but it was the first sign of trouble in seven weeks and came shortly after changing over to Russian diesel. Luckily there was no traffic and a breeze so they continued under sail. Nikolai pumped up more fuel with the plunger on the filter and after a few attempts on the self starter the Sea Panther picked up. At low revs it continued to run with some harsh grumbles but no more explosions.

'Kastroma in a mile,' said Vitali just before noon, pronouncing it with an A in the first syllable, and the emphasis on the last.

It was a hazy morning. The crew were busy getting ready to clean filters and put the last reserve of GND ('Good Norwegian Diesel') from spare cans into the main tank, They also shifted kerosene from its big jerrican into the small red bubble for topping up the cooker, re-filled the outboard engine with petrol, and put water into the main tanks under the bunks from the jerrican deck cargo. This involved adding chlorine tablets to a container for consumption by Milo and Vitali. There was still a division of opinion on this. Nikolai wouldn't drink the water which had the pills in it; Jim liked it with his own supply of American ones.

Ropes were readied for tying up as town houses came into view through the mist and the mouth of the Kostroma River opened on the north bank.

Crowds were still on holiday afloat in a scene like a May Bumps Day at Cambridge. Boats laden with feasting families lay at anchor, singly or rafted in up in fours; other circled aimlessly.

People were washing clothes and themselves, swimming, wind surfing, rowing, and sailing.

Children were jumping off the roof of a rickety wooden hut on stilts at the river's edge. Nikolai explained that it had a bath inside for winter use, with furnace able to keep it clear of ice.

Hundreds of boats not in use rested out of reach of floods on a curious series of wooden scaffolds six feet above the summer water level.

On the Kostroma River's western bank stood a long low white building with a frontage of perhaps 400 feet and a round dove cot at either end. From afar it resembled a huge Irish country house like Mount Congreve. Then one saw that the windows were more like gun ports, small and mostly high up. But the bright red central door was big enough to admit a carriage and four There was a turret above it with green spires and over its right shoulder the five gold onions of a sobor. This was indeed the monastery of St. Ipaty, dating back to 1100. Down went the anchor.

Entering they found that as at Tolga, the front or river wall was part of a hollow square on the lines of a fort. Inside were flower beds amid plots of rough grass – lawn mowing seemed virtually unknown in Russia.

Kostroma is the heartland of the Romanov family which provided many Tsars. In early Tsarist days it counted as the fourth most important religious establishment in Russia but under the Romanovs it became second. Zagorsk only near Moscow was more revered. In 1613 Mikhail Fyodorovich was crowned here. In 1649 St Ipaty was destroyed by fire and later patched up. The gates are called after Katherine II in honour of her visit. All the stone houses and walls are 17th century.

The monastery suffered again under the Communists in a period of destruction between 1957 and 1972. Recently it has been extensively restored. Among the thousands of documents preserved, a few were on display, striking among them a love letter from Tsar Nikolai to Alisa Gessenskyv of August 25th *1823*. It must rank with the letters of Napoleon to Countess Marie Walewska.

Many more Romanov records remain un-catalogued

The crew enjoyed examining the main Trotisky Sobor with its dazzling iconostasis – five rows, each containing six icons mounted in gold as a narthex or backdrop to the church nave.

Perhaps they found the arched colonnades with many murals of fantastic animals and fishes, leviathans, flying snakes and winged dolphins more to sailor's taste. More ominous were vivid pictures of The Damned enduring an ingenious variety of tortures. I will spare readers the details as The Blessed lounging comfortably on snowy clouds seemed happily unaware of the sufferings of their fellows below.

The day had become hot and humid threatening rain. Lightning and thunder rumbled and flickered on the horizon but the rain never came.

Kostroma itself is an attractive market town and as well as St Ipaty's has an open air Museum of Russian Architecture.

To see it Wild Goose shifted east a mile or so. While making fast beside the Yacht Club, Miles noticed that one of the mooring lines seemed very short and got an embarrassed look from Nikolai. Then the story came out – Nikolai, after failing to pull Wild Goose astern off the hulk on which they had gone aground, had waited until a barge was being towed up the river, creating a series of waves which were just enough to lift her. At full revs astern the engine had moved her off, but he'd forgotten about the 15 mm thick stern rope. It got round the propeller. The rope cutter which had saved them from several earlier foul ups had been unable to fully cut it. Nikolai made nine dives in smelly brown water to clear the remains from around the prop shaft. So of course Milo was able to give swift praise for a fine bit of problem solving.

The loss of length was not important as Wild Goose carried almost 100% replacement for all rope in use.

Long haired Hell's Angels in black leather patrolled the streets as Milo looked for the Market. It occupied an extensive low single storey building. There he talked to a woman stall holder.

'I come here only five times a year and that makes enough to pay for my own house. There is a lot of crime with children stealing the fruit and we have to mount a guard over the stands at night. The dacha owners take it in turn.' She insisted on giving them a big bag of strawberries.

A small bearded official Semen Ovchinikov of Kostromaskaya Oblast (ie the County Council) after eyeing Wild Goose from the tow path asked to come on board. His odour preceded him like a warm front on a weather map but he gave much information s about fish farming and the river in general.

'There is one downstream in a reservoir for trout and carp. Essential because in the river where there is no motion everything dries up and dies. This is what is happening to all the Volga. The river is noticeably worse than six years ago but people accept it calmly. The Volga still brings great supplies from south and north. It no longer fulfils the great part it used to play in our history but it is still important. People used to take boats and go up and down the river to Sanatoriums but ferries and tickets are too expensive;

people are strangled by prices now. There is no disposable income. But life is better here than in Moscow. There is no sign of organised crime being on the increase, people are safe to walk home late at night. But the trouble is now that hard honest work does not make money; it is corruption that will ruin the country.'

None of his family had turned back to the Church but he did not resent money being spent on the churches as they help people.

Much of Miles' and Nikolai's day was given up to cleaning three fuel tanks, four filters and numerous fuel lines. The diesel in rusty cans they had bought from the bargee at Cherepovets seemed to be the trouble. They pumped it all out of the starboard tank and dumped it. The good Norwegian diesel, saved for such a situation, took its place; but what would happen when that was finished?.

Here Nikolai's expertise was invaluable. Miles knew little of diesel engines but was doing his best to pick up all he could before the looming crew change when Nikolai would be leaving.

Reassuring was the skill which Nikolai told him could be found at local garages. Spares are so difficult to get that Russian mechanics are much better at fixing defective parts than their western peers.

The Sports Society Boat Club beside them was a wooden building of two storeys built in imperial style in 1966. Now the paint was peeling and several windows smashed. An earth closet stood in grass beside it, surrounded by torn newspaper. More interesting than the club was its Director.

Miles talked at length to barefooted Ivan Gregorivoich. He had no use for shoes even in winter. Picking at his toes he told of the four times his tank had been set on fire in WW11. As mechanic he was lucky to get out of the burning turret each time and survived to serve with occupying forces in Germany as a Captain. Now 75 he looked no more than 60 and told Nikolai of his girl friend of 40 and active sex life. Swam twice a day in the river, even in winter. His recipe for long life is to starve himself twice a week, eating nothing all day.

Nikolai stayed up to fish most of the night under the full moon with this man of incredible activity. They caught catfish (som) with long whiskers, squeaking as they were landed. This is a famous fishing place and the record for catfish is 32 lbs. Everything in Russia is huge.

Supper was cheese omelettes. A peaceful night alongside followed, guarded by relaxed river policemen who patrolled with collars slackened and hats pushed onto the back of their heads.

Wild Goose motored reluctantly away from the easy going atmosphere of Kostroma Boat Club and headed towards the fuel dock. Horrors! The engine suddenly faltered, then stopped just as yesterday. It failed to restart. They anchored at once took off the covers, got out the tools, transferred fuel and cleaned filters once more. She kicked into life. Better to keep her going, now so they cut out the fuel stop and headed on for Plyoss. The engine had plenty of power but was grinding horribly.

Milo managed to get Watermota who had supplied the engine on the radio and let them listen The friendly voice of John Potter, the manager, said it was almost certainly just bad fuel.

'Very unlikely to let you down. Keep the revs low. If she stops again you could fit the spare fuel pump we sent with you.' Relief! Proceed at 1,000 revs which meant 4 knots instead of five and a half but as they say in Ireland, 'Slow and aisy goes a long way in a day.'

The river widened into a long stretch of open water.

Waterfront houses, artificial beaches packed with bathers, but nary a waterside restaurant or pub. … Further east of Kostroma the banks turned again into rich pasture, amid stands of tall birch and alder with good old fashioned hay stooks among the trees. The wind was ahead today and wavelets reflected the sunlight in eye blinding fires of glass.

A Meteor boat with its bow pushed up on a strip of sand disgorged many pairs of passengers. 'Might get a cool coke if we stopped', said Vitali. A run ashore and a brush with the natives, as Captain Marriot might have put it, sounded a good idea. Short walks indicated a great deal of serious lovemaking going on in the woods. Nikolai explained that this was due to the lack of privacy at home; a large boom in babies could be expected each year nine months after the start of summer.

As they approached Plyoss the river broadened out. There were Jon boats all around. Some had wives with them in the boat and they seemed slower than elsewhere to respond to waves. This was dacha, izba and tent country, the antithesis of big city living. Shipping seemed much slacker, not one in 20 miles, but many villages. They were almost always in sight of each other, emphasising the interdependence of riversiders – yet each village having a complete life and pride of its own.

The thickets on the east bank looked freshly swamped as though the water level had only recently risen. In fact the dam has been in place for a decade. The trees can live in many cases for twenty years with roots well submerged, and remain a lot longer as dead stumps. The feeling of being beset by moribund trees and the lack of houses or life in the swamps among them seemed to breed in the crew a sort of river mentality, especially at Wild Goose's slower pace. When a wee breeze came up astern and the engine was stopped as the sail began to draw, the silence was utter. The Sea

Panther started at once afterwards and it seemed that the fuel trouble had abated. One plane was heard that day, almost an event in itself. Cloudy again, big cumulus, isolated with ill defined edges, seeming to drift away into nothing. One could hardly believe they could look so random and beautiful.

There was an hour-long golden sunset but the disc never quite makes it to the horizon without being swallowed up in haze or smog.

Now on the right bank they suddenly came on sophisticated camping, a red flag to mark the site, towels spread out under the trees, fish drying racks, plastic sheeting, table, chairs in front of wooden huts, rowing boats pulled up on the sandy beach below.

Questions came again, 'At kuda?'. 'Where are you from?', the sailors way of saying, 'Who are you?' Milo, a born mimic, could now reply 'From White to Black' in passable Russian.

Wild Goose made an impression everywhere as Nikolai remarked because of her beauty and strong contrast to any other ships on the river. They tied up that night in shallow water near the floating Meteor dock at Plyoss. Immediately large black hornets started buzzing dangerously around.

PLYOSS, THE VILLAGE OF ARTISTS

Plyoss is a village famed for its beauty. It is well situated, its many curious and decorative buildings screened from the river by forest trees on steeply rising slopes. In old days it was guarded by an earthen fort of which traces can still be seen on the hill top above. Now the risk is no longer from nomad raiders but instead from too many visiting tourist ships. A walk along the towpath east of the ferry disclosed a lagoon with some shreds of the old life. Boats are pulled up there including some of the old Volga two man rowing skiffs, bottom up and apparently abandoned. They had pleasing lines and raised spoon bows and sterns but are out of use now as they cannot readily take an outboard. 'I'd love to have taken one home', Miles thought, 'but it would be too long to sit on deck, even if we swapped one for our wee punt'.

Plyoss is the home of artists and there is a fine gallery. It shows superb water colours by Levitan and Baksheev – dreamy, and rather sad, with scenes that are mainly misty.

Diesel was more in the crew's mind than art. But the Filling Station was closed. At least when Nikolai approached Rita the lady attendant refused him.

'Diesel is not sold; private petrol only; you have to get state cards for diesel.'

Nikolai, 'Please: we need some.'

Rita, 'I can't. We don't sell it to people who have no cards.'

Nikolai, 'I am a driver. I've been a driver for many years. Now I own a garage and I know it is possible; we are four yachtsmen and we got bad fuel in Cherepovets. If we cannot buy it here we do not know what to do.'

Rita; 'I don't want to loose my job for your 60 litres.'

Nikolai, 'If they fire you, I will get you a good position in Moscow'.

A car and bike turned up. She wouldn't deal with others watching. Nikolai looked steadily into her eyes, used all his charm and said, 'I promise to pay you well for your risk.'

Rita: 'It is very strange for me to sell diesel fuel. But you can have some for 15 roubles. The official price is six but nobody sells it at that.'

Game, set and match!

Wandering along the rough dirt streets they admired buildings smarter than any seen in two and a half months travel. Much of the woodwork was the decorative reesba fretwork so popular on old Russian houses, bare wood with all the quality of age.

Jim said, 'I'd give everyone five gallons of paint, a thousand dollars and their own house. And tell them to get on with it.'

Night Clubbing

Back at the pontoon they were invited into a small bar at the stern of a Meteor. At a table sat a clean shaven man with hair black as a sloe and brown eyes that danced like eddies in a peat stream. He introduced himself as Mark Ivanovo, a marketing manager and his friend as Lena, a slim blonde. She was an advertising executive from Moscow who was 'resting'.

'You can get here lots of hard currency food here,' they chorused, 'yoplait, yoghurt, smoked sausage, Campari and orange juice. We'll be drinking all night.'

Mark came from Ivanovo, after which he was named, famous for producing top quality flax for making linen. Asked about whether Communism had gone for good, he replied with enthusiasm. 'Yes. It won't come back, not in its old time form. I believe in the future of Russia. It will be a great country. It's a great country now! Of course we have some problems with politics and the situation of the rouble but I believe Russia is the unique country of the world and we have very great people and if they have more rights and more knowledge about how to make business, how to live and I think they will get it soon, we will be the greatest trading country in the world. I believe in this personally.

'For old people it is simple to wish to live as they lived. They had very little knowledge of outside life, and now they may compare with how the western countries live and how Westerners have their own ships and how they are able to travel round the world. But such a life is more complex and this to the old people is some problem. Some people would like things to go back the way they were. The majority of younger people of my generation have chosen the road the country is now taking. Older people prefer their old life which was very simple when they had their earnings and products at low prices. Now of course it is a time for the producer and not the consumer.'

Nikolai invited them on board Wild Goose. Lena brought a bottle of Algerian wine and insisted that Milo boil it with sugar. He took his eye of it for a second. Over it frothed and flames leapt three feet high over the whole stove. Initial alarm! … But the well placed fire blanket had it out in seconds.

'Algerian red wine, plus sugar equals fire', says the log. 'Poor man's liqueur we call it and it's good to drink', said Lena unabashed.

'This boat is like a museum', said Mark 'I'd like to come sailing with you'. But it didn't ring true So many pass that compliment and only the adventurous mean it. Also alongside was the Muscovskiy, a ship which served as a river ferry by day and a disco by night. By 1145 the downstairs bar was unlocked and flickering lights began to cast shadows along the deck. There was Bulgarian brandy on offer, white wine and berry juice, chocolates and eclairs. At 1215 a pair of girls arrived and sat down expectantly Olga looked as if she had stepped out of a Laura Ashley catalogue, Alice band, white blouse, blue stretch belt, tiny waist and flouncy skirt. Olga was in plain low-cut black. There was dancing upstairs all evening. Around the walls were posters about how to get sex calls from Germany and Denmark. Behind the bar a girl wrapped herself round a huge Russian engineer. The Wild Geese found good company and danced till the stars came down with the rafters.

Mark was eager for marketing ideas and told Miles to look out for a Romanov yacht next day.

Jim meanwhile good naturedly had stayed on board to make sure Wild Goose was safe. The rest of the crew got to bed at five and pulled themselves together after two hours sleep for breakfast. There was green algae and yellow scum in whorls between Wild Goose and the bank of the river, a sickly sight for overhung eyes.

It was a damp monochrome morning with slanting shafts of light where the sun filtered through the treetops.

An artist set up his easel on the tow path, remarking that it was a day of interesting contrasts. 'But the scenery is not entirely the work of the Lord,' he remarked. 'Smog can add to surroundings by adding a misty effect.'

He was an optimist. In minutes came the first rain for ten days and he scuttled off, swearing, 'Koorva' at the sky.

The engine grumbled from the start but they had got used to it now and didn't think she was going to stop every minute.

There was red Devonian sandstone on the right bank and open prairie rising away from the river.

PART TWO

BY MILES

THE ROVING ROMANOVS

'I expected to see the wagon trains rollin', rollin', as in the old Wild West songs. Never a fence or hedge. Havn't seen one in weeks other than around cottage gardens. Vitali singing a muppet tune. Lots of traffic on the river today and smell of lime off the land. Passed through the town of Kineshima at lunchtime. A new bridge being built. Everything looking grey and wet and the town a monument to red brick indicating the lack of building stone. Visibility right down in the heavy rain and the land a uniform grey. Piers seemed out of place as they appeared through the mist to be floating in from another world.

For the first time now the Volga banks are like the shores of two different rivers. The left or north bank open prairie with lone trees among villages standing on small shelves. The right bank high with fir trees. Sense of endlessness. You need only to look at a map of the old Soviet to see that what a tiny part of the whole is European. We're cutting across the bottom left hand corner which included the whole of Russia itself. The ex-Satellite States stretch 3000 miles east of where we'll be on this trip.

Air shudders with gunfire in the afternoon; were relieved to learn from a fisherman that it was from an artillery range. A twin tailed fighter aircraft came roaring down the river with a kind of high pitched scoring sound, turned towards us and banked away to the south.

And so we came to Yuryevets. The first sign of it was a beautiful white sobor gleaming on a grey autumnal type morning. Polished stainless steel domes and cupolas, beside a white tower in five diminishing square segments. Aspect spoiled by iron ladders up the sides. The other churches around seemed to be in total disrepair. High on a hill above the town a wooden church was being re-roofed.

Boathouses extend along the shore so close you couldn't walk between them. The city stands on a steep escarpment thickly wooded with scrub and small trees. Attractive houses set among them look out on a low wooded island called. Guess what?! Gorky. That's the commonest feature name on the river, like Seal Island in The West Highlands.

Imagine the realtors spiel. ...

'Attractive period wooden house recently renovated to include genuine earth closet'.

The scarp is on the inner bend of the river where it turns at right angles to run south. We look into a mini harbour but it's small and crowded. Anchor half a mile on where a steep hillside is cut off as with a knife, just beyond a coal dock. Almost the sense of being on a sea coast again because with the meeting of waters here, as the River Unzha comes in from the north east, the Volga is five miles wide.

We had wind and sheet lightning that night. I hung a wire over the side in approved fashion to act as a conductor in case it struck our mast but the flashes were far off.

It was 18th July now, a grey Saturday with a warm autumnal feel in air which bore phosphorous smells of industry mingled with wood smoke. Nikolai plunged off the bow for an early morning swim.

Scudding south all day into a featureless wall of grey bleak landscape. About 1640 tall white sails on the horizon caught the lookout's eye – a yacht tacking towards us against a tin forest of smoke stacks.

As they drew alongside us there was a great hail.

'We are private yacht; we have good meat and French wine; you are very welcome to Russia; Come and meet us'.

This was Betelguese, a white-hulled staysail schooner, a little bigger than Wild Goose, with blue deck, fine sheer, clipper bow, and steeved up bowsprit. By far the most interesting yacht we'd seen so far in Russian waters. A silk Russian flag flew at her stern, amid neat orange life rings. A figure in Hawaii trousers and golfer's white cap was talking as excitedly as if Wild Goose was a spacecraft from Mars. Beside him a wife in pink tracksuit, and son in jeans were busy with a video camera.

Captain Vadim Romanov's last shouted remark was , 'You will be sorry if you miss us, Captain!'

So of course we agreed to sail in company and berth alongside at Gorodets. The meeting was to brighten what had been a long and dull day.

'Come on board , gentlemen. I am crazy boy. Maybe you have heard something stupid about our country. All Europeans now, we

109

are no different. My wife is Elvira My son is Roman Romanov. I want he give his son this name also – Roman Romanovich Romanov. I have an account in Moscow International Bank.' Vadim was a tall lean man in mid-thirties with clean cut western features. He might have been taken for a professional golfer.

Betelgeuse's equipment was simple but effective for a lightly rigged 35 footer. The 12 HP engine shown us with pride looked a monster, weighing I should think almost half a ton; the bilges were full of oil. (But on that count Wild Goose can't talk).

The entertainment was five star.

Iced champagne was produced and conversation flowed. Vadim was 37 and had been born in Kostroma, on the banks of the Volga. Took a Doctorate in textiles and became a lecturer. Then a State owned company asked if he wanted to join in a private venture. There was a three million pound input from the West: the company was designed for 80% export, with 2,500 workers. He showed me his card,

Vice President of the Danish/Russian Joint Venture

Joint Stock Company.

Economic and Foreign Relations Direction.

'The company is the biggest Russian specialist in the linen industry. I deal with James Mackie (old friends of Milo's family business) from North Ireland. Kostroma is centre of Romanov family. My ancestors are also from Kostroma and we have the direct blood of the Tsars. Today we stopped at Chikalofsk, where a famous Russian flyer is celebrated. There is a special museum and a big hangar, also his private plane and some of the planes which he had during the War. We are lucky to have met today because I have only about two weeks maximum holiday. Most of my time I am in Europe travelling. My wife it not so happy because I am a very big traveller. Linen and textiles is a difficult business.' (Dad might have chorused, 'You can say that again!'). Ham, steak and new potatoes appeared on the table, followed by sweet biscuits, chocolate, sardines.

More champagne popped. ... Facts come tumbling forth as if spat from a Tommy gun.

'Only on TV are people told that Russia is hungry. It is crazy, don't believe it. Please be at home, it is very nice to meet you because it is so unexpected. You were running down wind and we were tacking and we wonder why the boat has such a funny name. I say to my wife, perhaps someone has done a good journey but I do not imagine you are from England. You must drink to our meeting and we must drink to our friendship, to our relations, to our joint adventure.'

Miles tried to change the subject, 'Tell me about this beautiful

110

ship'. 'She was completed six years ago by one very old man who copied it from another boat. It took him nine years to build; he used the skeleton of the old boat. She is a good sea boat. For me it is not so difficult to be sure of this because she is a typical sea boat. She is 12 metres long, 14 including the bowsprit. The whole interior has been made by hand. Sometimes I am crazy, I go over the Border each two weeks: some Russians bring back a television set but I bring back a chemical toilet for my yacht.' 'For what?' 'I say for my boat.' My wife says, 'You are crazy boy, you should bring a washing machine or a dress or something like that'.

I lectured for ten years and when things began to change economically took a share in the Russian/Danish company. Two factories in Russia produce Novorsibirsk looms, but I buy Swiss, Sulzer, which are much better.

Then the conversation turned to the Volga 'I was born when the river was just starting to be dammed. my house looked out on it. But the main trouble is that plants give dirties to the water. It is crazy but we haven't enough cleaning system and in the future of course it will be a big ecological problem. Now we have organised a special committee of cleaning the Volga.

Walking rather slowly and steadily, we returned from the bare inside of the day sailer Betelguese to the jam-packed interior of Wild Goose. Our minds full of Vadim, his food, wine and aspirations.

Another climactic point in the voyage lay just ahead.

Meteor Ferry

CHAPTER EIGHT

Gorky for a Crew Change

By WALLACE, *MILES*, GALINA and ARKADY

'High the domes of Gorky gleam
Islanded in Volga's stream'
With apologies to AE Housman

Miles woke rubbing his eyes on a misty Gorodets morning. The
Romanov interlude seemed a bit like a dream; but Betelgeuse,*
lying quiet and crewless, across the basin, and a tight feeling
behind his eyeballs confirmed that the evening had been real and a
good one. In retrospect it reminded him of the yachtie in the Scott
Fitzgerald novel who claimed to have had a party so wild and successful that 'I had to sink my boat to get rid of my friends'.

'We lay in until nearly ten o'clock before slipping our lines from
Gorodets Yacht Club and skirting past tawdry triumphalist towers.
All this was lost to view as we entered a cavernous lock below a
concrete bridge. Grey people and grey cars were passing over it,
under a sky the colour of smoke. As the water gurgled and fell, grey
backed seagulls and grey crows feasted on fish trapped on the sill,
enjoying a squabble with some like-minded grey pigeons.

'The whole mis-en-scene was monument to greyness. For a
moment I longed for the tinselly brightness of India where every
vehicle, post and poster is in screaming technicolour. This preva-
lent monochrome greyness, must be a principal reason why bright
church interiors and icons are so much prized.

'The cost of filling and emptying a lock in terms of power and
lost water is so great that it is very rare for small craft to be
allowed to use one solo. Now we shared with a curious "com-
poundable" craft, with a bow designed to fit by a huge copulative
joint into an aperture in the stern of an engine-less craft as big as
herself. At close quarters I was not quite sure at what moment the

---

*In 1998 Vadim is reported to have parted company with his earlier Danish
associates but to be living mainly in Denmark and trading successfully.

112

hinge might suddenly jack-knife and swat Wild Goose against the stone wall. Notice **Photography Prohibited**. *Jim proceeds unabashed.*

'As we emerged into the Cheboksary Reservoir a grey steel tanker Volga-Don 237 lay in a floating dry dock beside the channel. This gave a rare chance to see her lines, surprisingly sweet for such a long hull, and her sharp forefoot. Her bridge and accommodation was right aft and her beam must have been carefully calculated to give just three foot clearance on either side in a lock. A heavy wooden rubbing strake, scarred and shredded, told of contacts of un-gentle kinds. Her carrying capacity is a colossal 10,000 tons, usually of loose grain.*

The variety of Volga shipping is endless. All ships were state-owned until very recently but this has not inhibited the production of many fine designs.

River history reveals extraordinary past vessels with names which might come from the Hunting of the Snark.

Chaika (meaning seagull) the small open double enders of the Cossacks; Duschanik, Baidarka, and Barka were freighters towed by the celebrated Volga Boatmen 300,000 strong struggling along the towpaths before the day of steam. Kolmenka and Rechievahs had capstans driven by teams of horses to haul themselves upstream. Others to be seen were the Nolik, Gusyarna, Touer, Belyarna, Pashalik and Cabestan.

Nowadays more mundanely the traffic consists of chunky steel Volga Balts and Nefts, Dons with numbers instead of names, Amur container ships and many specialists like Rekamore river-sea motorships. They are distinguished at once as ocean-going by life rafts slung along the rail; the sort of craft you see in Port of London, Dakar or Copenhagen.

Of multi-deck cruise ships there are twenty for Intourists and ten for Russians.

'For details you should read the well illustrated *Russia's River Shipping*. (Roshrechflot, Moscow 1991). Cruise ships have it in their bookshops.

CRISIS

There was a very fast current below the Barrage as the river tightened in to its narrowest and shallowest. It does this at the upper end of each Reservoir

Nikolai was watching narrow-eyed a Volga Neft approaching from a bend less than half a mile ahead, her deck covered in pipes like intestines. Heavy anchors projected menacingly from her bow, looking as if rusted in position. In two minutes he would be meeting her. A stentorian Honk!! ... from astern drew his attention to a battered tanker about to force him into mid channel by over-taking on the inside from the port quarter He edged over starboard, and realised the two big ships were going to pass each other and Wild Goose on opposite courses at the same moment. There was just room to get through in midstream. Then a dredger suddenly sheered out from the south bank forcing the oncoming Volga Neft further out to the middle. Four ships converging at one point! It was Nikolai's moment.

Miles just had time to yell. 'Fenders out at the R R R ush!!', and dive for a bearing off spar. The sphincter of one crewman gave way, as suddenly Wild Goose was hedged in between walls of patchy rivet-studded steel, not more than twenty five feet apart. They were passing at a relative speed of over thirty knots. For what seemed a long minute Wild Goose seemed to stand still, as Nikolai wrestled with the tiller.

Contact with the tanker followed by smashed spreaders or broken mast seemed inevitable. She was 'flying light' with her tanks empty, her helmsman finding her hard to keep straight. The upper blades of her great propeller were threshing white water, showing a smother of brown foam as high as our heads. Luckily the revs were in the right direction and it was the wash that threw Wild Goose clear.

The river banks re-appeared and in a flash the moment critique was over. Nikolai gave a nervous laugh. 'You see; anything is pos-sible for a good Bolshevik!'. Miles licked his dry lips, and was going to suggest a dram to steady the nerves. But not yet. Round the bend the current was speeded up by a sudden descent into a woody hollow as though the river had fallen through a crack in the landscape The cry from the bow at the lower end was, 'Ware sand-banks!'. Some showed camel-colour on the surface, others loomed pale just underneath; the most dangerous ones lay too deep to be seen but lurking to catch our keel.

These were the remains of the pericartes or shallows we'd read about, the curse of navigators in pre-Barrage days. They'd been given chart corrections at the lock but were they fully up to date?

'Bash on regardless', says Vitali. 'Nishevo' in Russian. But Miles stood on the bow, scanning the surface, as old river hands do, for a change in the pattern of ripples, a twisting eddy that might warn of a shallow or the riffle that showed where the current ran faster.

'Port a bit'. 'Midships'. 'Hard a starboard! and so on, until at last they seemed to be clear.

They were at least luckier than passengers 150 years ago.

A traveller's account entitled *Mother Russia* gives an idea of the hazards.

'In 1850 there were a number of steamers on the river owned by the Volga Steam Navigation Company. Their tug Samson was taking passengers eastwards. Of all the rivers of Europe there is probably none so uncertain and difficult in navigation as the Volga.

'Seldom very deep, the channel is in many places devious and, as the bed is composed of loose sand, ever changing. Barges or steamers are constantly running aground and some are generally to be seen embedded. The first barge we were to tow, heavily laden with Siberian iron and western manufacturers for Astrakhan, was waiting at the side of the river. Having taken her in tow we proceeded until a sudden jolt startled us and we discovered that our vessel was hard and fast on a sand bank. The barge, which had considerable way on, should have dropped its anchor but failed to do so. It scraped rapidly past us, the tow rope, getting foul, swept over our deck and carrying away some of the funnel stays amid much confusion. It is a great danger to unwary loungers on deck when such occurrences take place. A mere touch from the end of the tow rope as it sweeps along will certainly break a leg and the whole thing is so sudden that occasionally there is great difficulty in getting out of the way.

'At last our boat floated off but only to drop anchor once more and wait for the engineer who had gone ashore. ... While gazing wistfully down the stream I was once more aroused by a sudden crash and found that another barge had fairly run into us, toppling over and staving the quantity of casks she had on board and very nearly breaking our rudder. We had to stuff flax tow into a large hole in the barges side. After having progressed 14 versts we anchored for the night. As the channels are so intricate it is out of the question to proceed after dark. There is a curious rule that no lights were allowed on board the craft after dark. Perhaps this was to avoid the risk of fire.

'Notwithstanding the difficulties there are upwards of 30 steamers plying on the river.

'They stop frequently at wood stations in which are piled large stacks of birch logs. Loading wood to fire the boiler was an occupation which usually occupied six or seven hours, to the shouts of shrill laughter from the bare-legged maidens who were carrying the faggots on board.

'The melodious chant of boatman in the evening floated across the waters, as with a measured tramp they warped their vessels up to their anchors. The most curious type of vessel known as a Rechievah contains some 300 tonnes of grain. It is propelled by 80 men or in some cases horses, working a turntable on deck. Seven or eight boats are lashed one behind the other to the barge which contains the horses, and the whole looks like some gigantic river monster working its way up the stream. On the deck of the leading barge a covered stage is erected which serves as stables to as many as 150 horses and they work the huge capstan by which the boat is warped and round which they perambulate as in a threshing machine. Boats are continually employed carrying anchors ahead and sounding the channels. With this cumbersome contrivance however not more than 20 versts are made a day and the voyage to Rybinsk occupies six months. The whole convoy carries some 5000 tonnes and extends to some half a mile. Now these horse driven barges are finding it very difficult to compete with the steamers.

'They were at a distance a pleasing object with elaborately carved triangular sterns, spacious decks that projected over each bow in a stage, and a pedestal painted and decorated with flags and erected. Here six feet above deck stood a booted and sheep-skinned figure leaning over a tiller almost 40 feet long and able from his elevation to see how he could most easily run into everything that came in his way, much to the detriment of a huge pair of eyes that were often painted on the square bow. They probably proved as much use as those of anybody on board. One enormous square sail was the additional propelling force for when the wind served.'

Once out of the area of pericartes Miles found it a relief to have hills on which to rest the eye after weeks of dreary flat level. Their appearance on the south bank marked the approach to the third city of Russia. This still appeared on our Air Map as Gorky, the name given by Stalin as a reward for support by the greatest of Communist writers before he died in 1936. The city has now officially reverted to its more euphonic original name – Nizhny (pronounced softly as neeshny) Novgorod. New Novgorod that is, the prefix in deference to old Novgorod, an even more ancient trading town 50 miles south-east of St Petersburg.

Nizhny on account of its array of submarine, tank and fighter factories was prohibited to all foreigners until 1991. Gorky still seemed to be the name in common use.

The city has grown outwards from Woodpecker Hill, a great defendable scarp on the right bank overlooking the junction between the Oka and Volga rivers.

The hill is crowned with an enceint of castellated walls and rectangular towers, a strong red brick kremlin. The crest beside it is lined in buildings of white, almost classical style. The water front, the first planned one we have seen, is red brick Admiralty with long rows of white columns, giving a sense of solidity But main impression from the river is of contrast – abandoned incomplete buildings with projecting rusty iron spaghetti – smudged concrete walls hung with tendrils of disintegrating motor tyre fenders fester below cool pyramids of pale poplars among modern glass windowed office blocks and ancient churches.

Wild Goose tied up at a wooden Tsarist style Yacht Club on the Oka River at Roosa. The building looked even more run down than the last one at Gorodets. Expecting to be met by Arkadi, the crew were dismayed to be told there were four other Yacht Clubs in the vast city. Arkady was a man with a vital role – he was to take over as skipper from his friend Nikolai. No sign or message.

Vitali talked to the crew of a modern yacht beside us. She had the tasteless lines now favoured, for speed, by designers all over Europe. Her bow silhouette was like a Stanley knife blade, her deckline straight with none of the lovely curved sheer of older champions. Her mast was of taperless alloy. A race winner no doubt but as West Country fishermen used to say that an ugly yacht is no more interesting than an ugly woman, no matter how fast she may be. Our large neighbour was owned by a Trade Union and had ten topless Russians on board. 'Very small spik English', said the skipper. He hadn't seen anyone looking for us.

Then a man of about 40 appeared in dark horn-rimmed spectacles under a white cap with a neatly trimmed moustache, wearing a silver watch and a black T-shirt inscribed Challengers of Highway 750.

'Call me Arkardy,' he said with the long Russian A. When asked how he had made contact, he said, 'Miles, there is never any problem in Russia. No trouble locating you; news of the voyage has stretched down the Volga; everyone knows there is a British yacht on the river'.

Approval grew as he produced fresh music – an HMV recorder and cassettes, as well as a bottle of liqueur vodka from his brief case. A resourceful lad clearly but with limited English, and not much of a mechanic. The change has come just when Nikolai's skill with the engine will be most missed.

The bad news he brought was of worsening civil war in Georgia and many civilian casualties.Vitali had been in an understandable state of worry for the last few days as his family were on holiday in what appeared to be the war Zone. Then Galina, from the Moscow Explorers Club, walked onto the pontoon with several suitcases. She had met Milo the previous April and formed a picture of Wild Goose as a spacious 60 footer so she had brought her eleven year old daughter Anna to share the expected stateroom.

A brunette of acute intelligence and winning manner, daughter of an Artillery Colonel, she would have been welcome by herself at any time. Now her arrival was both a pleasant surprise and a problem. Jim, never one to miss an opportunity, photographed the greeting at a range of about ten inches.

The first difficulty came when she revealed that Dimitry Schparo, her boss in the Moscow Explorers Club, knew nothing about her being here. When it had been suggested in the past that she join Wild Goose he had objected. The second headache for Milo was the question of room for Anna.

At the same time Vitali announced that he was definitely jumping ship. He felt compelled to go and see to his family's safety but promised to be back as soon as possible. Miles however observed that his packing was so thorough that a return looked far from certain. His going would leave the crew minus an interpreter

Bruce, having foreseen the near impossibility of voyaging without one, had encouraged Galina to make the rail journey to join for as long as she could manage, a week at most.

A fairly heated discussion ensued. Miles could not above all afford to fall out with Dimitry who had organised the whole trip and would be fixing the exit from Russia in another six weeks time. For once he felt nonplussed. Galina he needed, but no way could he fit a child on board. His trained and balanced crew was about to disintegrate, but 'Skippers cannot cry.'

It would have been disastrous for crew morale to reveal the depths of frustration he felt.

All he could do was kick for touch.

So an outwardly calm Miles made the new chums welcome and said the decision as to whether Galina and Anna could stay would have to solved in the evening.

Meanwhile Nizhny awaited exploration.

Galina recalled her arrival as follows:

> 'On Tuesday July 21st, the boiling humid day when my eleven year old daughter Anna and I arrived at the yacht club where Wild Goose was moored, I was taking aback by several things. First of all by the boat herself, I had imagined something much larger and smarter, that is one of the reasons I had no hesitation of bringing Anna along but when I saw Wild Goose I soon realised she was something special, probably the best sort of boat for the Russian roundabout: she was beautifully made, unpretentious, perfectly adapted for long distance cruising though not of course for racing and designed to last for ever. I soon saw that compared with glistening fibre glass palace boats an old one like Wild Goose would attract more of the right sort of interest, friendly curiosity of ordinary people and less of the wrong sort of greedy stares from potential thieves or corrupt bureaucrats.
>
> 'My old shipmate Nikolai was heading back to Moscow rather to my disappointment because I always thought he was an outstandingly competent and attractive person. In fact I was quietly proud of

myself for having introduced him to Miles on that freezing winters day six months earlier.

'But the man who took Nikolai's place on Wild Goose was also a very good sailor, called Arkady Gershuni. Just turned forty, he was bald and ruddy with a neat silver moustache and a calm reassuring manner. He was not so much of a of showman as Nikolai and knew less about engines but was the more experienced sailor and more senior in the Moscow Yacht Club. Like any two men who have sailed together Arkady and Nikolai had plenty of private jokes, almost a secret language in which they used to have their giggles. For example Arkady once said to me with Nikolai listening, "You know one of the best things in life is watching a real professional at work, the skill, the concentration, the sense of timing, the attention to every detail and nuance", slightly puzzled I asked as I was obviously supposed to, "You mean watching a boat builder or a wheel wright or a sculptor". "No", said Arkady in his absolutely dead pan way, "I mean Nikolai talking to a woman". That was typical of Arkady's quiet humour.

'For me the prospect of a weeks sailing with him, Miles and an unknown American to Kazan in the Tatar Republic was an intriguing one.

'All this was going on in my mind as I was introduced to Jim who lent a note of drama to the reunion by photographing furiously as though we were the Royal Family. Weighted down by his astonishing array of cameras "Jeem", as I called him, struck me as a screaming caricature of the American spy I had been taught to watch out for during my Soviet school days. He was one of the first real live Americans I had encountered at close quarters and I looked forward to working out what made him tick. Nikolai before he left drew me aside and explained to me that Jim was a dedicated photographer who had been given some very specific tasks to fulfil by his magazine. "You mean he wants to see ancient monuments, beauty spots, churches". "No, not exactly", said Nikolai "His top priority is to find the most graphical illustrations of our pollution problem, dirty streams, pipes in the wrong places, chimneys belching out fumes. He will be eternally grateful if you can find him a really stinking piece of filth".

'But the biggest surprise to me was the extraordinary change in the appearance and manner of Miles. When we had met the previous winter in Shparo's office he struck me as an easy going homely sort of fellow, a pound or two overweight and slightly awkward and diffident as he made his way round a city which was obviously completely new to him. By now he had turned into a real sea wolf with a big straggling beard, thin as a rake. His whole bearing was different, he was fine – drawn, taut, sharply focused, feverishly intent on organising everything, down to the last detail and maximising the chances of a successful trip. We were getting near the half way point; that's when sometimes, as Miles joked, things can get 'laxative'. The period when the skipper might loose his grip and take things too easy; just the time when something serious might go wrong: a broken mast, a serious engine fault, a row with a lock keeper or some other form of bureaucrat could still destroy all the progress that had been made.

'"I am afraid there simply isn't room for your daughter, I don't know how you ever imagined there would be", Miles told me rather sternly. Actually I didn't see the problem; Anna and I could have kipped on the deck pretty well where ever we dropped.

'My aim was to make life easier for Miles and not harder so I agreed to find some friends who could take care of Anna. To get through life in Russia you need friends in as many different places as possible with whom you could exchange big favours.

'And so to see the great dirty bustling metropolis of Niznhy Novgorod. A crossroads in our waterway system. The city was also one of the turning points in Wild Goose's journey through Russia. began. My arrival was only one part of a bigger change of crew which seemed to alter the whole atmosphere on the boat. As a yachtie of some experience I hoped I could offer Miles skills in sailing and radio communications as well as translating.

'Jim was delighted by the hotel room he had found. He spent half a day snapping the house where our greatest dissident Andrei Sakharov was confined. Nizhny was used by the Soviets as a place of exile where contact with westerners could be easily prevented.

'I told Miles and Jim how for centuries Nizhni had been a bustling commercial centre, none too clean or graceful but always a hive of trading and craftsmanship. Even religious buildings like the Church of the Nativity built by the Stroganov family of merchant adventurers seemed to say more about the ostentatious piety than mysticism. Since being opened to visitors the city has been doing its best to revive its old mercantile traditions. So far it still came over as a stolid no-nonsense fortress town, well symbolised by its giant Kremlin overlooking the Volga.

'We went for lunch to a popular Kentucky fried chicken joint called the Gardinia run by a dark mustachioed Palestinian American called Victor Khoury and his wife Mary who had been a commodity broker in Houston, Texas. There were posters of Tina Turner, New Orleans and of Arab whaling. "People here are super nice, super naive and super hospitable", Mary chirped up. "I love the Russian people, I want to give them everything". Not all that naïve was my reaction but the Gardinia was clearly most successful.

Miles and his crew had emerged from rural days afloat to a

sweltering urban whirl. The city was in shorts. Since taxis are non-existent Galina adopted the standard practice of hailing a passing private car. Its owner agreed at once to drive us around and a fee was fixed. The rusty grey Lada reeked of the gas by which it was powered. Miles felt a little dizzy, whether from this or the strangeness of moving faster than five mph for the first time in weeks. They viewed the hideous mile long facade of Kruschov worker flats which dominate the modern part of the city, a concrete cliff of ten storey identical apartments. Then he dodged through four lane traffic to the famous iconostasis in The Church of the Nativity at the foot of a steep hill by the river. The edifice was a whited sepulchre, turned inside out. Battered and unkempt on the outside but of ageless dimly lit beauty within. The stacked rows of icons had the form, colour and patina to be of intense attraction, a truly unforgettable sight.

From the hilltop outside the thin red brick Kremlin walls the crew had a view of 40 miles or more. In the foreground a fascinating sweep of curving river with tugs pushing giant log rafts, in front of scattered green meadows. Beyond the smoke of villages arose from flat land overlaid with a reticulation of dark woods.

To the north in haze stretched the dark shadow of unbroken Taiga – It was an awesome thought that the you could travel from here for 500 miles north to the edge of the Arctic tundra. without leaving the shade of a tree and by dint of constant bushwhacking.

Below left the low sandy point showed between Oka and Volga where for hundreds of years the Makary Fair, the greatest market on the whole river system, was held for weeks every summer.

Elizabeth Hapgood, an American traveller in 1895, wrote as follows:

'On arrival we were nearly torn to pieces by isvoschicks or droskyboys. The one we picked did his best to jolt us to pieces before arriving at the hotel.

'At the Fair a swarm of human beings seemed to have hived.. Their dwellings, aquatic and terrestrial, cover both land and water for a considerable distance. Immediately below us was a crowded bridge of boats. On the tops of hundreds of masts on each side of it fluttered vanes and gay coloured flags. Warehouses stood beside temporary wharves abuzz with business-like steamers and loaded barges. On the low flat beyond 150,000 people crowded into the smallest possible place, to be visited by upwards of 300,000 would buyers and sightseers.

'The variety of goods exceeds that to be seen elsewhere as there are so many advantages to counter the expense of transport. Tea from China, furs from Siberia silks and gold ornaments from

Constantinople, icons, accordions, brassware from Teheran, bayo-
nets and bedsteads from Birmingham, Leatherware from Bokhara,
Nordic figureheads. Not to forget sloe-eyed courtesans from Syria
and gigolos from God know where.'

(RUSSIAN RAMBLES, Elizabeth Hapgood 1895.)

Exploring among the grass and trees within the Kremlin walls
Miles' soldierly spirit rose at an array of Novgorod's planes, fighting vehicles. and guns. The coarsely made but war-winning T34
tanks were the prize exhibit.

The designers had not done so well on the Gentleman's Toilet a
duckboard an inch deep urine led to a row of holes piled in steam-
ing excrement. A look from the door was enough and luckily thre
were plenty of bushes.

Back on board as the log notes *Jim returned at 2240, excited, to
announce: "I wanna discussion with you, Miles".'

*He sat down uneasily and held his thumb and index finger aloft
firmly together. Then proceeded to tell me earnestly (as though to a
child) that he had spoken to the USA and arranged to call his son;
that he had a wonderful view down river and was going to shoot the
sunrise ; then (still agonisingly serious) that he needed a car at precisely 7.30 next morning. Nikolai, Arkady (the mildest of men) and
Vitali looked bored as he continued to hold the floor.*

*'Sarah, your wife,' he continued, 'very kindly called Pat, and she
very sensibly did not call Collect. She should total up all those calls
and let her know how much they were ... Pat is a qualified economist and she takes care of such things.*

That is my statement.'

*He wouldn't eat supper but stuffed some cheese down his throat
and then hassled about getting Vitali to go with him ... 'You gotta
see my hotel room, It's our first real view of the river. It's like the
U.S., just south of Kansas city'.*

By evening Galina, had found a friend to look after Anna.
Schparo had accepted her temporary loan as essential, and it was
agreed that she would stay on board until Kazan. There Vitali
promised to do his best to rejoin.

Galina recalled that Miles looked tired and up tight. Not much
wonder, you may say. Endless problem solving, physical effort,
and now this big crew change as the most worrying interlude so
far. Vitali on the other hand was continually amazed at Milo's
energy and remembered only seeing him exhausted twice on the
whole trip. At midnight he and Nikolai departed by train to
Moscow.

After weeks of the closest companionship their going left a
tangible gap that it took some time for the new chums to fill.

As Wild Goose was getting ready to sail next morning the Director of the Oka River Yacht Club presented himself.

'I wonder why Director, not Commodore or even Admiral,' thought Miles. He was a courteous man, bearing gifts and good wishes, a pair of traditional Russian shoes woven from reeds, collar badges and a mini club burgee.

These momentoes came home to Ireland eventually, but poor Wild Goose was getting more and more cluttered.

'Ships and men rot in port,' Miles said rather briskly as he nursed Wild Goose down the Oka river the following morning under threatening skies and a strong north-east wind.

This old adage was almost literally true; the paint on Wild Goose's hull had begun to blister under the water line from the filth on the surface of the river.

Now there was a new crew to be 'Wild Goosed'.

Arkady was quick to learn the ropes and neatly summarised the new establishment:

'Joining Wild Goose at Nizhni on July 19th I was the oldest of the crew and as the elder statesman tried to act as a calming influence, a steady hand at the tiller in more ways than one. Vitali probably found me an old bore but I hope he respected me. I think I succeeded in reassuring Miles that none of the bureaucratic difficulties he encountered would be insuperable.

'In a way perhaps I am a living example of the principle, that there is a way round every obstacle. I had made a moderately successful career as a metallurgy engineer with a Diploma from the Institute of Steel, despite the fact that advanced metallurgy, along with journalism and theoretical physics, is one of those sectors where Jews like myself faced huge discrimination in Soviet times. Rather like Miles I was strongly influenced by my father, a professional officer of the Soviet army. I never saw him in civilian clothes until I was six. He encountered his fair share of prejudice but never complained about it or let it stop him making a decent unspectacular career.

'My journey on Wild Goose began on a note farce when Miles told me to put purifying tablets into all our canisters of drinking water. Because I have a hard time reading English instructions I managed to lace the water with contact lense cleaning fluid instead. Once I realised my mistake I threw in some purifying pills and the mixture tasted perfectly good. Miles forgave me and he acknowledged my expertise in other forms of colourless liquid. Essentially there are only two sorts of Vodka good and very good, I once told him. He solemnly recorded this important piece of Russian folk wisdom in his notebook.

'But we did not need any artificial stimulants to enjoy some of the sails we had on our way eastwards towards Kazan. It was a week of flying spray and flickeing sunshine during which the river, now shallow, now deep sometimes tree shaded, at others in oblique light, showed a range of colour that was almost unbelievable – every variety of green from deepest emerald to palest jade, every shade of blue from sapphire through aquamarine to what at sunset became turquoise and later vermiliion.'

Galina too enjoyed the colours and the sailing:

'This was the start of a week in which to my delight we spent most of our time under sail. The four of us would huddle together in the tiny cockpit with most of the steering done by me or Arkady. Those long sails gave us plenty of time to set the world to rights and to thrash out with Miles the purpose of this voyage. He was a formidably conscientious skipper and host, Delicious meals, different every night, sometimes nicknamed "Culinary Rembrandt", came from his galley efforts. And he did a lot of physical work on board himself. He was determined to return the boat in perfect condition to his father. To be honest I think he should have delegated more work to Arkady and myself. There were times when we Russians literally had to force Miles to stop worrying about the boat and take some time off to write.'

As they drew clear of the city, 'Jeem', as Galina called him, burst forth again.

'There's a road like that along the river in Pittsburgh that only a few of us old timers know about.'

'Look at those road workers. They still use the same dam' brooms they were using when I was shooting here in 1955'.

Miles' log became staccato – 'threatening skies and north east wind. Our waterline filthy with acidic oily scum. Good to be moving again. Engine sounding rough but rugged.

Six days to Kazan, then South!

CHAPTER NINE

A Week Under Sail

By WALLACE, *MILES*, and Galina

'The Kirk is an anvil that
has worn out many a hammer.'
John Knox

23 July

MAKARIEF BY MOONLIGHT

After making thirty miles in eight hours they tied up late at a floating ferry pier.

It served a building that drew the eye like a magnet – the gleaming whitewashed walls of Zhultavodky, a 14th century convent appearing as if carved in ivory. It reminded Milo at first of a low elongated Taj Mahal.

The Solovetsky kremlin in the far off White Sea, the Church of the Resurrection Kizhi Island and now this were the most strikingly beautiful of all the structures they passed. Snowy towers and walls surmounted gently sloping chalky ramps stretching down to the water. They looked like the scarps of a Vauban fortress – scarps which once protected the walls from erosion when the Volga flowed swiftly They knocked on the main gate. A sleepy sacristan in shabby black robes answered after some delay and said grumpily that it was too late. As he attempted to close the portal Jim got his foot in it and brandished a fistful of dollars in the old man's face. But the only reaction was a dignified withdrawal.

> 'I had to admit', said Gallina, 'that we were not a very pious looking lot. Miles in shorts, Jim the image of an American spy and myself with a kerchief over my head as a makeshift covering.' As we rowed back Jim remonstrated with me, 'You'll never be a reporter. You have to insist, you have to make yourself obnoxious, you have got to use charm, persuasion, money, every trick in the book. Otherwise you'll never make it.'

At midnight the crew rowed out midstream to view Makarief's pitchy conical roofs limned against the afterglow across a river that glowed silver grey, like the water in Vermeer's Delft.

Later all was milky under the moon. Utter peace for a good night's sleep.

Bangs on the hull at 0400 drew Miles from his bunk as from a well of treacle; it was the wharfinger to announce that Wild Goose would be in the way of a ship due at 0725. The floating dock was the now familiar two-story pontoon, garish in red and green, incongruous off the river gate. It was shaped so much like a Noah's Ark that it would not have been surprising to see a giraffe's head poking out an upper window. Miles had to let go the lines and motor away in an extraordinary manoeuvre preceded by much miming and drawing of diagrams, necessary because Galina was asleep and no one wanted to wake her.

It was hardly worth going to bed again, so Miles waited for dawn light to photograph. In the cool of morning sick fish circled aimlessly on the misty surface.

It was so silent that from the cockpit he could hear Arkady licking his lips thirty feet away on the bow. Then in a magic moment the sound of singing from Matins stole over the water. Full daylight showed the four round tower bastions which Galina called Cillia – they had wooden witches hat roofs , surmounted by what appeared to be tiny dovecots. The walls linking them were slotted for arrow fire and pierced for what looked like cannon. Ingenious defences that had saved this dream-like place from all enemies except The Bolsheviks Two churches stood within. One, unusually, was over the main gate , as at Solovetsky. Inside was a small building with a strange black domed roof; by it were the cells for the nuns. The Troitsky Cathedral dates from 1664, an outstanding monument with frescos from the 17th century. Already there was a photo exhibition of its history.

By nine o'clock there was a woman keeping the gate. Milo asked for books or postcards. 'Books, books! Nobody ever reads any book here, we haven't time'.

A dozen nuns, mostly old and severe, were attending another service. Each in turn applied oil with a brush to her forehead after kissing an icon, kissed the priest's hand and bowed. Makarief had only been open for about six months and the Metropolitan of Moscow was already asking permission to restore seven neighbouring churches. The manner in which these few elderly ladies had contrived unaided to re-introduce a little order into lawns and gardens and to renew the air of peace and contemplation that had formerly existed there stemmed from faith almost beyond praise.

The nuns would not have been available for conversation until eleven so Miles decided to push on. The anchor chain, as it came up cold and dripping, was covered in tiny snails and winkles. The misty morning had given way to bright sunshine as they headed south for Cheboksary. Some organised forestry for the first time appeared on the bank – rows of seedlings and saplings and neatly piled pit props. Further north trees had been so numerous and the forest so endless that re-supply was left to natural regeneration.

LIFE ON A LIGHTER

The following two extracts are taken from the account of a journey in the years 1821 by a Captain, Royal Navy, John Dundas Cochrane working his passage down river.

Vessels of the Volga one hundred and fifty years ago

'I am now on the magnificent Volga. The lighter on board which I had embarked did not depart for thirty-six hours but I felt too much of the sailor in me to quit: working my passage, nothing was demanded of me but to row the boat ashore for the captain, and now and then supply him with a glass of vodka. This I was content to do till I found that a little grog and tobacco, was followed by the demand for still more, which my purse could very ill bear. I was therefore well pleased when the anchor was weighed, and we descended the stream; but so slow was our progress that we kept the heights of Novgorod in sight for two days, being frequently obliged to anchor, with the repeated dunning of, "Vodka, Batyushka". ("Gin, master").

'The vessel I was in measured about two hundred and fifty tons, perfectly flat-bottomed, and drawing but five feet water. At length, losing sight of Nizhni Novgorod, we passed many islands and villages, the latter always on the right bank. The left was uninterrupted low heath. The strength of the current I calculated at two knots and a half.

'The variety and singular appearance of the different craft on the Volga, not a little surprised me, as well as the innumerable different ways in which they were propelled. The present season of the year, immediately preceding the Fair, is the best for the navigation of the Volga, when barks from one thousand tons to the size of a canoe, all promiscuously float together. They are generally provided with one mast, which, in the largest, may equal a frigate's main-mast. The weight of the mat-sail must be prodigious, having no fewer than a hundred and sixty breadths in it; and yet the facility with which it is managed will bear comparison with that of the Yankees, with the boom main-sails in their fore and aft clippers. They are generally worked by from fifteen to forty people. The rudder is a ponderous machine, extending astern twelve or fifteen feet; the tillers I have ascertained from measurement to be from thirty to forty feet long, and all worked by the hand.'

'The soil on either side is clay and chalk, and the wood fir and birch. The inhabitants of the villages are the inoffensive and ignorant Finns, a race of people more approximating to the character of the Gallegos in Lisbon, than any other class of people I have seen. Their great content, and small possessions, are in both a prominent feature. We reached Makaryev, after a tedious voyage, vexatious from the annoyance of the horse-flies and mosquitoes. I was fairly put to the alternative, whether, during my sleep, I would be suffocated or devoured. I preferred the former, as smacking more of humanity, wrapping myself up close in canvas.'

In 1992 there were not many mosquitoes and still no obvious pollution in the river. Miles could not remember seeing a single piece of midstream litter in 800 miles but what lay on the bottom no one knew.

The willing Arkady kept busy swabbing the deck. Indeed he and the other Russians used such vigour that the deck scrubber which usually lasts several years on Wild Goose was worn out in three months! Then he scraped off and varnished bits of the doghouse, while Galina gave womanly help to Milo for what in Ireland would be called a 'good redd-up'. It involved the emptying and cleaning of every locker, a stock take and re-stow of food and gear.

Progress was laborious into a stiff headwind, the mainsail drawn in taut amidships and the bow thrusting aside an endless low cascade of muddy tea-coloured water.

BARMINO, THE (ALMOST) DESERTED VILLAGE

So to Barmino, a once thriving traditional Volga pasiolak (large village) which had been dying for 30 years. It had been a big place with a several streets but people were forcibly moved out just before the Barrage made the river rise.

A Collective Farm had followed for two generations with its own cannery for meat and fruit. In 1983 the village church was burnt down, perhaps on Government orders, a unique wooden building 300 years old. Retired people now lived where there had been for centuries kulak managers and hard worked peasants. The shop which used to supply goods to passing river traffic lay abandoned, the Cannery likewise. A sign reading 'Forward to the Victory of Communism' lay broken with the star askew The cold store, where spring ice and snow, compacted two metres deep, was once kept for use through the summer, lay full of rubbish.

A pair of ravens (Grach) croaked in disapproval. There remained at least one super abundance – fruit of many varieties.

Wild Goose's arrival drew a crowd. It had done the same at many a western island from the Blaskets to St Kilda. Sometimes a nuisance, but more often a convenience; it gave instant introductions of the sort open only to shipborne arrivals.

An early conversationalist was Yvgeny Ostroumov, full of village and river lore.

> 'The river level has risen four metres between 1981 and 1985. Fishing once fed the village – now when they pull in a net, all they get is mud. No fish since the flow ceased. It used to take 45 days for the water to pass through from here to the sea, now the pace is so slow it could scarcely be measured, might be a year. Impossible to bring the river back to its previous level but people are campaigning strongly against any further rise. Enthusiasts are already predicting that all the electrical stations would be removed from the river, but when nobody knows when. Now many things are broken'.
>
> Yvgeny was born 80 miles away but since the age of 16 has lived near the river. 'I remember it as narrow and lower; people drank the water. It was very fast – very strong current.'

'Would you let your son Anatoli swim in the river?'

> 'Well, boys are boys! But not too often'.
>
> The river here freezes at the end of November for six months. April 22nd is the date for navigation to open. Sometimes in winter icebreakers carve a course through it but in the spring the ice moves itself. The Volga Neft ships can cope with ice up to a foot thick and break up the big pieces.

Miles asked about commercial fishing. 'None. Somewhere there are a few small crews but it depends on the authorities; generally it is forbidden because numbers are declining. Before the 70's there were boats which took fish to the official shops – Lyesh and Soudak. Of course it is forbidden to catch sterlet. You can take one home but if an inspector sees you it is a 500 rouble fine for each fish.'

'Is there any difference in the quality?' 'I don't think so', he replied. 'The flesh has not gone soft but there are just smaller fish'.

Galina recalled seeing at Volgograd in 1975 shoals of fish trying to get into the spawning grounds. There was a pass round the hydro electric station; about a quarter of the fish got through; the rest came close to the station, but couldn't find the pass. A lot of fishermen caught them as they circled with rod and hook, no bait, just 'fishfly' (ie foul hooking) and a flick into the bushes.

The dachas, isbas and isbuskas of Barmino were particularly fine with antique fretwork shaped as butterflies moons and flowers round the windows, corner posts and gables. TV aerials on roof tops were in strange contrast.

Some intricate windows frames were painted blue, but the streets were deserted.; perhaps the pensioners were resting. Wildflowers and herbs bespangled the grass, thyme and rosemary, cornflower, larkspur. Convolvulus was growing through the bottom of an upturned rowing boat. Cockerels crowed but overall the village was fighting a losing battle with nettles, so that if the winter did not come along, housed and all would be digested by nature.

Bits of old beds, broken planks, ruined gates and the ugly air of abandon reminded Miles of a visit to Gola Island in Ireland a year after the population had left.

Galina translated some Russian wit as a pair of kids bleated from a tabletop. 'Their mother was called Thatcher, a hooligan, very difficult.'

Can we see her?

'No. We ate her last week!'. Further away from the boat Vera Konstantinova, peered through a muslin curtain in her underwear. Her attitude totally hostile and her dog snarling to warn of intruders. 'What do you want?', said Vera suspiciously. Vitali at this point came in with a not altogether helpful translation. She says, 'You can see my garden but I like to keep my private parts to myself'.

Galina described the scene; 'Jeem looked so American that of course people were suspicious. He was always brash, taking close-ups of people without permission. The crew were not happy with it'.

Miles was very worried, frequently having to use his utmost tact to de-fuse such situations; knowing that, to quote Lord Dufferin, 'There is no hatred so intense as that you feel for a disagreeable shipmate.' (*Letters from High Latitudes*. 1856.).

Galina explained to Vera, 'We just want to take a picture'.

'But you must ask. There are some more beautiful houses than these. People like me feel ashamed to have not such a beautiful house. I come here for five months because the goats need to be milked'.

During the War she was in Belorussia with the army. Her husband after that was boss of the landing place here. He and a friend, she related ,built all the isbas. There is no comparison between the river now and fifty years ago. She would not swim in it at all; it is not dangerous, only unpleasant. She'd been a pensioner now for three years but still working as hard as ever. 'When you work at home it is worse than working away because you never stop'.

Vera gave them a can of goat's milk and a basket of cherries. Galina explained

> 'Russian people are always friendly to foreigners, and to strangers'.
>
> 'I love talking to these people, because they have a special dialect typical of ancient Russian unlike Moscow or any other city where the language is spoiled. Here they speak with the letter O perfectly pronounced typical for the Nyznhy region. They say Korova whereas in Moscow it is Karova. You can tell exactly from which city someone comes by their accent.'

Further down women were working at beehives in white coats and long hats with veils, and flour sacks over their hands.

They talked to another dacha owner, a craggy septuagenarian ex-Air Force helicopter pilot who had flown British Hurricanes and thought very well of them. He had graduated in 1943 and then became an instructor. Here he had built his own house over a period of 17 years. His father's house had been near the river but too close to the edge and eventually fell in. He owns a tenth of a hectare which he acquired when it became possible to buy land; as a regular ex-Service man he didn't have to pay. He took us to a balcony overlooking the Volga. 'The river used to clean itself', he remarked, 'It used to flush out the thaw lakes on either side, now they just remain stagnant'.

Back to Wild Goose, laden with gifts on the fairest of afternoons.

Lev Mityagin came alongside as they dinghied out, anxious to show off his 27 foot yacht Fortuna, afloat by the pier. She had been built by his own hand in four years. 'Mostly I used pine but friends in the Black Sea sent me bits from other ships.' She had a bow like a Grand Banks schooner and lots of varnished wood but seemed lightly built with a bowsprit that looked as if it would break off in your hand. He was clearly a keen sailor and natural craftsman but Galina, as they pulled up the anchor said that 3000 roubles was a 'terrible' price to have paid for the pine (Sasna) for the boat.

The afternoon passage showed vast meadows of short grass on the south bank punctuated by fine stands of dark pine. Axes flashed from figures at work amongst them.

Milo was glad to see 500 foot hills rising behind them; he'd been born in sight of mountains and was a climber as much as sailor.

The north bank was afloat with islets, tufts of rushes and entanglements of dead trees. It might have belonged to a completely different river.

HERE BE PIRATES!
Insect Island, *by* Fukino

They decided against stopping in the lee of a dam wall on the north bank by the village of Mikhailoyskaye, finding the water too deep. Instead anchored off an island close north east of Fukino. The object as usual was to find somewhere out of the current, sheltered from the wind and over a bottom firm enough to give the anchor a grip. But this time the chosen spot was far from comfortable as Wild Goose rode bows west into the current and the east wind blew the dinghy up to bang against the stern. There were swarms of white stinging flies. Miles logged the place as 'strange and rather frightening'. They were at the west or upstream end of a scrub covered island shaped like a lobster claw with the nippers facing east.

This left them exposed to the current but handy for the village which lay just out of sight over a hill.

As dusk fell there was a feeling of isolation and danger. Rustles in the island reeds, Milo began to think, could be brigands choosing their moment to emerge. A dozen swift oar strokes in a skiff could bring attackers up to the gunwhale.

Not wishing to share his feelings with the crew, he took his ancient 12-bore on deck on the pretence that it needed to be cleaned. He worked at it on the coachroof to make it clear to a concealed observer that the yacht was armed.

Perhaps what he sensed were vibes from dead followers of Stenka Rasin, the Robin Hood of the river. He kept it in a state of terror during a peasant revolt before the days of Peter The Great. History has become intertwined with myth. Stenka and his fellow outlaws moved from island to island, Miles had been told, on a felt rug.

After a period of total silence, Miles decided that an anchor watch was no longer needed. It was a relief to put the insect screens over the hatches, see that the scuttles were closed and turn in.

Friday 24th July; Fears, real or imaginary, were dispelled by a silken dawn and the comfort of men fishing nearby. Might there really have been a brigand lair on the island? Thefts of cars at this time were endemic in the country, and often accompanied by violence. But for car parts swift disposal was always at hand whereas a foreign boat would be almost impossible to re-sell. So the risk, although there, was probably not all that big. Minimal to a well-armed and alert crew.

EXPLORING A SWAMP

Miles had a shower, then decided to move away from Insect Island to the left bank and explore the swamps, what Americans would call stump fields. Air maps showed them extending for up to ten miles north. Thick grass at the edge soon choked the outboard so they rowed in silence past entanglements of dead birch where seagulls perched among fronds of greens. When they landed on the islets insects crawled all over their bare legs but curiously the water in the shallows was clean. Yellow water lilies dipped, big fish showed bow waves as they moved aside, mallard rose, terns hovered, buzzards soared, all to the background of grunting and screeching of young herons standing up in their nests and flapping wings. Rising fields with hay stooks showed quiet beyond the floods in contrast to the riot of bird life among the rushes.

Crossing the south again the river was popply, with wavelets slurping over the dinghy bow, but that wasn't worrying a fisherman fast asleep with his legs and arms over the sides of his tubby green Jon boat and a hood over his head. Mikail Kalmykov was affable once awake – he came from Azamas near Kanash (names here had a fine ring to them) and was an inter-city bus driver. He was sure his three belled lines would soon bring a catch. This was a good spot because of the depth of the river. When he caught sterlet he kept them in spite of risk of a fine. 'To me a boat is freedom!'

BREAKFAST WITH FISHERMEN

An encampment on a sandy spit among willows on the south shore was the next attraction. Behind it reared huge piles of lime for fertilising the fields, and road metal which had been dumped by barge. Some fishermen lay asleep on the sun warmed shingle, others were mending nets or drying fish to take home. They were on holiday from Azamas – fathers, sons and brothers. The fishing was terrible, they said, the sort of story you hear from anglers anywhere. A steamy fish smell came from a huge pot suspended over an open fire. A small boy offered them soup. It was warm and welcome; fish grilled over an open fire and set on damper bread followed and vodka to wash it down. The boy was vague as to fish names but the scene on the spit was not unlike that described by that sporting American, Elizabeth Hapgood:

> ***Russian Rambles*** 'The sterlet soup was a deep gold colour, almost orange, with rich fat, utterly unlike anything we had ever tasted'. The unfortunate fish were plunged alive into the boiling water, even the head being esteemed part of the delicacy. The scum is not removed but stirred in as fast as it rises. Other sterlet were speared alive on willow wands and roasted over the fire. After eating a steak or two she agreed with her Russian hosts in counting the sterlet as king of all fish.

133

In 1895 she watched the fisherman tow out a net 250 yards long in a great circle and draw it ashore on halters made of the soft inner bark of the linden tree and win a cartload of fish for half an hour's labour.

These latter day fishermen were curious, asking Galina directly how much money she was being paid by the foreigners and whether the yacht carried liquor. They laughed when she told them that the boss was a surly fellow, now on board sleeping it off.

They pointed out fields behind the camp, very rich grazing forty years ago, now giving poor growth and getting worse.

At noon it was off again under engine but a good breeze from the ENE gave them a fetch under sail in Force four. The north bank was 'floating forest' (as it is curiously called, really trees with roots deep under water) continuing for many miles. At 1340 they reached the confluence of the Sura near Vasil Yursk. There were steep slopes behind it with houses peeping through trees. Every village, as Miles remarks, looks attractive from the Volga. Away beyond lay high forested hills, blue green in the haze with dead treetops poking through. It was warm and sunny with massive cumulus clouds sailing overhead and the crew in Volga mood felt in no hurry to get on to the city ahead. At 4.45 they steered out of the buoyed channel to pass close to a village at the mouth of the Soomka river which didn't exist. At least it wasn't mentioned on the chart and all its houses seemed to be deserted. Beyond it was a church with a tall slender bell tower, background to a curious little cameo A car pulled up; eight figures emerged, one in black, one in white, and walked down to the river. The bridegroom (he in black) picked up his bride, who allowed him a brief hug on the river bank. Then he carried her, struggling fiercely, to the door of the church. Kicks, blows and lacerating scratches were exchanged. It looked like fighting for real until the party disappeared inside. This was our introduction to the Mar-iel Republic and its way of wedding.'

They passed the city of Kosmodemyansk, Capital of Mari, to starboard in a channel which seemed a huge confusion of flashing buoys, leading marks, side channels, and island studded swamp. The city appeared as robbed of its waterfront by veritable cliffs of cement. The sheer volume of concrete in this and other parts of the river bank was mind blowing. The only similar things Wild Goose had seen with such volumes were the submarine pens built by the Germans in Bergen and Brest to protect their U boats from the RAF.

Miles elected to anchor just beyond the city in a widening of the river. Deciding on approaching a strange port whether to tie up or anchor, and just where to do either, is one of the recurring problems of coastal sailing. At anchor the risk of pilferage is lessened. And it avoided the risk of running aground ñ fairly high as most small Volga harbours are for craft drawing a lot less than Wild Goose's five feet. Set against this is the convenience, if tied alongside, of being able to step ashore for a leg stretch, shopping or sightseeing.

On strange coasts I've often felt under acute pressure, tired at the end of a long passage when faced with the problem; the sort of pressure that has made my wife and me get into irrational arguments. One longs above all for just one familiar harbour to make for. In Russia Milo faced the quandary daily.

It takes luck as well as skill from a skipper to reach right decision, and if he asks for advice he will get as many opinions as there are crew on board. This time he got it right and the holding was good and the water undisturbed. There was a brief visit from some friendly local sailors who guided them to a small market ashore. The crew were looking forward to new intersts – visiting on the morrow the capital of the Mari Republic, about which Rita of the Cruise Ship in civic pride had told them so much and after that the Chuvash country and the Tartars. But Milo's Deck Log entry carried a note of weary frustration, *'How can you write anything interesting about a place in four hours ashore?'* That was all the time they'd be able to spare next day.

But why worry? As they settled down to sleep wood pigeons coo-ed a lullaby from fir trees on the bank. It was comfortingly familiar; 'Don't cry so, Susy; Don't cry so, Susy, Don't.'

The mischievous deities of this area, which the visitors had told them about, neither plucked the anchor out of its holding or went bang in the night.

Milo called the hands betimes to see what Kos had to offer.

Poacher attempting to boat a large sterlet. He stopped as soon as he saw Wild Goose approaching.

CHAPTER TEN

The Locks of Cheboksary

By WALLACE, *MILES*, GALINA and Arkady

'So all you Gods that love brave men,
Send us a three-reef gale again!
Thorkild's Song … Kipling

A bright clear morning, Saturday 25 July, saw Wild Goose motoring a mile back up the river to Kosmodemyansk.

Miles on Arkady's suggestion headed for the 'beeg sheep' pier. No woollies in sight, so he deduced that big ship was meant and tied up as requisite.

A vast Market Hall was first en face. It was filled with double life size portraits and lengthy names of winning workers, often enshrining also the name of the picture framer. Much of the information was in Tatar; even Galina was foxed. But a rusty unpainted Hammer and Sickle gave a message of new moods. Milo, rested after a good night's sleep, began to note the surroundings.

Eyecatching on a front line stall was 'Erotic Folk Tales of the World – Issue Number One, Ukraine'. Beside it were Bibles, tape recorders, glasses, shirts and videos, pairs of fur lined leather boots 800 roubles, fur coats 5000 roubles (£10), all at random among the meat and vegetable counters.

The people were reasonably dressed and healthy, the buildings poor and decaying Two women and a boy man were carrying a pathetic elderly man with the narrow face and hollow eyes of an Aids victim. There is a chronic lack of wheelchairs in Russia

The men had almost Eastern slitty eyes, the girls tightly bunched mouths, small eyes and noses. A woman with breasts like a pair of melons leaned over street stall trying to sell us caraway seed.

'You buy Pifta Oil from scianic pine?'

'What's it for?'

'Very healthy, it is very good for your looms (sic). For example I use it just as 'flu is starting. You just take some, just smell it and in two days it is enough so that you are absolutely well.'

'People are aggressive here because life is clearly difficult', said Galina.

As for Jim he was breaking cultural barriers in his way as we sweated through the cracked stalls He enjoyed showing off his newly acquired Russian phrases. 'Spasibo Bolshoy' and 'Dobroye Rutro', he would shout cheerily in his very best American twang, demonstrating his effortless mastery of expression. 'Thank you very much' and 'Good morning'. Occasionally he would confuse his listeners by getting the two phrases the wrong way round but as Galina said you had to give him full marks for effort.

We'd hoped Rita might be there to show us around but she was off at work on the river. So we plodded up a rutted cinder track among the pine trees to visit the Folk Museum. A fascinating collection of rural houses – one 15th century wooden house had intestine stretched over windows, more efficient than I had imagined. There were many esoteric Mari tools and weapons. But no reference to the wizards and warlocks Rita had told us about at Kizhi.

Arkady shrewdly comments: In a country where up until very recently we were supposed to be forgetting racial differences and merging as a species called Homo Sovitecius we observed how every ethnic group was remembering its half forgotten peculiarities including little known minorities like the Mari and the Chuvash. Only a few years ago they had been blending imperceptively into the Soviet whole. In this bustling market town for example we were whisked off to admire the communities traditional crafts and architecture. They played haunting music on an instrument called a gusli (psaltry) and showed us traditional implements for spinning flax which Miles instantly recognised. 'You seem to know all about our people's artifacts', said the Lady Curator rather surprised. 'That's because I descend from eight generations of linen weavers in Ireland', Milo retorted. I think that confused her even more.

LEAVING THE MARI

Too soon it was time to go. The wind was strong now. Gusts bundled them down the path to the riverside. Miles, always a little worried about Wild Goose when she was out of sight, was glad he'd put out plenty of chain They were relieved to sight her just where they'd left her but tugging fiercely at her cable. It needed all Miles' skill as an oarsmen for the wet business of dinghying the crew on board one by one. Then with a reef in the main and the wind blowing straight on shore, it needed smart work on the anchor chain and jib sheets to keep clear of shallows astern and get her head cast southward. Wild Goose was quickly on her best point of sailing, beam wind and rail not quite awash, making six knots for Cheboksary, 45 miles south.

The cockpit of a yacht is a good place to chat. With attention fixed on the flutter of sail, an oncoming wave or another boat people talk away without having to look into or avoid each other's eyes.

Now Galia told the crew about her background; her father had been a senior army officer, something to do with missiles.

The distrust of foreigners was drummed into us every day of our lives. 'Are you still suspicious of westerners', Miles once asked. 'No; just a bit bewildered', I answered. However well I learn English I always feel there is some unbridgeable gap between our world and yours, even when I get to know people well as a radio ham. To be frank dealing with westerners my strong sense that you are different from us is one of the few things that makes me feel any identification with this country, whatever it is called now. I never felt that the word Soviet accurately described me and I don't feel totally Russian either. I feel more akin to the Indians or the indigenous people of the Russian Arctic. Miles shared with me a strong desire to move outwards to people other than his own countrymen, to explore and he also felt very powerful ties to home to the island he had come from. We had some amusing moments on Wild Goose but certain matters were absolutely sacred, his wife, his family, his private life were subjects on which joshing and teasing were absolutely taboo.

Once exasperated Miles took me to task. 'You seem to have an endless capacity for gloom, depression and the apocalypse'. I answered rather sharply and said that most Russians had plenty to be gloomy and depressed about but I tried a different tack, 'I think a few westerners would find our reality hopelessly difficult and frustrating'. It is true that our lives particularly in the last few years had been desperately hard, harder than I can make you realise but we have our own way of coping. We have a stubborn fate that things will eventually get better. Our religion tells us that pursuit of earthly happiness like all human project is doom but at the same time our religion is also the beginning of all joy. I am not sure what he meant, he certainly was a joyful old soul himself even though he had been fasting for five weeks he looked even thinner than you Miles.

The speed and sensation of rushing through the water brought Arkady to life.

On first joining he'd been quiet but now he began to sing and talk in animated fashion with his arm round Galina.

There was wonderful progress all afternoon, as the wind backed further aft and freshened, spray showered over the cockpit and sheets of brown water volleyed away to leeward. In the squalls that came out of flying saucers of dark cloud approaching in procession from the north. In gusts Wild Goose heeled sharply, to put the lee deck two planks down. Every loose item in the cabin slid or jumped out of its place.

He who runs may read, or hug, but if he does so he will most certainly jybe. And so Adik did. As he let Wild Goose veer momentarily off course the wind got round behind the mainsail. The great wooden boom kicked up, then swept across the cockpit with a mighty Wham! It scared Galina and spoiled the courting as it came up against a running backstay with a jolt that could have taken the stick out of a less sturdy craft.

But Wild Goose's rigging is well oversize, and nothing carried away.

Recovered Galina was ready to rib Jim when he made critical comments on the shortage and quality of loo paper in a land so rich in timber.

'What do you use for toilet paper?' he asked

'That is the great secret of every Russian. What would you use, Jim, if you ran out of paper?'

'It just wouldn't happen – Pat would always see to it that we had a supply in the house.'

'Well, just imagine for once, just imagine what you might use if she just once forgot to have a supply.'

'It just wouldn't happen. Pat is an economist and plans all that kind of thing very carefully.'

The only thing to do was change the subject.

CHEBOKSARY

At 9 pm they were abreast the town of Cheboksary which lies six a miles short of the site of second Volga Barrage. An anchorage beckoned in a well sheltered cove but this was voted too far from the chances of a telephone. After a further search a hungry crew let go in an exposed deep water berth thirty yards off a steep concrete ramp by what looked like an abandoned Yacht Club.

Miles had recovered his spirits by now and undaunted by the surroundings managed a celebration dinner for the end of another Reservoir – vodka sours followed by a huge beef stew with carrots and potatoes. Then cheese and a variety of fruit.

The Skanti radio seemed unable to reach UK , so at 1130, he and Galina rowed ashore to telephone. After a long wait on hard brown benches in a State Office equipped with inkstands and quill pens they got calls through to check on arrangements at Kazan and the care of Galina's daughter. It was long after midnight before they could turn in.

Got *water from a spring in the morning*, Miles recorded, a curious entry How, one wonders, was there a spring , so close to a city, one that looked potable to the cautious Milo. Was it polluted and the cause of later lassitude and illness. Maybe they considered spring water as better than any piped supply.

Cheboksary, capital of the Chuvash Region and situated at south end of its eponymous reservoir, is unremarkable as a city. But it is historically famous for the sturdy independence of its Turkic people's and their ancient mode of dress.

The population is around one and a quarter million. The country, lying on the boundary between the Taiga and the Wooded Steppe zones, is divided about half and half between dense pine forests and agriculture.

In the 19th century the Chuvashes used to affect curious stove pipe hats and the girls had a reputation for great skill and stamina as stevedores. Now many of them man the passenger ferries which ply the Volga in steadily increasing numbers.

Some Chuvash dresses were on display. much the most interesting items in the inevitable Palace of Culture. Beyond it lay a Fashion House linked to an Academic Drama Theatre for good measure.

Miles noted: *'Shades of the early Chicago Mayor who said "We ain't got culture yet, but when we do we'll make it hum!".' Behind the Art buildings are factories producing machine tools, tractors, pipe laying machinery and even some fine linen! I wonder if Dad could learn anything from that'.*

We then motored six miles down river to the Barrage in most unseasonably cold weather.

Jim was in imaginative form.

'I can't understand why these guys aren't all driving Mercedes. If I lived in England, I'd wanna buy a hundred thousand acres here … this is the kind of place that makes me wanna write poetry.'

HOW GIANT TWIN CHEBOKSARY LOCKS WORK

A huge expanse of concrete under a network of electric cables reared ahead marking the end of the reservoir

We entered the left hand of the twin locks behind two barges and an oil tanker, got through by 1130, then anchored in the shelter of the breakwater dividing the east approach. This was so that Galina and I could see how the Barrage and locks were managed. Her charm got swift admission – firstly to the Control Box which slides across from above from one lock to the other depending on which is in use. From it the watch keeper can empty 90,000 cubic metres in six minutes and put them back in twelve.

'If he'd pressed the wrong buttons we'd have been sunk,' said Galina.

Then we were led to the Hydro-electric Multiple Operation Room – like the bridge of a ship with flashing lights, endless dials in grey casing, festoon blinds, and a woman sprawled asleep on a sofa. It can produce one and a half million Kilowatts from eighteen turbines but seldom more than four are in use and these only in daytime. There is not enough water to work them 24 hours so they used to suit times of peak demand. We could hear the low2 hum of mighty generators making the building almost vibrate.

Stanislav Kalmykov, Chief of Lock Operations, invited us into his office. He wore a Humphrey Bogart in an open-necked brown and pink shirt, hardly moved his mouth and found it hard to smile but talked non stop with infectious enthusiasm.

'There are up to seventy openings every 24 hours. That means one every 20 minutes. We have calendar bookings for the passenger ships but usage is down fifty percent on last year – so many ships laid up due to the high price of diesel. We needed the twin locks badly a few months back when one was clogged for weeks by a sunken ship.

'But also having the two allows traffic to pass in both directions at the same time without delay'.

Then with a look over his shoulder, 'It was a great mistake of the Government to cover such a large area of good land with water – an ecological tragedy. Now the water is becoming stagnant and everything in it will die and all cities will receive bad water to drink. In the past people used to plant vegetables and crops along the river, then the land was irrigated by floods in the spring. That made for a big harvest. But not any longer.

There are more catastrophes coming. There is no fish pass for sterlet in the Barrages and it is purely chance if they get up through the lock.

The bosses keep changing things. Before the completion of this Barrage in 1985 the reservoir went all the way from Gorodets to Tolyati, another 250 miles.

Now they make big threats to raise the level again. If they do, ther'll be a much greater problem. There is some current still but if the Barrages are higher, there'll be no current at all.'

'Can Russia solve this problem?' I asked.

'Our Government can solve nothing!'

The raising isn't only for extra electricity; they planned to create a greater Volga with more and bigger ships. But the system is still not viable; hasn't paid for itself yet.

Still too shallow in places for Volga-Balt, Volga Neft, Batisky, and

141

Rekamore ships. The locks are minimum twenty seven feet deep, but the hold-ups come from shallows in the river. They change position all the time.

'How important', we asked Stanislav, 'is the Volga today?' 'Very important – for oil, coal, ore, sand, and wood from Tatarstan, Baku and Samara. The railway isn't capable of moving the volume that comes by river.'

Finally he smiled, opened a drawer in his desk and poured out three stiff vodkas. Then he gave us a chart of the next reservoir and lots of pilotage hints.

A good man, bold critic and a great lover of his river!

They returned on board to find visitors. Milo was in better form now and warmly greeted Valentina, a top marathon runner, and another bronzed and muscled Galina. They had swum out to Wild Goose in bikinis and clambered on board via the bobstay. Russians take their athleticism very seriously. We refreshed them with tea.

Then like that Boston whaling skipper of old who circumnavigated the world wothout catching a single fish, we had 'a hell of fine sail'. The smokestacks of Volsk shot by at seven knots.

I never tire of looking at the banks; now the right is best, cliffed, with wadis breaking through and dark wooden dachas everywhere. The left bank duller with low sandy islands and beaches but enlivened a glimpse of a wild boar coming down to drink.

This, par excellence, is a voyage of looking forward, never back. Never retracing passages or revisiting coves, as one does when exploring an archipelago. Every day is different. Fine by me! Most anchorages are at their best first time. It's unlikely I'll ever be here again. And there's a Sesame round every bend ahead.

THE HALF WAY POINT

At 18.40 precisely, by GPS position and checked on the chart on a straight stretch of shimmering Volga, we reached the half way point on the passage between the seas!!

We had slowed down to four and a half knots under all plain sail. Suddenly at the witching moment came a gust and Wild Goose spurted up to near her seven knots maximum.

'The girls at home have got hold of the tow rope!' said Jim.

I'd been waiting for this moment and out came the hoarded ingredients of the Galway Blazers very own Cocktail – Bushmills whiskey and Pouilly Fuisse.

That soon livened up the evening. We've seen a lot of the Volga now and begun to feel like experts.

During an extended Happy Hour we tried listing the things that we hadn't yet spotted.

We hadn't seen any large private houses along the river. No 'rich men furnished with ability living peaceably in their habitations', which a country needs according to the Old Testament. Not surprising, as for one thing annual spring flooding would have tended to keep such houses well back from the Volga, and for another rich men or big houses in existence in 1919 would have had short shrift at the hands of the Bolsheviks.

No forts had appeared, other than the Kremlin at Nizhny Novgorod, and a small one at Plyoss but plenty of monasteries with defendable curtain walls. We'd seen how the Volga divides the Continent neatly between the taiga and the more open Wooded Steppe but it shows little sign of having ever been seriously fortified.

Like any other big river it has of course acted as a defensive line. Now once again after the 1991 break up of the USSR, the Volga encompasses the state of Russia neatly.

No riverside pubs or eat houses had tempted us to pull in for a quick dram. The Sappers whose motto is, 'Time spent on licenced premises is rarely wasted,' would have been at a loss in these waters. Soon perhaps the embryonic facilities on some of the floating ferry stations will be extended. Then Irish pubs, like those already offering excellent Guinness in St Petersburg, will spread to Volga side what their customers soon come to look on as the bare necessities of life!.

No signs of a lifesaving organisation, although statistics show hundreds of deaths by drowning annually and rescue service are claimed to be in place.

We'd seen no burlaki or Volga boatmen laboriously man hauling colossal loads on clumsy ships with ropes made of lime bark up stream against the current.

But that would have been expecting too much.

Few small birds had appeared in the marshes further west but this would be more than compensated for by the burgeoning bird life further south. But Iceland and Black Headed Gulls, to be seen on all parts of the river, a thousand miles and more from salt water, gave feeling of comfort and familiarity.

Celebrations continued at a gentle pace as the hours drew on and Wild Goose sailed smoothly south. If any objections to our presence arise now, Miles noted , it will be easier to send us south than back north, so odds of getting right across must now be better than fifty fifty.

Towards evening on the right bank the sunlight continued to illuminate the trees on the hills, leaving the land below between them and the river shadowed in velvet folds of light and dark. It's quite different being on a south going leg; you get this lovely play of light

143

and shadow. We are now sailing about south east and the sun sets to starboard and not over the stern. The hill silhouettes and movement of land are again reminiscent of Salisbury Plain.

The spirits of the crew were soaring at the rapid progress. The land was low to the south and standing up on the coach roof they could see enormous skies over as great stretches of open. steppes ahead At 10 pm Miles picked a tributary creek on east bank, noseyed slowly up it, watching the echo sounder read lower and lower, then turned to port parallel to river. This gave a berth neatly protected by a line of shallows from the wash of passing traffic. They let go off waterfront of a town he judged to be Zvenegovo.

Vodka and curry in the cockpit, under a brilliant sunset leaving a long orange track on the surface of the waters, crowned the halfway festivities.

THE SHIPYARD OF ZVENOGOVO

There was no movement where we lay but we could hear tugs roaring past us during the night.

Ashore early in sunshine to find Zvenegovo to be a town of 14,000 people, presenting its best side to the river. Izbas lined along shore. Women bricklayers were at work creating what was almost a suburbia. Houses with neatly packaged privacy, faced a strip of tarmac with sand either side labelled River Drive 2201.

A tout begged us for cigarettes, saying the shops were closed. When we were unable to respond he spat what a Prison Officers would have called 'verbal'. Galina described them as Russian prepositions.

In the library on the Ulitsa Lenina a mother spoke to us, 'A priest comes here to baptise and hold Sunday School', Little children love it, especially bible story books with pictures. Older kids prefer sci-fi and animal behaviour.'

She directed us to the office of the Alexi, Director of Butikov which we learned is the oldest ship building yard on the Volga. It is named after a local worker who became a hero of the 1940 Finnish War. The Director's office was bare, containing nothing but some plastic sailing ship models , a bronze of Lenin against a red background and a strip of carpet no more than the size of the desk. He conducted conversations with increasing heat on two telephones while scanning his visitors with close-set black eyes from the depth of a beard that had once been fair. 'Looks like a rat peering out of a ball of spunyarn,' Nikolai whispered to me as we waited. 'Truly sailors are an international fraternity'. Long ago I'd heard the same comment on the lower deck of a Royal Naval cruiser.

Then Alexei banged the phones down and began to explain. They used to build sailboats but after 1865 started to produce steamships and engines for them. 'Now we build steel tugs and have a workforce of 2,000 including 20 nationalities, half on the shore and half working directly on the ships. We export ships to Hungary and to other rivers in the Soviet. Also we've just built the first oochega gastinitsa, a flotel with 20 rooms and its own engines. I designed it as an independent ship which can be positioned where there is business. It has a sauna, bar, a restaurant – quite luxurious. The first flotel is for Moscow and the next one will be for Kiev'.

Another creation is the OT or Ozerny Talcatil. It means lake pusher with a square bow and claws for linking onto barges or log rafts. 'We build one with 2000 horse power engine in eight months. In winter all this space is covered with ships laid up and everybody works all year round on repairs. The workforce puts in up to 16 hours a day all year round and receive all State vacations'.

A tour revealed men making slides for children and dacha stoves (Ssh!! State secret, Why?), rolling pins, folding chairs and tables, rocking chairs and pedalos.

Other gangs were ship breaking and loading the scrap steel on barges for Cherepovets A fascinating and unexpected plant.

Alexei claimed that the first ever specially designed motor tug was built on the Volga. There is no doubt that much ingenuity over the years has gone into making special ships for the Russian rivers for example the early 19th cent raketas propelled by horse-driven capstans. But claims to originality are so much favoured by Communist propagandists that they must be taken with much salt. Stanislas' proud display of his plant and its versatility made one of the great mornings of the trip.

KAZAN, HERE WE COME!

At 12 noon we hoisted the mainsail at anchor, put one reef in and sailed on for Kazan. It would mark a major turning point in the voyage. Arkady grasped the tiller with one hand and Galina's waist with the other while Wild Goose made six knots.

Galina was laughing with Arkady about remarks in a book she'd found in Wild Goose's packed book shelves.

Wallace (no relation) had written in 1930 'The Soviets should not be blamed for everything. Some things have not changed since before 1911'.

One thing that hasn't lay just ahead. The smoke of trains on the famous Trans-Siberia Railway could already be seen. Another came from the bank, revolting smells with a strong mix of sulphur.

Within an hour the bridge above Kazan was visible, a milestone

145

in itself, The trains puffing across under coatings of soot were bound on a six day journey to Vladivostock.

As they admired the bridge four barges shot by two on each side with a mighty HONK, HONK, HONK, as if to emphasise their superior load carrying power.

'You get quite used to seeing thousands of tons of metal slipping past the ship less than 20 metres away. The helmsmen were competent and usually gave a cheery wave.

There are bare hilltops beside us now in folds like bedclothes over a sleeper and with moghuls on their faces.

At 1830 the wind began to die so the engine was put on and we motor sailed past an archipelago with houses on stilts among them. Far away to the south land began to lose its trees It was quite bare at the mouth of the Svarga river. There lay a pretty islet with two churches and a monastery. I'd love to have stopped and added one to my collection of isles visited in six continents.

Any island on any horizon anywhere draws me like a magnet. An infallible cure for insomnia is to recall visits to them one by one. I've rarely got through more than a dozen before dropping off.

Not much later on Tuesday 28th July we arrived at Kazan, capital of the Tatarstan Republic which had elected to stay in the Soviet Union after the split.

We might learn on the morrow how it was adapting?

Isba with bark-roofed byre attached

CHAPTER ELEVEN

Three Days in Kazan

City of Tatars and Many Massacres

By *MILES*, WALLACE and Arkady

*'When waves with fire and blood were bright
And gunfire thundered through the night'*

28th July

Our mood seems to be tied to the temperature and the speed of progress. Today we feel flamboyant. Arkady shouts that a notice tells us we are now in Free Tatarstan!

Under clear low sun we anchor at 20.30 off a septic island near the main ferry port. After stowing the sails we relax in the cockpit to try to take in this city, the greatest port on the whole Volga system. *Our first impression was of high banks intersected by deep ravines, the crests topped by dachas and flaming chimneys Its dominant trading position is hardly surprising when we worked out that that traffic comes to it from two Volga tributaries, its own Kazanka River, and much more importantly a few miles south with the mighty Kama, the histiorical routeway to the Urals and Siberia, navigable for six months of the year for a thousand miles to Rudnichny.*

Today the word Tatar may be most familiar in the Western World to diners who ask for steak tartare,, called from the fancied preference of Tartar people for eating their meat raw.

The city, founded some miles up the Kazanka River before 1400, now covers some 15 miles of the eastern side of the Volga.

Kazan is oil and soil rich, for it lies in the Wooded Steppe zone of chernozem or Black Earth.

This belt of dark soils runs in a band hundreds of miles broad from the east in Siberia to the west in Russia for 3000 miles and is next in economic importance to the rivers themselves. Seen by us in the evening sunlight the earth had a sheen like the coat of well groomed stallion.

147

A LITTLE HISTORY

Arkady told us that the Tatars are a Turkic people, descended from the Mongol horsemen of Genghis Khan. His Golden Horde stormed out of the east in the mid 13th Century, slaughtering most of the Bulghars and absorbing the rest. Thereafter they posed a threat to the whole of Europe but Ugodei, the son of Genghis, able as he was, did not quite have his father's fire. And the whirlwind western path of conquest slowed. Kazan became a state or Khanate in 1436, an uneasy vassal 400 miles east of Moscow, while other Tartars hordes remained her principal enemies.

Since then Kazan has been a garrison town, guarding a vital east/west route.

In 1548 Ivan IV, aged 18 and not yet Terrible, made a first attempt to bring the Kazan Tatars to heel. Unseasonably warm weather in February swamped roads and softened the Volga ice so that his siege guns sank on the way down river from Nizhny Novgorod.

That attack ended, as historians relate, with Ivan literally in tears A second attempt on 1550, based on a prefabricated wooden fort floated down the Volga erected on a hilltop on the Svyaga River which we had passed that morning was more successful and the Russians of Ivan the Terrible entered Kazan. But the garrison Ivan left behind was too small and the Tatars retook the city.

The most famous date came when Ivan, now even more Terrible, approached with an enormous army in 1552. Things went badly at first. His general complained that, 'at dawn wizened old men and women lined the city walls and broke wind in the Russian's direction. Then straightway astorm would rise with tremendous rains, but only over our army, ruining the rations and sinking ammunition barges'.

But a sliver of the True Cross rushed from Moscow stopped this magic flatulence.

This little comedy was about the only one in the city's history. It fell after its wall were mined. Mass death by torture followed for the garrison, then Russian colonisation.

'The city of Kazan is built on bones, the stream of Kazan runs with blood' are lines of an old Russian song. Miles had already begun to compare Russian history to the peeling an onion – the more you peel, the more you cry.

But for English Merchant adventurers the fall of Kazan had a good effect. As Arkady described it to Miles: 'When your fore-runner Richard Chancellor, the first English to enter Russian via the White Sea, called at the Court Ivan the Terrible Tsar was still savouring his victory over the Tatars.'

148

'That must be why Chancellor found the Tzar in such good spirits', said Miles as he showed him a page from the old Elizabethan seadog's impressions of the Kremlin.

> *'Moscow itself is great, I take the whole towne to be greater than London with her suburbs but it is very rude and standest without order. There is a faire castle, the walls whereof are of brick and very high, the one side is ditched and the other on the other run of the river called the Moskava which runneth into Tatarie and so into the sea called Mare Caspium. Within the castle there are nine fyare churches and therein are religious men. The emperor can put two to three hundred thousand men into the field in battle.'*

'Chancellor's English seemed even stranger than mine,' was *Arkady's reply.*
Changing to the present century, he related:

> Kazan was until recently a closed city because of its plant producing Mig 29 fighters, helicopters and the Konkordski.
>
> Now the Tatar ethnic consciousness is being revived in something more that a few shabby exhibitions of folk art. In fact at that moment it seemed quite possible that the state of Tatarstan would be added to the list of flash points of racial tension. If so we could be instantly in a war zone
>
> 'Don't forget, it's only eight months since an event which, for most of our lives, we would have considered unthinkable – the disintegration of the USSR. – The unbreakable union of free Republics – as our National anthem used to call it – has broken into its 15 constituents parts. Some people think that this unravelling process will go further as various bits of Russia strain at the leash.
>
> And if that happened then Tatarstan, a sort of symbolic homeland for about seven million Tatars scattered liberally across the ex USSR would presumably be one of the first to go. As the Tatars begin to rediscover their language, customs and Moslem religion, some of them dream of reversing the historic defeat by the Russians.

Jim not to be left out pulled out his American tourist book to quote as if a gem of originality that Kazan 'is where east meets west and old meets new'.
We had a comfortless night rolling in the wake of passing ships disturbed by the dinghy banging. and echoing loud hailers from the Raketa Station half a mile away.
Close by lay a barge with evil smelling contents and water slapping hard under its overhung bow. It looks ready to sink within an hour from the rust holes just above it's waterline. Miles struggling

to get *Wild Goose* to lie more easily during the night took a line to the barge. The bargee returning at dawn with bloodshot eyes took violent exception to this encroachment, with scowls and oaths.

'I retaliated by cutting our line and got some satisfaction from this international sailor's insult which means, 'I wouldn't have my line back on board after it has touched your filthy ship. But I doubt if Boris got the point'.

The scepticism the traveller develops is immense. Can anything ever work? Can anyone ever be trusted? The scale itself is part of the Russian problem But the domestic is ever with us.

At breakfast Galina asked for thinner bread.

Arkady counters: 'Your poor husband, are you difficult to live with?'

Galina, 'We don't live together, I told him he would have a difficult time if he married me but he would not listen.'

It was a relief to move into a 200 yard wide pool, dodging a fire float and two ferries coming out through a channel only fifty feet wide.

There were curved rows of buildings round the basin and canals leading off it, lined in stone and capped with wrought iron railings. This bit was reminiscent of St. Petersburg. The biggest channel was almost dry, crammed with rubbish. 'Boots, bicycles, old tyres and mothers-in-law,' said Galina.

I had to shout instructions for mooring against triumphant loudspeaker music from the red painted station but most of the railway tracks were covered in rust, and there were packs of mongrel dogs living in a rusty red train.

Jim hurried off to check in at the Hotel Tartarstan. Later I heard him tell a fellow American, 'We've come here to put Kazan on the map', and found myself hoping that a few lines in the National Geographic would be the only form.

A crowd round Reception watched the film 'The Rich Cry Too'. Faded postcards of cats were on sale, mixed with Tartar dolls, mini-sledges, woolly hats and inflatable canoes. A huge consignment of boxes in the lobby contained refrigerators.

We were shown a bedroom resplendent with a brand new one. On the first floor the cleaner lady was a decrepit seventy year old, and the smell of rubbish overpowering. On the next the concierge was a huge woman whose blouse looked as if was ready to give up an equal struggle; she had violent pink stockings and obviously had not used a razor for years.

'Because of the risk of Aids' said Arkady. The menu in the hotel seemed to exist only to show what was off. Cucumber and tomato salad was Hobson's choice. The restaurants in town had all closed by ten o'clock.

Down by the ship again amid heavy eastern smells we were almost talked into buying a lorry by an Aeroflot pilot who was selling them as a bargain at 230,000 roubles (say £500). He had bought from the State at 150,000 roubles and flown them in ten at a time in his plane, having arranged a monopoly in the area. Said he'd fly one out to the West for us!

Kazan had clearly just taken delivery of a large consignment of Adidas look-a-like tracksuits in blue, green and red as though the city was preparing for some great athletic event. Indeed there was one coming shortly as the taxi drivers told us. An International Congress of Tatars.

The city covetted by Ivan the Terrible has become an industrial centre. The early factories were based on soap, canvas and hides. Now they make anything from space craft to computers and medical equipment.

Going ashore meant climbing up a vertical steel ladder to emerge into streets that within a few blocks seemed to hold a jumble of every one of the hundred nationalities that comprised the old Russian Empire; and a few more beside.We jostled with high cheeked Mongolian clansmen in grey felt caps turned up on all four sides, their faces of the yellow tint that every European pictures as Chinese.

Cossacks on good horses and Cossacks who looked as if any horse was beyond their means but still of proud bearing ; Kalmucks from the backwoods who'd just come up to town and had never seen a white face, dirty bearded Bulghars, foxy faced Muscovites, Greeks anxious to buy dollars. Tall Varangians with Scandinavian features and blonde beards and deep-chested Chuvashes with the shoulders of stevedores mingled with teenagers in designer jeans. When Arkady and I stopped to eat tasteless bread rolls and sip vodka, youngsters hung around the table waiting to pick the leftovers off our plates.

Traders bound for the market pushed past with fruit laden wooden wheeled carts and barrows past rows of shabby cars that stank of the bottled gas they used for fuel.

Lorries honked, drivers swore. Among it all well dressed ladies drew aside their silk skirts to step round frequent puddles.

Rita

At the quayside in the morning Rita, the pretty Cruise Ship hostess, with Natasha her friend greeted us with a cheery 'Haroch!'. They had left their home town of Yashka Ola at three am and changed twice to get here. Rita, may I remind you, is a very sweet person, with short dark hair, wide set dark eyes and a curvy smiling mouth.

*She** at once helped me by using the telephone to make contact with Vitali in Georgia. She then checked about obtaining charts of the Sea Azmov (as Jim insisted on calling it) ,and got permission in advance for entering the Volga Don Canal. That done she fixed dates for the next big crew change due in Rostov.*

Natasha, her friend, seemed intrigued by me, the first non Russian she'd ever met, 'Until now,' she said, 'Westerners were as strange to me as men from Mars.'

So when the work was done they were both keen to make up for lost time and a good party developed in the most convivial atmosphere of Wild Goose's cosy saloon.

The accumulated laughter and camaradie of fifty ears of voyaging seems to have been absorbed into her very timbers and comes echoing back at times like this.

Galina had been busy on other arrangements and came back to the boat after dark in a private car, supplied at no cost because the police were surprised to see a woman trying to get home so late by herself. There was a strong police presence in the streets at night. I'd arrived convinced that the Tartars were aggressive, but on the whole they proved to be extremely friendly.

Bed at 0130. Very tired.

30th July A busy day if ever there was one. Up at 0630 on a still sunny morning. Managed to get a train ticket, from Aeroflot of all places, for Galina in evening ; all earlier trains fully booked.

To market for an hour until 0940. Then call on.

KAZAN EVENING NEWS

Khazbulat Shamsutdinov, the Editor, in brown specs, short sleeve blue shirt, jeans and trainers, spoke of increasing organised crime and active fighting starting in the cause of free Tatarstan. 'It's getting worse. Newspaper sellers have been killed. Youth crime is another problem'.

Khaz arranged an expedition for Miles and Jim to see the pollution on the Kazanka river; a nightmare endless flow of thick yellow and green oily scum making its sluggish way unchecked and officially unnoticed into the Volga. He had written in his paper of the special dangers of the organo-phosphate components. The factories where the seepage originates are said to have been converted from making nerve gas to producing components of agricultural pharmaceutical

---

*Bruce and Wallace met her on the Cruise Ship Tolstoy in 1995 and hope that one day she will come and visit them in Ireland. Her husband is an engineer on another cruise ship and they have two children who are looked after by her mother when both parents are away on the river during the tourist season.

products. These would include sheep dips, one example one of the products that has caused a high suicide rate among Western sheep farmers.

Jim photographed with relish at close quarters the waste from the combined outlet of an EX dynamite and a Bio-Chemical Warfare factory discharging into the river. He returned from his inspection of the gooey mess with a look of triumph, and convinced that his pioneering work in the field of a clean Earth had taken a major step forward

If there was a day that could be identified as the one on which a tired Milo got a whiff of some of these vicious pollutants, this was it.

He got back on board at 1330 to find the brilliant news that Vitali had arrived, having sorted out his family affairs in Omsk before travelling several thousand miles via Moscow to rejoin. His return was a credit to his perseverance as well as to Miles' ability to attract loyalty from his crew. He had all his mother's Dublin charm and a way of getting everyone to feel involved in decision making.

Jim and his gear had just been collected from the Hotel. He greeted Arkady with a question.

'What's the most depressing thing about being in the Third World?'

Arkady thinks, 'Poverty?, Secret Police?, Restricted Travel?'

Jim: '… Waiting in a bedroom for your international call to come through'.

'What did people think about your beard,' Miles asked Vitali in a jocular manner. 'Some people told me I looked more attractive, more serious', he replied in a tone of solemnity. 'Even more attractive?', asked Galina incredulously as she packed. He ignored her and continued his deadpan explanation. 'I told them that I don't find it comfortable to shave every few days. I do not need it for the handsomeness of my face.'

Vitali then picked up a forecast of strong winds.

To get things shipshape for this and open water ahead, Miles spent the afternoon on pleasant sailor's work, correcting the tension of the rigging and checking for loose shackles or bolts, stranded wires or chafed ropes. Then came the less agreeable one of clearing the engine filters once more.

After tea Galina hugged the crew in turn. Then almost tearfully she helped slip the shorelines.

Such is the comradeship which with a good skipper develops on a small boat. With glistening eyes she watched as they pulled out Wild Goose to the anchor laid out in mid pool to keep the hull clear of the rough pier face; then waved her handkerchief as they uphooked and motored away towards Ulyanovsk.

She was to start back to Moscow at 8pm. Miles missed Galina as much the most accomplished and witty of the Russians to have lived on board. A career girl working for the Moscow Adventure Club and later privately for tour operators and Motorola she keeps in touch and has been a welcome guest at our home in Ireland.

As Wild Goose gathered way Miles, in neat swift pencil, noted in the deck log :

Time 1710, Barometer 1010, Wind Calm.
And finished with an unusual flourish.
'South at last, by God.'

The fisherman we nicknamed 'Neanderthal' at Goroditshe.

CHAPTER TWELVE

Green Scum

By MILES

The very deep did rot, O Christ!
That ever this should be!
Yes, slimy things did crawl with legs
Upon the slimy sea
             The Ancient Mariner

SOUTH FROM KAZAN

So on 30th July they left Kazan ...

Ahead lay four great semi-stagnant vodochranilisce. Dams to you; English is lucky to have the equivalent in single syllable.

Each dam is almost two hundred miles in extent, a four or five day passage since the curfew on small craft makes night passages illegal. Each dam is named after the city at its lower end. Distance to Roscof and the sea about a thousand miles, and days to do it, thirty.

First dam would be the Kuibyshev, alias Samara, which reaches its terminal barrage at the start of the Samara Oxbow. This is where the Volga is forced to make a mighty U-turn, forty miles east, round a 2000-foot massif.

After this comes a twisting and narrow dam, extending past Balokovo (You can guess what Jim called that) and Volsk, to end at Saratov.

Then the slightly wider Volgograd Dam which runs south to the city ever famous for having spoiled Hitler's plan to conquer Russia.

Past it a boat climbs over rocky hills by the Volga Don canal. That was an engineering feat which defeated Peter the Great and Sultan Suleiman but was cracked by the Communists at the cost of vast human suffering. It was that canal that made Wild Goose's voyage possible. By making it Stalin islanded Russia.

Then on the Don the Tsimlyansk Dam close to sea level leads on to Roscov and open waters.

155

For a skipper already weary, the dam* descent looked almost damnable, a tough unknown obstacle course through odiferouis water. The voyage was right on schedule. There could be few rest days from now on but Milo with a well-trained crew was beginning to feel confident.

It was soothing to be under way again, to settle down in the cockpit with forearm resting on the tiller shaft and palm on the carved goose head and catch up on Vitali's news.

'Dacha country', Milo wrote, 'which makes us feel at home. Wild Goose old and wooden, is like a floating dacha.'.

The river was quite different in character nearly two miles wide with the banks roughly equal in height.

A small cable ship under Azeri flag from Baku on the Caspian met us, heading north. Exchanging salute with a dirty bearded skipper we felt that no more than a sharp turn to port at Volgograd would put us well on the way east. From Astrakhan we'd be on the Golden Road to Samarkand.

We turned inshore at 2030 when Adik (we could use Arkadi's family nickname now) spotted a cosy guba or cove on the west bank where we'd be sheltered from the north gale if it came.

The evening remained tranquil and we had time to watch the long day wane and the lights begin to twinkle from the dark huts of Grebini village. Then gusts began to whip the river into jagged snakes of foam. The squalls ceased as wind came in vertical torrents and we hastily moved below to eat dinner off our knees. The dinghy started banging from the wash of ships passing out in the channel while the Radio told of The Olympic Games in full swing, and up to form. Three Brits. been sent home for failing drug tests.

Framed in one round porthole was the surprise of the day, a French style chateau, with decorated dormers and Mansard roof. A fisherman, who came alongside with a present of perch and stayed for a vodka, related how it had been built by a homesick Marquis long before the Revolution. The ruins of the distillery he had set up stood beside it. The village cemetery hung on the edge of crumbling cliff.

'Their days are numbered', said Vitali aptly.

---

*Long although they seem to a five knot yacht, none of the Volga dams in terms of capacity rank in the worlds Top Twelve. Measured by the thousand cubic metres the Kakhovsk on the Dnieper is second in the world with 182,000,000 but it is dwarfed by the world's largest, the Victoria Nile in Uganda, which is thirty times larger. Russia's Bratsk and Veya Dams rank in the top twelve for capacity.

By power output Russia has four dams in the top twelve. The Volga owns none of these as it lacks rapidity of fall but Mata Volga would surely take the cake for Foulness of Water in its Dams.

At dawn the forecast gale still hadn't arrived; in fact it never did. The weather here as at home is much given to bluffing. Now the sun was setting up his backstays, oblique shafts of light illuminating far-off tree tops with pale searchlight beams, a sign usually of wind to come.

On the breeze came smells, the warm hum of cow you get in a milking byre, fresh horse manure, and the crushed grass odour that greets you when looking out from a tent at dawn. There were open fields of corn along the banks and a sense of richness.

As we got under way a new form of traffic roared overhead – transport aircraft lumbering low and using the river as a navigation guide.

We were bound for the huge Kama Volga junction. The river was now four miles wide, with pines on the far shore over broad swathes of yellow sand. The blue river surface, tessellated by sun and breeze was frequently marred by the creamy wake of speeding hydrofoils.

By 1600, three miles from the junction, the east horizon sank back to barely visible tree tops behind black smudges of smoke from coal-burning steamers in mid channel.

Hull down they showed the curvature of the earth's surface.

There was a feeling that we were demonstrably on the eastern edge of Europe and that some drama should mark the fact, but with no wind and no waves, all that greeted us was swarm upon swarm of white flies.

Soon the waters of the Reka Kama were making whorls and swirls on the surface as they flowed in from the north east, having come from eastern lands afar.

We glanced over them into a misty blue distance without any great desire to go upstream for a looksee. Now at the confluence with 25 miles of open water to scan five freighters would be in sight at a time and a procession of Meteors dashing along the horizon. The air was filled with the warm, damp smell of wheat, a golden line across the south eastern horizon.

By watching the echo sounder we were able to cut the corner by keeping the west bank close aboard, like a jockey with his leg over the rail; it was steep as if sliced with a knife revealing fine layers of sandstone of a pale camel colour under reddish soil. The forests were thinning out.

Jim expecting rain prepared meticulously with generic soap and clean towels, and sat stripped on deck all expectant.

The altruistic Arkady stuck to the helm for hours, saying, 'Miles, you write book'. Vitali spent the day singing, and teaching Arkady English 'Wonderful', 'Beautiful'. Red, I overheard, is synonymous with beautiful in Russian. That explains a lot – the garish scarlet colours of many churches!

Stronger thoughts were forced onto Milo, with his interest in things military, by the vast array of earth and water – a realisation of what a formidable barrier these rivers have been for armies. He could see more clearly than any Sandhurst lecturer could explain the virtually impossible task Napoleon faced trying to conquer all of Russia. and the truth of the advice given himself as a young soldier: 'Never be separated from your kit. Never volunteer and NEVER march on Moscow'.

By 1640 it began to rain but Jim had covered his flesh and gone below. There was lightning on the far horizon. This landscape is so big that one can see other people's storms and not be part of them.

At 1750 we anchored in 'safe Harbour'; that's how its name translates, ten miles south of the Confluence. Not a bad name but Wheat Port would have been better: we are in the lee of a low island, surrounded by corn covered hills. By invitation we 'saddle-bagged' alongside the good ship Volga Neft 42. Captain Nikolai Nikolaevich Dimov and his wife Lilia entertained us most kindly with vodka and cakes, showed charts and gave directions for getting on to Rostov.

His group of twenty 12,000 ton motor ships is the biggest on the river. He has sometimes taken crazy risks of being beset on late autumn voyages. One has to imagine the river in winter 'When frost stays the waves that dance', as a two thousand mile strip of ice, twenty feet thick in its northern reaches, three feet here.

We woke to the light echoey sound of the water between our bilge and the steel hull of NEFT 42 The bay was covered in streaked lines of algae. Admirable were graceful egrets fishing daintily along the shore, pruning their feathers often to retain their white purity. But a green dog trying to shake off clinging emerald scum after a swim caused much laughter.

THE BULGHARS

The captain had pointed out that the city of Bulghar lay close to the far bank and that we were in the territory of yet another culture. This point is where the river suddenly narrows. and the good harbour we lay in made it a natural stage on an east west trade route. The shores around us were, he showed us, full of evidence of old riverside settlements of Bulghars. They set up a Khanate of their own here in the early 900s, several centuries before the onset of the Golden Horde of Tatars. Some Bulghars were Muslim but stumps of wood near where their ships moored are remains of effigies of Gods of an older religion. They built a fort here to protect the caravan route to Khiva south of the Aral Sea. It was an international market with a currency of sable, samite and slave girls instead of gold.

158

Sometimes red-haired girls came from as far away as Ireland,. They might be bartered here to go on to some lecherous merchant prince in Samarkand. So Begorras and twinkling Irish wit spread eastwards far and early.

On these whale-back hills around us many a bulging Bulghar merchant sat on a silk covered couch with boys and girls for sale around him. And agents watched to make sure the Bulghar King collected one in ten of the bodies purchased.

Miles found that the layers upon layers of history around him broke the boredom of the daily slog. Without it at times they could just have been motor boating on humdrum waters in the flat lands below Seville.

'Wish we could find a brace of slave girls going cheap', said Vitali, as he washed up breakfast.

SATURDAY, 1st AUGUST

We motored in dull style south all day in extraordinary light. Sometimes water and sky so melded that the Volga is like a sort of Gulf Stream between two invisible lands. Then slowly the Volga tightens in again to become more clearly a Reservoir, the right bank two or three hundred feet high.

Suddenly a fisherman blared at us on his radio, twitching his short rod aerial like a conductor's baton. Couldn't get his meaning until we fouled an almost invisible line of buoys supporting a net. A bellow of 'Full Back Engine' from Jim got us off. Just! We hoped the net cutter on our prop. hadn't done too much damage to his net. Another skipper laughed his head off at our antics as he leaned out of his wheelhouse, trying to steer with one hand and blow a steam syren with the other.

Low walls or 'wing dams' project from the shore hereabouts, a little above water level but sometimes below it as a way of reducing erosion. Difficult to see in bad light, so yet another trap for the unwary.

A Green but not Green Peace World

An Imperial Eagle with white shoulders and bright yellow feet perched near a bulky nest in a treetop. How Dad would have loved to stop and shin up to it.

Sunlight made golden circles on the river as it shot sharp angled beams through steeply wooded hills to starboard. All day the algae became thicker, in patches at first, later as an unbroken uniform green. It felt as if we were motoring across pea soup. Ships passing showed pale green bow waves.

In the widest parts, ten miles or more, land to the east was so low as to be almost invisible, leaving us in a subliminal make-believe

159

world. Only our track cleaving the green slime astern remained clear for a while. Arctic terns took advantage of our passing to catching fry in it and big fish jumped for flies.

Right bank is sheer knife-cut dropping steeply into the river from a great height. Photographing as from a nid du pie at the masthead I could see healthy pines on open land beyond the crest. The near ones are sick, slipping progressively into the Volga. All stages of the process are portrayed, upright, keeling over, halfway down, lying in the water – like shots from a flick book.

There are small islands to the east stretching into apparent void. A half mile long log raft passed towed south by two tugs. Not so long ago it would have been guided only by men with long sweeps That night we talked about islands.

Our nightly conversations flickered sometimes without subject and seemingly without end. Now it was on the number of islands in the Volga. There are no official figures. To get a total of course it would be necessary to define what is an island and at what level of water in the river. But Arkady said by any standard it must be many thousands. Sometimes on a bend thirty or more isolated pieces of land would be in sight at once, each an island by the Scottish definition of being 'large enough to be inhabited or support one sheep'. Vitali agreed as to the attraction of islands and how an otherwise ordinary patch of scrub becomes an entity, demanding exploration, just by being surrounded in water. Islomania is a world wide disease. Wild Goose's bag is several hundred islands visited.

Bird noises come echoing out of the forest and rushes. Booms of bitterns, yaffle of woodpeckers, croaks of a Booted Eagle harried by small birds. Another big 'hook beak' bird sitting on a log gave a very distinctive cry, 'Kyak, Kyak, Kyak', like a dog yapping. Its chest is pepper and salt so it is perhaps a Spotted Eagle. And many smaller birds, strange to eye and ear, flit across the river.

Some ships still fly the old Hammer and Sickle Soviet flag. It was hauled down for the last time in the Kremlin less than a year ago so I suppose it's an economy measure until they tatter to pieces.
We anchored in a place with no visible name thirty miles short of Ulyanovsk – after nine hours on the move. In this time had made forty five miles. Shouts and barks come from the shore until late.

AUGUST 2nd:

We woke to the sough of clear water running over stones down from a spring set among beech and maple

Goroditshe, as we found our anchorage to be, is a curious combination of a Fishing Station and a Recreation Village. Landing beside the ferry pier we found spiral fossils at the water's edge *where the bank had collapsed. Some of them were shell shaped up to six inches across. Proof that this mighty plain was once under water. Vitali produced the Russian equivalent of the saying that 'seeing is believing but touching is the God's honest truth'.*

A fisherman with receding forehead, beetling brows and ape like jowl shouted something as we headed for a collection of houses half-hidden in trees. Short and bent, with wiry hair and a wall-eye below a savage cut, he wore a long canvas smock and woollen trousers with a gaping rip in the seat. We nicknamed him Neanderthal and gave him a cigarette as he scratched his toes inside worn out flip-flops.

'We fish all night in summer and sleep only three hours. Got this cut from a gaff when fighting to land a big som' (Catfish).

We watched the boats coming in, some empty, some with gun-whales almost awash, the fishermen ponderous and slow moving as if sated from a huge meal. The tiny pier became crammed with vehicles and as soon as a catch was weighed and loaded onto a lorry the driver planted his elbow on the horn stuck his head out of the window and cleared a lane for himself with oaths. There were SOUDAK (Pike) being taken in carts away from the pier to a local processing plant, also sappa. The latter were soft fleshed and almost translucent under the gills, but we didn't find their English name.

'It's all collective', said our friend. 'Wee boats working in pairs, told where they can and can't go and what size they can catch. 'Fishing's terrible; the Communists have spoiled Russia,' empha-sising by punching his hand with his fist. The absence of thought policemen was refreshing.

Only the successful fishermen were calm and aloof, walking up to the village with the steps of kings.

The sharp smell of old fish is a strong memory from a woman as she made sterlet soup over an open fire. Her odour was as putting off as the soup was tempting. I wished I'd had some of the pills Beryl Smeeton carried labelled 'To be taken before dining with the natives'.

A House of Rest (Dom Otdikha in Russian), a combined Spa and Sanatorium stood just up the hill. Trades Union financed at the time, it was being changed to a commercial enterprise.

Russian buildings have an extraordinary capacity for looking decrepit. The Sanatorium was Corbusier style architecture in pre-formed concrete, disfigured with cracks and peeling paint.

One sure thing I observed is the way the Volga creates a micro climate by bringing fresh damp air to the shore. You can see a very distinct line between clay away from the river and the good dark soil near the banks. When we returned to our dinghy Neanderthal

161

said, 'Watch me!' He started to row standing up facing forward in what was meant to be a demonstration of strength but after a few strokes fell flat on his face! Roars of laughter!

DEPRESSION

There was more thunder and lightning as we motored away at 1250. Soon we could make sail and put the engine off. At 1745 not far from Ulyanovsk we became anxious approaching a bridge which appeared near collapse. The whole bluff it sprang from seemed to be disintegrating. Sailing hard and well heeled we seemed to pass only by the thickness of paint on top of the masthead lamp. A whole neighbourhood can be seen as slowly sliding into the Volga as wide scars gape, scrubby trees tilt and houses sit at crazy angles.

Signs of efforts to build a new bridge appear but the whole looks like a post-earthquake disaster area. A small white ferry collects workers from midstream piles. A raw concrete road with displaced slabs winds through hills. In the river under a lowering sky a swell almost on the scale of sea waves fizzes as it breaks along the shore.

'Very difficult, not to feel depressed, partly the weather, I suppose, but home seems a very, very long way off.'

Vitali afterwards told us that the atmosphere in this Kuybyshevskoye Reservoir is known for its oppressive effect, a combination of the foul stagnant condition of the water and rotting vegetation on the banks tainting the air. Sir Samuel Baker, African Explorer, noted the same depression on the upper Nile brought on he thought from the stench of rotting papyrus.

Milo did not of course communicate his feelings to the crew. He had learned from Miles and Beryl Smeeton that private doubts and fears are not for discussion.

We passed thankfully at last through the lock at the Barrage, then found our way into a tiny harbour not more than a metre deep, dragging our keel through soft mud.

ULYANOVSK

This town is called after Lenin's father, a superintendent of schools working for the Tsar., Before that it was Simbirsk, where ships used to be laid up in the winter before the river froze. Reputedly a place of pilgrimage and holiday for those wanting to see where Lenin man was born, it had a fin du saison air. A big man with a brown beard and fair hair, in dirty track suit trousers and a Shetland sweater, took our lines. He looked as if he had been slightly overdone in an oven but in the cabin he was all smiles and introduced

162

himself as Sasha Vashislav of German blood. We were snug alongside a stone breakwater and our heater made things a little more
cheerful on this drizzly chill evening. There was even a welcome
from the Harbour master.

'We are eight metres lower than the big dam here. People live in
fear. Special groups of militia men look after the foundations'. We
could here the hum and whine as the load varied on the great generators at its base.

Jim went off to get a hotel room. The rest of us had a Goulbiaka
of mixed fried fish with Sasha and his family. He helped us buy
bread and vodka, by showing his registration card. There was a
cash shortage, so got change in practical manner in slices of
bread! Try that next time you're in Sainsbury's.

But for all the privation, there was a separate queue for War
Veterans and Diabetics.

When Sasha arrived in a taxi next morning the tyres were so tired
that the owner had to pump furiously every 200 yards.

'What brave guys you are,' he said. 'Sometimes new eyes see
more than old. What do you think of this place?'

That gave a cue to pass compliments on the kindness of its citi-
zens.

He took us to the Great Temple to Lenin which surrounds the
three houses he lived in.

We admired 'the honourable paper that young Volodya brought
from the gymnasium.'

Sasha and his partner Olga Nikitin worked at repairing videos.
They wanted to buy a restaurant but found too many problems just
then because of the risk and the expense of registration and the
palms to be greased In the process.

Brief stop at Great War Memorial overlooking the river, back to
boat having bumped into Tim Hewell, the BBC reporter.

Sped south pleasantly all evening under all plain sail towards
Tolyatti. I listened to conversation on BBC Radio about Country
Life, and making wills. Vitali spent the afternoon chasing flies with
the same athleticism he gives to his picture taking.

Found an abandoned wooden boat floating in middle of lake.
Wonderful evening, great platforms of land rising to the west, curious pattern of squares in crops. 'In England we have crop circles,
in Russia you have crop squares. I wonder why?'

English lessons continue. ' "Vun-der-ful". "Brave". "Braw". Is
that how Scotsmen really say it? We are looking forward to
Istanbul. There you will see stomach dancers. We'll eat Kolbasa.
Maybe that will make you do stomach dances.'

The girls at home certainly have got hold of the tow rope now
and are pulling hard. Top speed of nearly seven knots but couldn't

quite make Sengiley so decided to anchor along the lake shore where Nikolai might have remarked there was nothing to lay except the anchor. The reflections faded away as the light went and we were left off a gently sloping shore, bare grassland rising to trees on the crest of a 200 foot hill a mile or more away. There was a lovely biblical scene of hundreds of sheep grazing on the shore, boats rowing up channel, high pitched ululating tone of crickets in the grass, great wafts of cow manure. The sunset although lost behind the hills was clearly pink again and spoke of better weather.

Using our Tilley lamp for the first time now the evenings are getting shorter.

Felt like Carruthers in the Riddle of the Sands as I wrote by its steady light.

4th August: At four am a fuzz of mist ringed our craft at a discreet distance. I woke again later to the sound of eagles croaking as they hunted over the water. It was a crisp, cool, cloudless day with light breezes from west north west. Low headland disappearing in fading grey blues to an empty horizon as the Reservoir widens out to over 20 miles. There is a curious feeling of being in a great bay or wide sound between huge rolling islands. Land to west is like a billiard table, so smooth and already cut for hay. Pines stripped of their lower branches lean at crazy angles.

Away at 0620 with thick grey clay being scrubbed off the anchor as we passed a small chalk mining village. Babble of Russian between Vitali and Arkady. The dawn wind filled our sails for an hour then it was engine on as the reservoir narrowed and widened again near Sengilley. Great platforms of open land again over mud cliffs. Ramps of spoil come down to shore in places. Jetties in very poor repair stick out into the river. Fences overhanging the drop. Many deadfall branches washed into the green shallows. Ploughed land lies in huge swathes extending several miles over the hillsides. This is the black earth, the most fertile soil in the world. Here again you can actually see hectares of black chernozem where top soil is turned up.

By 1320 we were motoring across a lake, green striations still on the water. Chalk cliffs close to starboard, wind lines on the water. Water towers punctuate the landscape. Zhiugli Hills look as if ice-capped where the chalk shows on top like the hill above Loch Torridon in Scotland. We talked to three couples in a small wooden yawl with dipping lug rig all in a bad state with drink. 'Bolshoy Bodun', they said, meaning big hangover. The only people we saw all day.

Suddenly a thin strip of dachi appears on the bank then four smokestacks and cooling towers rise out of the river, capped by a line of black smog. Our pleasant wilderness is becoming another

164

industrial disaster area. At Tolyatti we selected one of nine small yacht clubs but got it wrong and grounded badly coming in stern-to. The level of the reservoir was rising and falling by the minute in alarming fashion. So when it was up, we moved to second basin and anchored at dusk with our bows to the jetty by the romantically named Heeik Chemical Yacht Club.

THE DETROIT OF RUSSIA

This then is Tolyatti and the start of the fifty mile oxbow of the Samara bend. It is an unfamiliar but pleasant feeling to a have bare high shouldered mountains all round after weeks when we might have felt like joining The Flat Earth Society.

It is also the Detroit of Russia. We were met by Sergey, a friend of Sasha our Ulyanovsk supporter. He sea-jacked us, instantly to see the world class Autovaz Plant where all the Ladas come from.

There 100,000 workers, including some ferocious ladies, produce 740,000 cars per annum. Introduced as a journalist of renown I was invited to drive at ninety miles an hour round hairpin bends on the test track. After weeks at five knots on Wild Goose my reactions were suspect, so for me they cleared the track and it was a lot more fun than go-karting.

We goozled at three hundred chocolate coloured cars being assembled at once in each of three lines, one coming off every twenty two seconds. More eye-catching was a blondie driver asleep, legs astraddle on her forklift and other girls being kissed by their boyfriends behind thin screens while radios blared and cars rolled by unexamined.

This was followed by a forced tour of the city to admire a Brobdingnagian International School of Architecture, and office buildings of immensity hard to take in. A tractor on top of one tower looked like fly-sized model until you saw a man driving it.

I felt like murmuring Morgenstein's lines:

> 'The architects meanwhile made off
> To Afrik or Americoff.'

Down the Reservoir the Russian Giganticism continues. Cooling towers ten miles away looked big enough to be close up. You think you have an idea of scale and then a tiny yacht sail comes into the picture. But everything, mark you, is available!

At dinner in a small private restaurant Sergey pointed out the local mafia.

'If there's anything you want', he whispered, 'Engine parts, fuel, electronics, just ask'.

165

'Lady friends too!'

I thought of the yacht skipper approached by a pimp in Port Said who replied testily, 'I don't want your sister. I want the harbour master.'

Pimp: 'Weell ... I think that could be arranged!'

Breakfast on the Yacht Club verandah in cool hazy morning sun at 0700; only to discover that we had crossed another Time Zone and that it was 0800. Sergey arrived dressed in so precisely the same clothes as yesterday as to leave some doubt as to whether he'd ever been away. But he'd come in the first official registered taxi we'd seen since Norway. We drove to the bank where Sergey worked as the Commercial Director's driver. Lev the Director told us that he had organised the first independent Bank in Russia. That was less than three years ago, and it already had 1.6 billion roubles of money in circulation. But changing our humble $50 bills at a decent rate seemed a problem.

Policemen at Murmansk and Gorki had done better! New car models being tested were paraded for our approval. There were lots more goodies to view Tolyatti. We knawed the nail of hurry and slipped at noon.

Volga traffic.

166

CHAPTER THIRTEEN

Round the Bend

By WALLACE, MILES and ARKADY

'At Stavropol ... the river turns southeast towards the Urals thus forming what is known as the bend of Samara. On the right hand are the Jigoulef Hills, a most beautiful range varying from 400 to 600 feet and clothed with wood out of which jut promontories crowned with blue limestone. Here and there the steep slopes are cut by deep ravines which open out into little valleys in which nestle villages bordered by bright green sward.

Russia Past and Present. Wyman and Sons, London, 1857.

Stavropol is former name of Tolyatti, re-labelled for an Italian Communist who introduced motor manufacture.

Wild Goose had to be poled through soft mud to get out of the basin at Tolyatti.

'Like a gondola,' said Vit.

'Some Gondola!', retorted Miles.

As they emerged a huge cruise ship at twenty knots burst out of the smog which veiled the river, making a wake big enough to swamp any open boat. It sprouted fifty aerials, far more than needed for ordinary navigation. Many officers on these ships are from the Russian Navy and it is widely assumed that they have a military surveillance function.

This was indicated when at one port the crew were invited onto the bridge of a cruise ship. In the midst of a friendly tour some fresh radio traffic came in and the captain immediately ordered 'Clear the Bridge!'.

Sun began to burn off the haze by 1100. In water, the sickly green of anti-freeze additive, we had to kill time for half an hour in hot sunshine before entering the lock. Around us was another complete city of high rise apartments and scores of cranes. Pyramids of

sand seem quite small from the water until you get the scale by seeing a caterpillar vehicle crawling over them. A hundred-foot crane
lay on its side, collapsed load like a broken lemonade straw.

We were called in by easy going officials who had been asked by
Moscow to check where we had got to. In the glaring white of lock
side buildings the heat was explosive. Public Holiday crowds
gyrated in the excitement of freedom and high summer as we
passed out of Lock 21 into a mile of narrow channel.

Beside it women in white coifs were painting the bottoms of
ships set up on jacks over their heads. Vitali imitates them by wearing a footballer's T-shirt as a sun hat over his head and looking like
Mother Teresa. This is the biggest yard we've seen yet. Dozens of
ships are laid up, their serried masts and rigging making attractive
patterns against the treed hillsides.

Another hour's wait until at last the Guardian let us through the
next lock on our own. The gates recess sideways like stage curtains.
Vast wharf with opening arches. The concrete blocks of the lock sill
flung back the heat as if a furnace door had been opened. The
ascent brings us into a different world. Hills on both sides hug the
channel, their cladding of trees stopping five hundred feet below
the rocky peaks.

Wall to wall blue haze to east, broad sandbanks on the right.
Stands of pine, casting their scent strong, over the river showed
bare areas grown up with scrub like patches on an old jacket.

A small, rather sorry-for-itself church stood like a tear-drop on
meadowland, white with pale blue cupolas like onions upside
down. Cattle knee deep in the river, gaping mouths of old mines in
layered rock. In scenery like this we motored all day and anchored
in lovely evening light remote from habitation under white limestone cliffs.

DISCO IN THE WOODS

Arkadi recalls what happened next: 'One of the highest and happiest moments of the Russian voyage for Miles. On the evening of
August 5th after a sweltering summer day Miles surprised us all
with 'Let's go dancing.' We had no land transport so, short of doing
a jig to the sounds of Vitaly's guitar, the opportunity of this activity
seemed limited but Miles was adamant and sure enough we pricked
up our ears and heard the strains of rock music somewhere in the
middle distance. It was growing dusk but water holds the evening
light for long and we could see showy figures on the shore. We
landed and walked through the woods in twilight past tents and
A-frame houses. People of all ages were gyrating and love making
in semi-darkness.

After several interrogations by suspicious locals we discovered the source of the melody – the summer camp for twelve-year-old girls which was having its final night of celebration. But how were three bearded males looking like wolves in ship's clothing to infiltrate .

'We'll have to hang some noodles on their ears,' I said using a Russian expression for telling fibs which Miles found intriguing. I located the stern Communist matron in charge of the camp and told her that Miles was a famous Irish writer who was doing a comparative study of child rearing techniques between England and Russia. That seemed to do the trick; we were ushered into a stuffy conference hall where End-of-Term speeches were being made. Miles was formally introduced and with perfect manners reciprocated with words of his own, translated laboriously by Vitaly, about the importance of international friendship. Clearly charmed by their unexpected guest the Mason presented him with a fine print of a Russian oil painting. Then it was time to gather round a huge bonfire where dozens of spindly-legged girls gathered at the feet of this exotic, glamorous figure who had arrived as it were from outer space. They peppered him with questions about his homeland, wife, family and past. He in turn tried to question them about what they wanted out of life. Did they expect to go back to Communism, were they ambitious to make money or see the world? 'We want Barbie dolls; bring us a Barbie doll from England next time you come'. Somewhat bemused, Miles replied that he would be sure to do so.

Then as a diversion he sang a song

'I've been a wild rover for many a year.
I've spent all my money on whiskey and beer'

They joined the 'No, No Never chorus'. Then the rock music started again. The innocent nice tunes from the 70's. It was time to show off our prowess at jiving. At the age of 40 plus I admit I didn't find it easy but Miles was a natural. I remember his blonde, bearded giant head bobbing up and down to the music, towering above the kids as they gazed at him in awe and admiration. All the tension and strain of the voyage, all the struggle to understand Russia and its peculiarities were instantly forgotten as he moved to the beat. He was loving it and girls loved watching him. Vitaly and I were enjoying it too.

Now four years later the image that remains in my head is of that joyful, jiving figure, radiating happiness in all.

We got back relieved to find the dinghy untouched and turned in dog-tired. The hills were too thickly clad to encourage a morning climb.

Next day Miles was 'thinking long', in Irish vernacular, about home and the limpid waters of the Aegean where he could watch the anchor spiralling downwards to the sea bed as we ploughed through the fields of algae. 'Oh for the smell of salt sea air'.

WILD GOOSE'S FARTHEST EAST

AUGUST 7th:
Our air map shows the next city as Kubyshev, named after a Bolshevik leader, but now reverted to the euphonic Samara.. On the slopes of the Zhugli Hills among apple and peach groves the white walls of apartment blocks vanish into blue haze. A cool wind is very welcome. but brings faintly some un-natural chemical smells. Big trees grow straight out of beach. Six fat women in folding chairs stare at us from on water's edge in front of candy stripped awnings We anchor off the Soviet Yacht Club at the cusp of the circuit of the Samara Bend – fifty degrees, ten minutes and five seconds East of Greenwich. A sobering three thousand five hundred Nautical Miles from home.

The Yacht Club, guarded by snarling dogs, was busy with preparations for the Balakovo Race, due to start south from here in two days time. Arranged a car which we had to share with a passenger so corpulent that there was scarcely room for one of us beside him in the back. Drove into town past to the Kirov Statue and Memorial. Lunch in a restaurant where Fatty told us over treble chins.

'The Volga is the most important thing in my life. One and a half million people depend it.' That seemed an underestimate and judging from the way he shovelled rice down and drank Kumyss for which Samara was anciently famed, ne would have thought it took second place to food in his personal horizon. Then drove out of town to see the countryside – long fields of barley and of rye.

Samara, founded to guard the river in the 16th Century, remains a garrison town, protecting extensive oil refineries. Khakhi lorries and Red Stars much in evidence. The modern part of the town is windowed concrete cliffs all too familiar in the Gorky style.

At the War Memorial four weddings were taking place simultaneously; most participants were smoking, some carrying bread and cheese and vodka as a picnic. 23 couples already married, 17 to go, clad in everything from evening dress to cheap tart's minis. Weddings very seldom go to church because there are so few available, only two in the city orf well over a million people. The women have no head dress but some have veils. Most of these were covered in flies. The old women look very unhappy at the constant chatter of those waiting.

A dewy morning followed, river covered in haze through which hundreds of small family boats could be glimpsed. We motored past

170

drifting green Jon boats. Colossal buildings for half mile down left bank. Paddle steamer on right bank, Women washing clothes in the river despite green algae. Hot day cooled by southerly breeze. Vitali is painstakingly repairing a clapped out guitar.

'Not only for me but for you to have some music'.Yesterday he was withdrawn; today back in his earnest mode of touching companionability. He put his hand confidentially and warmly on my knee and said: 'I try to hellup you'. With careful catlike movements he trimmed his beard and moustache but made a tiny cut in his cheek.

'Where is the poteen? Please put poteen on the cut.'

This was the remains of the bottle of the Irish moonshine whisky which we had brought but it had been reckoned undrinkable even by the Russians. In the evening Vitali starts playing his new guitar. A dog started howling in protest from the shore. Arkady rolls his eyes and says 'Stradivary'.

Then Vitali says, 'I shall wash bort (boat). They say this scum very bad for hull and it is getting all over the topside'.

Family canoes curtseyed in our wake off the village of Stary Zagora.

We anchored off another small derelict church on high open ground above right bank. Vodka martinis gave strength for a run ashore at this narrowest point on the Neck. We climbed up a track winding by the waterside then crossing a hill shoulder which diverted a bubbly stream. The church interior was bare but undefiled. The track was overhung with bush Lonicera Tartaria honeysuckle which flourishes here, tree ferns made Gothic arch tunnels . Through the gaps the view was stupendous as we joined a road leading upwards.

The Neck itself is some 25 miles wide but it is here split in two by a tributary running south from the Volga on the north side of the great bend. From the road running along the crest I could see twenty miles north to the smog of Tollyatti and to the south east a toy Wild Goose gyrating at anchor, beyond her mile after mile of swirls of current and left bank marshes afloat with islands. Any of them might have been home to a Lady of Shallot.

On our way downhill we were invited onto the verandah of very grand and fretted Sauna House, occupied by an extended family who offered us excellent local brandy, quiche, bread, cheese and fruit. Chocolates for which Samara is famed followed. Then the talk turned to an update on international news and good advice on the river ahead. Much refreshed by the spacious surroundings and warm family atmosphere we made our goodbyes and got back on board at midnight.

By 0700, survivors in Jon boats were out in force. The day was bright with occulting beams of sunlight coming through the trees. We motor sailed most of the morning. Drowned forest and stump fields to port; right bank trying very hard to be a steppe but not quite. Clumps of bushes lay in the hollows across an open landscape rolling in gentle undulations to the eastern horizon. Passed under a bridge near Oktyabrysk, very carefully spilling the wind from the sail so as not to be going too fast in case the mast should catch. The minimum 12.4 metres marked on chart would have caught us below the upper spreaders. The average water level is marked in white paint on one of ten piles and today luckily it was low.

AN UNEXPECTED HAMMER

Reached Syzran Meteor Station at 1400. The town lives by river traffic and oil refining; at a tenth of the size of Samara is small enough to be friendly. There Arkady sent a telegram to his daughter, while I received two gifts – from the pier master – a large glass of vodka which I had to drink at one gulp, and having passed that test a sledge hammer. It was a genuine hammer-and-sickle-sort-of hammer, with not a ghost of a spring in the short handle and a seven pound head. A good weapon if it came to fighting, and useful on a boat where wedges often have to be driven on the old time sailor's principle, 'If it won't go, force it!'.

ANCHORAGE BY THE NECK

   Left Syzran at 1740 and anchored under another derelict church at 1930 at the foot of golden grass hills seen over river bank oaks Had Hawaiian supper of risotto, then ashore. Visited church and then set off by myself to climb the ridge overlooking the south western end of the Great Samara Bend. This made another utterly memorable evening. I traversed a Pushkin landscape of rutted cart tracks among tall pines, deserted except for eagles sparrow hawks, and magpies. Suddenly the Volga spread out below, a seven-mile wide corkscrew turned pale gold by the sunset and sprinkled with a fantastically beautiful pattern of tufted islets and tiny ships at anchor. In my bunk by 2230 but the excitement of what I'd seen kept waking me up. At 0300 I bleared up the cabin steps to have a phosphorescent pee and look at the dark land under a the star filled sky and the lights of ships in channel. Went back to sleep but up again at 0600 and set off alone to the crest of the hill to see the sunrise over trees descending steeply to the river. The sun came up like a red balloon out of the forest steppe, the light an exact reversal of last night's, making a view at first barely recognisable but even more striking.

Islands which had been green and bosky were dark silhouettes ringed in the warm gold of a river shot with fire.

Staunched a mammoth appetite with breakfast of Compo ration porridge mixed with drinking chocolate before setting off for Khvalensk.

'Miha!' (Big eats!), said Vitali as he watched me wolf it. The hill top view stayed as a brain haze in my mind all day.

Under sail all morning. It would be hard to exaggerate the delight of gliding along under wind power, in contrast to enduring the drum and heat of the engine which in these latitudes made the cabin almost untenable. Time then to sip a vodka and enjoy the broad swathes of gently rolling yellow grassland hills to starboard, as we snaked along a buoyed channel within the wide waterway. Steep hills abeam, the last we'd see before the Caucasus, looking a-crumble in a most un-natural landscape. The land seemed embalmed in soft eggshell light under skies of drowsing turquoise over delicate strands of settling mist.

At 1800 came a very unusual sight, a pre-Revolutionary land-owner's house on the cliff edge and boats beached on a slipway below it. That made a combination interesting enough for a whistle stop.

The erstwhile abode perhaps of 'Rich men furnished with ability', missing on more northerly reaches.

The Georgian house now holds a Post Office and Rest Centre with the bar and cafeteria of a holiday camp set in lofty panelled rooms. We were greeted by troops of strumming girls and student playboys.

Arkady picked three that he fancied to take out sailing. And so we went 'yachting' for two hours, setting the big patched bal-loonatic jib and ghosting slowly downstream with young Sergey playing his guitar in competition to Vitali in the cockpit.

Something good by which to remember Khvalensk.

A quick supper of tinned stewed steak and smash finished the day. Rations were getting very low but Jim's Pemmican Packs seemed to last for ever.

The leading competitors in the Samara to Balakovo Race passed as we got under way. Then many ornate modern houses appeared along the shore, homes of merchants who used to live in town.

THE BALOKOVO BARRAGE

After motoring all day with big yachts in company we were lucky to be allowed straight into the lock at Balokovo. In a small pool below it we anchored off a jetty belonging to yet another chemical plant. There we exchanged compliments with Yuri, a hirsute Slavonian

173

Estonian entrepreneur of sinister bearing. His face looked the cover picture from The Joy Of Sex. He claimed to be on holiday from Estonia driving his Mercedes 230 but was closely watched by three bodyguards in an accompanying car. They helped us ring up to arrange a helicopter for Jim to get aerial shots of Volgograd and to make a rendezvous with Anton, Bruce's doctor friend in Saratov.

Boring breakfast of bread and jam. Now having to buy food every 48 hours as our stores are virtually exhausted. Serge, who had followed us by car, took us first to a Nuclear Power Plant where we failed to gain access. (Can't say I minded; they'd had a near miss Chernobyl boil down recently) so went to see a State Farm, a 'Solhoz', as distinct from a collective farm. Amid clouds of dust school children were gathering tomatoes and cucumbers. Spoke to Director of 700 acres of vegetables, then into town for bad lunch. Bought kolbasa through Sergey's wife because meat shop was closed.

AN EVEN MORE UNEXPECTED PRESENT

Back to boat where Totyana and Vitali Yurana, the owners of a spectacularly ugly home-made yacht invited us for a drink. Brought them back to Wild Goose for supper. She is a poet and he is an ex-Rocket Troop captain turned Ecology Lecturer. He gave me the most interesting present of the whole trip, the bone of a dinosaur. It was black, light and brittle, about 15 inches long, with knuckle-like nobs at each end, a toe maybe.

They were good company in which to celebrate another big reservoir left astern and be warned about some of the hazards ahead.

An evening walk showed some earthwork traces of the original 18th Century Balakovo. The construction of the Barrage and hydro electric plant in 1970 began a change which has transformed a once pretty village .Huge chemical plants followed, a marine diesel factory and then a nuclear power station. The population is now quarter of a million and growing A bitter price to pay for what is called progress but down by the river with the concrete cliffs shrouded in mist and only the distant hum of turbines there was still peace.

CHAPTER FOURTEEN

The Longest Bridge and Shortest Canal

By MILES and ARKADY

Who hath seen the beaver busied?
Who hath watched the bluetail mating?
*Who hath lain alone to hear the **Wild Goose** cry?*
               The Feet of the Young Men. Kipling.

MONDAY 13th AUGUST
Cock-a-doodle-doos echoing out of mist broke into my dreams of
an Irish farmyard. The disagreeable realities were Jim's snores, the
rumblings of a town he had already nicknamed Bollocko, (for once
I concurred!) and the sulphurous stink of the water in which we
floated . Wild Goose's waterline looked as if we'd sailed through a
cesspit. The harbour's surface was slowly circling surrealist whorls
of green and yellow.

Glad to be off, we motored out into the river to where the current
coming out of the Barrage ran with us at nearly two knots.

Swiftly we passed Maiden Island where the Tartars once kept
their most beautiful captives in secluded harems. Deadeye Dick
and Mexican Pete would certainly have made a stopover with little
chance of Eskimo Nell to arrive and spoil the fun but there was no
one with which to share the joke.

The next city Vol'sk (not to be confused with Volzhsk just east of
Cheboksary) was obvious ten miles to the south west by the clouds
of limestone dust with which it was whitening the landscape. Small
chimneys visible in the distance expanded into a chain of huge
smokestacks. Long clouds of smog drifted from them above us to
the north west. Behind the stacks and cement factories reared con-
ical mountains of limestone. The low and sandy east bank, looking
much the same as it must have done a thousand years ago, was pro-
tected by the Volga from the industrial slum to the west, on which
one could imagine it looked with horror. At 1645 on 13th August we

175

passed through the narrow entrance to the harbour of Marx. I was curious to find out the extent of remaining German influence. This was an outlier of the pre-war German Autonomous Republic. Catherine The Great, German herself, had peopled it by sending thousands of her fellow countrymen down river.

There was no room to swing at. So we anchored fore and aft between a red Channel buoy and the city shoreline. A lean, stubble-bearded young Marxist called Misha, with hollow cheeks and a pony tail, offered to help our search and took us in turn to the Library and House of Culture. I almost agreed with Jim when he said 'Frankly, I'd prefer to see the Lincoln Memorial'.

Then we got to the home of an elegant lady Eleonora Alexandrovna Gert, the most active of the surviving Germans. She had tales to tell of narrow escapes from death in Siberia during the forced evacuation ordered by Stalin in 1941 and of returns and reunions. Her talk was reminiscent of Highland Clearances in Scotland and hearts 'that never forgot the Hebrides'.

Marx was closed to all foreigners for reasons of national security hence all movement prohibited until the start of petrestroika. Since then tens of thousands of Germans have accepted the invitation to return to the Fatherland. Others have poured back from exile in Siberia and started to reclaim land left derelict by collective farming.

As we walked back in darkness through dusty streets the only visible German trace was a broken down Mercedes under tow. I felt utterly exhausted. We were careful to use minimum light from head torches only when boarding, but lots of mozzies followed us into the cabin and wound their sleep-defying sultry horns all night.

Rain pattered hard on the deck and dripped through seams opened by recent heat. I dozed on and off, and rose at last feeling awful. Up anchor at 0800 and motored away into bright haze on a cool and overcast day. We faced another with fifty miles to Saratov. The rain had left the decks filthy with cement dust. (Some of it must have got into the engine air intake. We found pistons badly scarred later), Now an enthusiastic deck wash went on punctuated by gobs and snots as we passed congeries of dachas perched on platforms of marl. I got two good hours sleep in the fo'cstle and felt a bit better. By midday the cloud was beginning to break up and it became warmer.

The Satellite Navigator tells us it is only 946 miles to Istanbul; as the crow flies. I wish we could do the same. By teatime the headwind became stronger and I risked increasing revs to 1300. Still feeling bad so took it easy below. Arkady steered quietly and uncomplainingly. The water is now covered in light hairy seeds as maples and aspens begin to turn into autumn colours.

176

All is going unnervingly well, I tell myself, and it looks as if we are going to reach the sea unless my health cracks up, or something serious goes mechanically wrong on the last leg.

SARATOV

At 1800 we reached Saratov after ten hours and anchored below the struts of a what is claimed to be the longest road bridge in Europe built in 1965.

And beautiful are its clean efficient lines with five spans each 500 feet long of reinforced concrete. Saratov was built in 1590 as another fortress to protect the river from nomad raiders. It was the capital of the German colony until the Nazi invasion.

Afterwards Nemsi, the Street of the Germans, became The Street of Kirov. This leading Bolshevik who died mysteriously when challenging Stalin in 1934 is now commemorated widely from the ballet of St Petersburg to the eastern boundary of Russia. Today Saratov's million inhabitants straddle the Volga; many of them live by processing the logs arriving in rafts from up country into wooden furniture and houses, others make aeroplane parts, grow corn and rye. We landed on the right bank near the Ferry Terminal on a dirty beach beside a sewage outfall. The filth pouring from it didn't seem to put off the bathers packed in various intimate postures.

I went straight to the hotel to find a message from Anton Surmenev, Bruce's 27-year-old surgeon friend. He turned out to be a real charmer and one of the kindest of all the many we'd met. Had a relaxed dinner with him and Jim, and enjoyed a good night's sleep in a comfortable room.

Next morning Anton conducted us round main Plaza where the variety of architecture is unbelievable. The Art Gallery is one of the greatest in Russia. Radeeshev 1749-1802 is one of the most displayed artists, also Ayvazovskiy 1870-1906 celebrated marine painter. The marvellous portrait of Catherine the Great with lace in her hair is on display. In the 1970's Party bosses used her personal priceless plates and bowls, for their private entertainment and weddings, throwing it at each other and smashing it in the fireplaces. People uncovered the stealing and some of it was returned.

Arkady recalled:

> During our walks around the town we frequently encountered wedding parties which Miles tried to photograph but because people in the town were not used to westerners they started to scowl. Miles put them at their ease in his own way by making strange noises and facial expressions until they could not help

177

*laughing where upon he instantly started snapping them. By that
time they didn't mind.*

This is a city with a real heart to it. We were threatened at times
by young stupid guys known in Russia as Ghovniks but police soon
battoned them off. Several churches were in process of restoration,
some being almost totally rebuilt, others with new frescos being
painted above the doors.

Already five are working, although some not yet complete.

We got no view of the city for it was hidden in thick cement haze.
Dinner with Anton and his brother Leosha at their parents' flat, a
great kindness. The main dish of stewed sterlet, called I think ras-
varenyar, was the finest dish of the voyage and eating it in a private
dwelling a rare treat. At midnight we went for a pedestrian tour of
the city down the mile long Kirov Ulitsa. It was a-buzz with
crowded night clubs, coffee shops and restaurants.

I was up refreshed at six to photograph a church near the hotel,
seen in golden light, washed red brick work, green roof and pale
blue domes.

Breakfast in a coffee shop with two engineers from Hamburg
who emphasised the remaining German influence which has
brought them lucrative contracts both with locals and from some of
the Germans who maintained business links here after moving
west. This in spite of occasional anti-German demonstrations.

The ringing of the bells ended our conversation; the rhythm is
faster here than at home and has an eastern flavour to it.

Looking north I could see log rafts with houses built on them for
families and domestic animals and the green islands we'd passed
limned black against the pale gold of dawn.

We got a taxi to Anton's Hospital State Number Eight, where the
equipment looked primitive but medical skills are clearly high. His
respiration gear is fifteen years old, but it works and the waiting
list is only a few weeks.

Then he showed us the house, now a library, where his merchant
great-great-grandfather once lived.

'Only one in one thousand can make money honestly today in
Russia', he said, looking at its ornate facade.

'In the West people are prepared to work hard to make money.
Here many people want to make it by doing nothing and getting paid
for giving permission. Many good ideas fall down because of that.'

This came a little wistfully for he had earlier revealed that as a
highly qualified surgeon he earned less than $15 a week.

A couple of years later Anton wrote to Bruce:

'My family and I have a pleasant recollection of Miles, we somehow *found a common language very quickly, and although I speak little English he told me about some of the historic voyages in which he had taken part and gave me a sample of his very particular sense of humour. One of his newly learned tricks was a perfect imitation of a Russian bureaucrat when angling for a bribe, "Dat ... Yees, that should be just poossible".'*

Then it was time to shop in the magnificent central market, glass domed in 1915 in imitation of the Great Hall in Paris. There was incredibly a choice of excellent bread, some interesting drinks, and good cuts of beef and pork.

By the time we got back to the boat a great party invited to see us off had arrived plus a film crew to do an interview. Masha, Liosha, Anya, Anton and others had to be got across that beach still swarming with humanity in all its naked variety and on board by dinghy.

Katya brought a guitar and sang us off with her eyebrows.

Very sad to leave but we had to pull away at last, dodging the racing fleet competing for the Lower Volga Cup.

Anchored fifty miles south of Saratov at last light. That comes before nine now after a very short twilight.

I only hope I remain healthy for another three weeks. It looks doubtful at the moment. Early to bed.

Monday was another beautifully bright morning with pearly light, and a cool breeze, warming quickly with the sun. Up early half rested, to set an example to the crew, for yet another a long passage. We must average fifty miles or risk serious weather trouble in the Black Sea. The coast is still one continuous band of marl and limestone cliffs, collapsing into the Volga by a slow subsidence.

The surface is green and blue gunge so thick you could spread it with a knife. It slaps along our sides like paint. We anchored at last on a small alluvial fan where a little stream ran down in a gully from the steppe.

Into my bunk on deck with Forsyte Saga and a few dozen passing ships for company. Pretty necklaces of lights came up from villages invisible during the day.

TUESDAY 18th AUGUST:

KAMYSHIN WHERE PETER THE GREAT FAILED TO BUILD A CANAL LINK

Away after a rather sleepless night. 0950 – passed under bridge at

179

Kamyshin with only a couple of feet to spare. Moored stern to a wooden pier building for a whistle stop to sightsee and shop. Complete cover of green algae is becoming the norm. Vitali telephoned Nikolai, an ecologist, who kindly showed us the thing we most wanted to see – a wide but short trough in the steppe, marking the start made in 1696 on the Peter the Great Volga-Don Canal. This, a hundred miles north of the present canal, was to use the Kamyshinka and Ilovlia Rivers over a distance of seventy five miles. Peter built Kamyshin as a fort to protect the workers, then his attention was diverted by wars in the west; after five years work ceased and was never recommenced.

It was on the same lines as previous attempt by the Ottoman Emperor, Suleiman The Magnificent, about 1540, also unsuccessful.

The delay of 400 years in the completion of the Volga Don link seems longish but it is dwarfed by the record of the Corinth Canal which Wild Goose used on her return voyage. That contract started by the Emperor Nero was not completed until 1600 years later.

Kamyshin looks a pleasant place, situated in a gap in the Volga Uplands. With only 150.000 inhabitants it can boast the biggest cotton plant in Europe, also a factory making engines for Cheboksary tractors.

Got away again at 1300 – hazy now, sun not quite so hot and the apparent wind as we motor keeps the boat a bit cooler. I passed the time by starting to strip the doghouse for varnishing. By 2010 we'd had enough and anchored under crumbling cliffs so similar to last night that it is hard to believe we have actually moved at all. We are now in steppe country although there are still small patches of scrub and trees in the gullies. Supper of savoury rice and pork, allegedly Chinese ; it had no ill effects.

Another sleepless night. Dinghy banging as wind weather cocked. Up again at 0545 to get under way. Almost a relief. Motored into grey blustery morning with fresh southerly breeze. Sun came up bright red visible for only a few minutes before being swallowed by grey dark overcast. Flying spiders setting up shop in the rigging, spinning their webs for green flies. Limestone stands out against slate grey clouds. Land and sky a study in fifteen shades of grey. Wind died when the sun came out and came up again after lunch from south west. Steadily increased so that in the evening we had a storming sail under double reefed main and staysail in Force Six. The Volgograd Reservoir, up to four miles wide, erupted in white horses, steep enough to swamp open boats.

We hailed one whose owner was baling frantically, but he refused our offer of help.

Volgograd (Tsaritsyn for three hundred years; Stalingrad for 36 years) is said to have forty miles of river frontage; true in a way

180

but there are plenty of rural bits interspersed. We reached the northern moles at 1615 but then had to kill an hour dawdling while Arkady tried to get through to a lockkeeper on the radio. Then I put him ashore under trying conditions, a leap onto a jagged wall in an onshore gale. Collecting him again was worse but he'd got the go-ahead and as I write we have just begun to descend the last lock on the Volga!

Poplars cast attractive shadows against the steep lock wall, A train chugs across just in front of us over the lock.

Once through there is sense of the freedom of an open river – no locks between here and the Caspian; we could carry on to Astrakhan!

Instead we make it where Hitler's armies failed and enter Volgograd.

We anchored downstream of the gigantic Motherland Statue where four or five yachts lay on moorings off a marsh. Vitali and Arkady nipped ashore and found a private car whose owner was only too keen to drive us into town for a small fee. There we met Alexander, the National Geographic stringer. Jim stayed ashore with him.

THURSDAY 20th AUGUST:

Vitali went off early to telephone Moscow for news of his family. Now blowing from the south Force Five but we lay peacefully to the very strong current. The river looks extraordinarily clean. The consequence of the dinghy going adrift here is at least different; it might end up in Baku. I double check the painters often for chafe and absence of Mullingar hitches.

Alexander came to the boat at 1230 having made arrangements for a helicopter from the State-run Ecological Committee.

Arkady recalled the Volgograd visit in very human terms:

'Since August the 14th we had been hearing news on the radio which gave Vitali every justification for worry. War had broken out in Abkhizia, a lovely sub tropical stretch of the Georgian coast which in Soviet times we used to associate with bathing and orange groves and summertime frolics. His wife and daughter were on holiday there in the region of the capital Sukhumi which had rapidly turned into the battlefield of one of the bloodiest and dirtiest of our post-Soviet wars. The final two weeks of our voyage were over-shadowed by Vitaly's worry for his family and made us realise how lucky we were that Wild Goose herself had not been passing through an area of open fighting.

'At Volgograd Vitaly looked pale and preoccupied as he led us round the shuttered brickwork of Flour Mill number 17. The build-

181

ing which has been left un-repaired is a memorial to the 200 days of fighting when 300,000 Germans and 800,000 Soviet soldiers died. This battle was the turning point of the Great Patriotic War Russia fought against Nazi Germany.

'At every stop in our final journey down the Volga Don canal through the Cossack country and across the big ugly expanse of the Tsimlysk Reservoir Vitaly tried to telephone to get word of his family but the only news was that there was no news. One good thing which came out of the crisis was a reconciliation between him and Jim. Jim had been a hard taskmaster and Vitaly had never realised at the outset that he would be working not for one but two highly demanding westerners with different priorities. Now Jim went far to dispel any resentment by the sympathetic and fatherly way in which he reacted to the news about Vitaly's family. "I know how I'd feel if my wife Pat was caught up in a conflict", Jim said. At one point he offered to provide a National Geographic helicopter to fly Vitaly to the place where his wife was.

'"It is very kind of you Jim but I just wouldn't know where to start looking",

'Vitaly replied, "but I could tell he appreciated it. These moments of human decency and concern were, I suppose, the high point in a very tricky relationship" '

FRIDAY 21st AUGUST:

THE VOLGA DON CANAL

Up at 0545 and sailed past Volgograd in its grim splendour at six and a half knots for twenty miles.

The city is facing a new enemy: pollution. Between the Volga*

---

*The Headman of the village of Dubovoy Obrog beside the ponds Aleksandr Krupenko told Jim Blair, 'Our wells are polluted but we still drink from them. There is no alternative. The water we use to irrigate our land is tainted too'.

It was estimated in 1992 that from the Kirov district of Volgograd alone 40.000 cubic yards of untreated sewage poured into the Volga each year. In the same period steel chemical, fertiliser and alloy plants dumped in twelve tons of mercury.

Over the river as a whole 3000 factories were dumping ten billion cubic yards of contaminated waste and other effluent each year. On some stretches Petro-chemical by-products had reached a hundred times the allowable limit.

Until recently most of this activity was cloaked 'for reasons of national security'.

Since then Friends of the Volga Groups and others have been campaigning for closer supervision.

Figures from U.S. News and World Report April 13 1992

*and the canal we glimpsed a landscape as horrific as any video
'nasty', where a huge chemical plant has spewed effluent into 50
square miles of settling ponds. Jim seems to be busy already photographing from his helicopter the hideous pattern of glutinous
orange and brown. Sources are various. Some comes from a
converted chemical weapons plant now churning out detergents
and pesticides. Much of the killer cocktail must finds its way into
the main river.*

The wind bore heavy traces of these fields of obscenity across
the cockpit of Wild Goose as she approached the Volga Don Canal
but her crew were too busy to take much note. What could they
have done anyway?

*We reach this dramatic watershed with satisfaction but not with-
out some regrets on my part at leaving Mother Volga after six weeks
on her broad bosom; the fruit of many months of planning. But the
anticipation of getting to the Don and achieving a direct link to the
Mediterranean soon overlays nostalgia.*

*It's a glorious morning of low light and long shadows once we
leave the city and its ordure. Healthy if unkempt rural surroundings, scrub to starboard, tall trees on sandy banks to port.*

*Good second breakfast, aways a favourite meal on The Goose,
with English tea provided by Stas. We reached the entrance to the
Canal, did a reconnaissance of the basin outside it, tried to anchor
in a gusty Force Six opposite the huge statue of Lenin but found no
hold for the anchor. Then the fun started. Berthing under sail in
strong onshore winds and narrow waters is not done in the best circles but Jim was overhead and streams of instructions coming by
VHF. We entered the Canal, tied up alongside, lowered the mainsail, shook hands with the lock keeper and were greeted by a small
curious crowd. 'Again please!' We made sail, moved back out into
the basin, sailed smoothly in, tied up, shook hands with the lock
keeper and were greeted by a dwindling incurious crowd.*

'Cloud got over the sun at the vital moment. One more time'.

*The lockkeeper was smart. He'd disappeared by now, so I shook
hands with a bemused onlooker. Up and down that canal eleven
separate times we went under orders from Jim in the helicopter. It
would have been risky to enter the lock under sail once, let alone
repeat it, but Jim was insistent. We had to do our best and managed
to avoid damage All a wasted effort as none of the shots was ever
used but we were not to know that.*

*On the banks there was much contrast; industry in the back-
ground, ponds nearby with wildfowl and open steppe ; then areas
of filthy shore and broken boats on hillocks, intact dachas and*

derelict dwellings. We had plenty of time to admire them before we were allowed to lock in.

This canal, I read and re-read in the Directions, was completed in 1952 after four years work. 63 miles long, 15 locks, it climbs 289 feet from the Volga and drops 144 to the Don. Water supply is maintained by three reservoirs – Karpovka, Bereslavka and Varvarovka occupying 28 miles of its length. The main freight is coal going east and timber moving west.

At 1540 we entered the first lock behind a passenger ship.

Arms reach down to sell us apples and tomatoes. Cruise passengers wave.

'Where are you going?,' they ask.

'White to Black', Arkady shouts. 'We have already completed 2,500 miles of our 3,000 mile journey. We mist make the sea within nine days!'

1620: Second lock. The lock filled but we were told to wait. Eventually got to third lock, then motored along a six mile straight to the next, during which we fell astern of the ferry. So we entered fourth by ourselves in very blustery conditions.

There we were told brusquely to go back to the Volga.

Only after much argument and maximum persuasion by Arkadi did the lockkeeper say we could go through and then telephone the boss of the canal. This we did to find him absent but Arkady managed to convince the keeper that there had been an oral agreement about permission a month ago between the Director of the Canal and the Moscow Adventure Club

What a relief! The real reason they were objecting was because it was the weekend and they wanted to get away home.

'If you act like a sheep, you get treated like one', said Arkadi.

We anchored in a small widening in the canal beyond Lock Five. Vitali and I set off in the dark on a lonely road and managed to get onto a bus and from there managed to get a taxi to the Intourist Hotel for dinner with Jim and Stas.

AUGUST 22nd Saturday:
Lock five. Dining room not open until eight so walked round the Square of the Fallen Heroes and back to a restaurant at 0800, Spoke to The Volga Weekly with a circulation of 60,000; visited Red October Steel Plant, one of the biggest in the world.

JIM BOWS OUT

Jim came to the boat to collect gear. No one has ever made such thorough preparations for quitting Wild Goose – or been helped so eagerly in doing it.

He left us his Bosun's Chair, life jacket with flashing light, a kit bag so large and waterproof as to double as life raft, elaborate medical supplies and ten dozen 4 oz Pemmican Packs (his personal rations in case there had been a famine), but alas no generic soap or intimate wipes.

Found Vitali at the house of a friend Igor Ragcheev. He appeared in a dressing gown accompanied by two vicious dogs that I had difficulty in stopping myself kicking. Gave us coffee and showed us photo album of his army days. He drove us to the Motherland Statue, hugely impressive, then we got a bus to the centre of the city to see the ruined mill preserved as it was when a key point in the fighting, Panoramas and Museum relating to the battles during World War II. Women in red coral dresses had gathered for the anniversary of one particularly ferocious air raid. These women are the Children of the Stalingrad Choir who meet every five years. As we got back to the boat it was blowing a near gale from the south.

Wild Goose yawing madly around her chain. Up anchor and motored towards Lock Six just in time to dodge big black bows appearing from the brickwork as the gates were opening. A rise of ten metres revealed bare hills and many dachas.

So at 1850 – August 22nd – we entered the last ascending lock of the voyage. From here it's really all downhill and downstream!. This time the Triumphal Banners don't just stand out. They are statuesque in concrete. On top of the pump house, stained with pigeon dung, is a fully equipped radio station.

Lock Eight: Weeping willows, pigeons, the same triumphant stone Soviet banners. Streams of people bent on crossing the lock gates are delayed until they close again. Huge insect-like arm puts restraining wire across.

Vitali was drying apricots on deck in the sun.

'I don't like to let people sit on them after they have sat on dirty water mellons', he said.

We were offered tomatoes, pears, plums from dachas. A pink neoclassical building seen through the trees was yet another Sanatorium. Should I apply for a bed?

Lock Ten sheers ahead: Two gazebos with eight Corinthian columns surround the pumping stations. Each has a circular top and massive black statues with pikes, swords, stars and laurels. Even a rear pump house is semicircular with portico in front. In the lock white froth six inches deep, street lamps, bird's busy feeding young in every crevice, ships passing in the night. Steady nerves needed to motor blindly into darkness of narrow channel as bright red sunset fades.

2235 – Anchored out of fairway just short of Lock Ten and went below for a sundowner.

The cabin seemed strangely empty in the absence of Jim and his vast array of cameras and boxes. There would have been room for a table now but the folding one had perforce been left in Ireland to save space, and we'd been eating off our knees for so long that it would have seemed strange to do otherwise. Arkady moved aft to Jim's bunk leaving Vitali to enjoy solitary state as Captain of the Forecastle.

Self portrait – Anton Surmenov, who was a most kindly host to Miles and his crew at Saratov.

CHAPTER FIFTEEN

Cossack Kindness

By *MILES* and *ARKADY*

'Once you ran swiftly, Don,
Yet now you flow so sludgily'
Then spoke forth the peaceful Don,
'What else but sludgy could I be ?
Far away my eagles are flown;
My eagles-Cossacks of the Don'.
(Old Cossack Song)

23 August
We radio to Lock Ten Control at 0700 to be told we could come
through with the big vegetable ship Konstantin Panchenko. Hoped
they might chuck us a few cauliflowers which would have gone well
with our breakfast cheese omelettes. On board supplies are becom-
ing monotonous.
  We content ourselves with the grace the old whalers used

'The weather's rough,
The meat is tough,
But thank the Lord
We've got enough.'

Lock Ten was every bit as glorious as Nine. Such structures deserve
names, not mere numbers. Columned ivory temples flanked the
approach, gleaming in the morning sun as it warmed stones on the
lock side to the right temperature for bare feet.
  Leaving we proceeded through waters so narrow that our wake,
drawing arrowhead ridges on the surface, made the rushes on both
sides nod as if in conversation about our passing. Two bags of for-
gotten Hula Hoops found in a forepeak locker added welcome
variety to our Noon Balloon. The banks are like a Bird Park; king-
fishers flash and dive, partridges whirr, egrets stalk and stab. Bushes
are a-flutter with finches and warblers. The shore line a-croak with
crows feeding among black and white sheep. Bullrushes, which Vitali

187

aptly calls cigar plants, nod above feeding geese. A twitcher would be getting vertigo from constantly turning round to see strange new targets for his camera. In curious way the un-peopled surroundings are quite reminiscent of the White Sea Canal. But colours of people and vegetation grow brighter as the weather gets warmer.

We reach Lock Thirteen, unlucky for some, but not us this time, at 1715.

No one is in sight; no voice booms out; the familiar cycle happens as if by magic. Gates open ahead. Gates close astern. Seconds later the level starts falling.

This is not so much a lock as a monument. The Control Towers have domed roofs. A huge archway, its supports decorated with discs in complex relief, spans the canal. 'Glory to our Motherland' is inscribed in 'Blind Man' letters round its cap band. Within the cap is a Weather Station. Above it a mass of anchors among swords and tangled snakes pointing skyward.

Passing underneath I remark that it gives an idea of how the Colossus must have looked, astride the harbour entrance at Rhodes, seen from the deck of a trireme.

'But this one has no balls', says Arkady.

The evening light picked out in silver the cobwebs in our rigging as it gilds a splendiferous Memorial to Airmen, Soldiers, and Sailors of the Great Patriotic War. The furniture of Communism is indelible; it will take generations for it to recede into obscurity.

That was our goodbye to the long awaited Volga Don Canal.

South of it a channel leads straight and tree-lined between white towpaths; an aquatic avenue reminiscent of the Bief St Jean in the French Midi Canal which Wild Goose traversed thirty years earlier. Beyond it twin breakwaters run away to the Tsimlyansk Reservoir. Their ends lie between more eight columned temples decorated with the protruding of bows of stone galleys as if celebrating a sea victory of Trafalgar proportions.

For a few moments just before sunset the whole vast expanse of water ahead seemed to emit diffused aureate glow, as though illuminated from underneath.

THE DON AT LAST

As we glide towards the Tsamlynsk Reservoir into which the Don has been constrained we see to the west low rolling hills separated by shadowed gullies. They form a perfect limestone amphitheatre facing the river. The arena at their feet is streaked with gurgling streams emerging from hidden valleys in which willows weep. Black goats with short high tails are being driven north on the flats beside the river by a lone herdsman.

To the east it is still steppe, covered in short yellow prairie grass, and sprinkled with bushy trees.

Banana-shaped boats are at work with fish drying on ropes stretched in the rigging.

We all feel the excitement of being on a river directly connected with the sea which we have been travelling so long to enter. Arkady expresses this, saying, 'I very want to Istambul go'.

We anchored that evening with only three feet under our keel three miles north of the main waters of the reservoir. Not a ship passed; only little fishing boats gliding by in fairylike procession as we close the hatch to the measured clunk of distant oars and

> 'The Don majestically still between its green fringe of reflected forest'.

(How could one match the descriptive powers Sholokhov in Quietly flows the Don).

Up at 6.15, overcast but silvery bright light. Through a bridge with a train crawling across it puffing black smoke into the clouds. It pulls carriages the type that used to bear the legend 'Forty men, Eight Horses'. From their red sliding doors people peer at us and wave.

We motor on into a huge featureless, mirror calm glow of whiteness.

After lunch in the cockpit came a light steppeland breeze to which we set some kites. But they soon frightened the wind away. Fourteen hours and seventy miles later, we anchored off a bare cliff on south east side of the Reservoir and rowed ashore. The dinghy grounded fifty yards out in sludge. Millions and millions of camari (mosquitos) blew their tiny trumpets round our legs as we ploughed onto gravel and walked across steppe grass. Bad news from Sukumi – Georgian Government sending in regular troops and using artillery. Many questions in my mind.

How is Larissa, Vitali's wife?

Will we get out of the country before war breaks out here? How low is the next bridge?

In the morning a faint breath from upstream raised hopes for the Meltemi, the north wind which dominates the Aegean all summer. It must start some place around here.

The after part of the cabin was alive with bright green insects. On deck sails, spars, dodgers, wires were all speckled green. Every crevice – under the liferaft, in the ventilators, under the spare oars – was stuffed with emerald newly hatched insects. Wild Goose must have been first thing solid they found to land on after hatching out of river. The only crew members who looked on this as a bonanza

189

were our spiders; their webs were full to bulging. We set all plain sail with insects spilling out of every fold as we swigged the halliards.

THE TOWN THAT WAS WRONGLY NAMED

We were soon approaching Volga Donsk at south end of Reservoir. It appears that its name should have been given to the one at the other end where the two rivers connect. I could imagine some Government official a thousand miles away in Moscow dreaming of his own little bit of Volga and allocating politically correct names to places he'd never seen. Then getting his cards mixed up.

But what Volga Donsk lacked in location it sure made up for in style. Entering its lock was like going through the Arc de Triomphe. Concrete columns towered twice the height of our mast. Pigeons looked like sparrows up top. The King Kong goalposts were crowned by horsemen flourishing sabres, banners, halberds, pikes swords, flails, laurelled banners, tassels, trumpets, posthorns, Maxim guns and artillery barrels. The pigeons clearly thought these had been designed to provide nesting sites and made free of such convenient facilities

This lock, the Guardian confided in us, in good times handles forty ships a day; this year maybe twenty. The basin is some 600 feet long by 70 wide, standardised perhaps with those of the far off St Lawrence Seaway. Even these substantial dimensions are now found too small for today's jumbo freighters.

Every tube and crevice above water in the lock walls was filled with spiders' webs. A man fishing with a television beside him marks the progress of civilisation – or does it? We passed under another bridge without touching but only just.

Should we, even at this late stage, unship masthead light or even the mast itself?

Then out of the environs into the Don proper. Dom Odikoffs on either hand and off them families in boats, Jerome K Jerome style, with radios, blaring and bored Montmorency dogs.

Slow rain at tea time, 'dry spittin' as they'd say at home; a prelude to a visible and audible wall of rain stretching right across river. We made a dash to get everything important under cover. Saw what looked like a baklan (cormorant), a welcome sign of being near the sea. 'These birds rarely go more than fifty miles from coast', our copy of Nature is your Guide avers. After happy hour anchored thankfully just down stream of the Nariman Narimanov, an Azerbajani ship heading north. Rain came on in torrents as we did so; doghouse roof leaking desperately. The crew won't melt, but how the hell do I keep drips off radio?

190

The sense of camaraderie is strong, now that it is just me and the two Russians. That evening we discussed future inventions to make shipboard life simpler. Vitali – a silent loo, Arkady a catapult which would infallibly flick used teabags out through main hatch and a way of preventing the dinghy banging on the hull. Mine is more complex, a silent engine, a sort of inboard/outboard so compact that you could undo four butterfly nuts and carry it home under your arm. Many a more serious topic came up for discussion. 'Shop' is the usually best form of conversation – an expert talking on his own subject provided no one is left out – Jim had often been worth listening to on his vast journalistic experience. Now Arkadi could talk of his engineering projects and Russian army life from inside; Vitali of The Canadian Arctic and military Service in the Far East.

It was warm until one a.m., then cool enough to get into sleeping bags.

Narimanov left at 0500, small tugs going past at 0600. Cool autumnal dawn, everything shrouded in soft mist so that the river disappeared into nothingness. Ashore the ground was covered in beech and apple leaves. The lowing of cattle and yapping of dogs resonated through the mist – we might have been in Ireland in the Bog of Allen. At breakfast Vitali was swatting flies with a rolled-up copy of The Times with the same athleticism he puts into his photography. I had to rescue his cameras from the rain last night. Low flat banks with mist still hanging in the trees after it has cleared overhead This is a friendly Wind in the Willows, Ratty and Moley type of river. The hills gradually disappearing to the north lay light as blue veined bubbles over a golden plain.

Just before the lock we saw a white eagle, probably a Bonelli's, in extraordinary flight like a white paper bag being blown in the wind as though totally out of control.

As we were leaving Nikolayefskaya Lock we met Volta-Balt 17 of St Petersburg whom we had seen in the Baltisky Canal seven weeks ago. The captain in Fidel Castro cap, mirror sunglasses, white shirt and stainless flashing teeth put his hands above his head in champion salute.

'Schastlivogo puti!' (Bon Voyage)

COSSACKS AT HOME

Next day after breakfast we approached a village, Straya Stanitsa on the chart, hoping for diesel. Price has not been a problem but the stuff's rationed and we're low. Disappointment. There isn't even a pier. We walk up rickety steps through the yard of a small wooden house and enter the most overwhelmingly agricultural landscape I have ever seen. Turkish goats with evil yellow eyes running through the village, haystacks, pigs, hens, ducks, oxen and horses – bay Cossack ponies, unkempt cobs, stallions, walers, mares with foal at foot, sway-backed nags. Horse ponds, rush awnings, drying hides. Then something we badly wanted. A baker's shop. Last loaf went and shop about to close as we got to it. Only just managed to persuade Lema Ermakov not to part with one of hers, she was so keen to be friendly. We were given embarrassing armfuls of pears, apples, peppers, damsons, apricots, onions, potatoes, beetroots.

Invited to an extended stay at this ancient Cossack village. Lena introduced us to Alexander, the Hetman, her father, also to her husband and eldest son. Made welcome with home brew kumiss and vodka in their house. Then it seemed to become an excuse for a family party. 'A bottle doesn't go very far amongst one', a dictum I'd last heard in Scotland, was the comment when cork of third one was thrown away.

The house was snugly made of mud brick thatched with reeds. A picture of Tsar Nicholas sat on chimney piece. Tall black sheepskin busby hats hung on walls, sheepskin poshteens from rafters. People had said that all the real Cossacks were dead but if so these people were real enough for us

This village, set in its vasty landscape, might have been the one place the Wild Goose crew had come so far to see. If we wanted reward, it was here.

The Hetman found us a rusty can containing alleged diesel. Thanked him profusely but privately resolved not to use it, even in extremis. The Cossack adults and children by turns had to be ferried out to see the yacht and sample the Bush, wonder at the loo, and clamber in and out of the forehatch. One teenager danced a mazurka to the tap of spoons on the cabin floor, kicking out his feet and slapping his legs.

'Tomorrow we go to round up sheep in the hills. I can give you a good horse', said the Hetman. It was tempting to stay.

We tore ourselves away after midday. And that's not just a figure of speech. I felt real pain at leaving such great people after such a short stay. To say good bye is to die a little.

A volley of shots was fired skywards in salute as we heaved up the anchor. Nice of them but I did have a rapid check for holes in the mainsail once we were out of sight.

Wild horses swimming hull down in the river their heads showing like kelpies in a Scottish loch was our last view.

Now less than ninety miles from the sea!

Soon had to give way to a barge bearing a tube fifteen feet in diameter, looking like a core for a nuclear reactor. The skipper on his flying bridge could barely see over the top. The river is very

Jim on assignment as billions of bugs bubble round the bow.

Pattern of islands by 'Neck Anchorage' at south-west corner of Great Samara Bend.

Same view – early morning. 'Like something fashioned from a dream.'

The Engeli Bridge at Saratov reputed to be the longest in Europe.

Some uninhibited inhabitants of Saratov swim out towards Wild Goose.

Sunbathers seem careless of pollution pouring into the Volga.

Hut double for bathing and clothes washing at Saratov. In winter fires keep the water inside free of ice.

Church being restored at by worker priest and his assistant at Saratov.

A gully in the chalk cliffs makes a secluded camp site and anchorage for Wild Goose.

Huge steel cores under tow by a jumbo tug emphasise Soviet giganticism.

Victory Statue towers over the Volvograd skyline commemorating siege of Stalingrad.

Volvograd skyline, the source of much pollution.

Monks in a stone boat are portrayed moving on rollers in memory of many portages.

Triumphalist towers mark the 1952 completion of of the Volga Don Canal.

Horsemen crown Volsk Don lock

Arkady often steered all day.

Cossack horses mix with cattle near the confluence of the Don and Donets.

Newly-hatched flies swarm in the Tsamlynsk Reservoir.

Dolphins welcome Wild Goose back to the open sea in the Kerchov Strait.

The mountains behind Novorrossisk Docks at south end of Caucasus look unfamiliar after nearly three months of flat earth.

Fishing boats throng banks of Don.

Minarets and lush vegetation at Amasra mark the entrance to Turkey.

Dodging a ferry amid the maelstrom the Bosphorus traffic.

Meanwhile, back at the ranch ... Sarah with Finnian, aged three.

Wallace, Molly Ronan and Miles as they appeared on front of *Milyet*, the Istanbul daily.

Bruce with Russian friend.

'A moment to treasure all one's days.' Sunset off St Sophia at the completion of the
Russia voyage.

'Thy dawn, O Master of the World, Thy dawn.'

narrow here, sometimes as little as 70 yards with only 45 yards navigable But it is forty feet deep: the eastern shore is deeply undercut by the slapping of passing traffic. Many birch trees again. Families of herons taking off from them at one time.

Konstaninovsky came abreast at teatime with a slogan picked out in green bricks on a red building. 'We will reach the Victory of Communist Labour slowly'.

The penultimate lock had only a ten-foot drop. Nothing remotely decorative about this, or the final one still to come. Cash must have run out before the designers got there.

Azeri ship called Poet Vidadi going home to Baku unladen. Cows and chickens at water's edge. Anchored for night just downstream of confluence with Sverkiy. Arkady went for a swim and looked as if he would drift away on the current but got in to the bank and worked his way upstream where it was slack in the manner of water wise ducklings

Near the confluence with the Donetz the river at dawn was covered with fine layer of mist which spoiled the reflections as it swirled gently and theatrically across the water.

The forests, meadows, lakes and clearings burned majestically in the pink fire of dawn.

In Sholokhiv's to mark the start of a very good day in several ways.

One: I found a bag of extra porridge hidden there since the Arctic.

Two: we came on a pair of small fuelling lighters tucked under the trees and asked for a hundred litres of diesel. Given willingly and didn't have to pay a kopek.

Three: Half an hour later at 0845 we reached the final lock of the voyage and got straight in. As we left a gaggle of Barnacle Geese flew off as if in salute from acres of wet fields. I felt like throwing my hat into the air and let it lie among them the ancient stumps .

No more locks ! We're at Black Sea level.

Shared the last bottle of Bruce's claret and some crisps in celebration.

As we clinked our glasses Volga Neft 42 who had befriended us at Safe Haven hove alongside.

'I am glad to see you. Happy Sailing', the skipper called, hands extended in bear hug! A Danish yacht, we were told, had been waiting by this lock recently for three weeks trying to get through, but no sign of permission so eventually gave up and returned south.

The feeling of excitement lasted all day. Food lowish but not desperate. Fishing boats anchored right across the river, each with four or five lines out. Gentle wind blowing down with stream to the south, herds of long-horned brown cattle up to their bellies in the river, sometimes joined by black-maned stallions with tropillas of a *dozen mares apiece. Tens of thousands of black crows in trees and all over sandbanks like a scene from the film* The Birds. *Droves of white geese along the shore.*

Masses of Dom Otdikhas with people waving and beckoning. We go straight sou'west for the sea heading past the northernmost meander of the river. People out with fishing rods, almost half way across the stream. Big bottle of Lambrusco for supper. Reading the Brendan Voyage *as I peel the spuds. Saw our first bass, a big one, splashing the water. Anchored near a small subsidiary channel in the short dusk. Tens of thousands of crows again, then a break, then joined by another flock, then alarmed by something and the whole forest lifted. peeling back into the sky like tea leaves. Ships moving back and forth all evening. Green navigation lights and white mast-headers seen through haze of wood smoke.*

Woke to view our surroundings a short distance up the Manich Reha. Three towers appear through the dawn mist and excite my curiosity – discovered they belong to very big church with its feet hidden in the trees. It has arched windows but all domes smashed and walls pitted with shell fragments. The building is not unlike a larger edition of the Monastery of Golgotha of such evil associations in the White Sea ; and just as there wagtails, among the most adaptable of birds, trot along its walls. We might for a moment be back in Kerelia. The harmonic lines of a one half of a bridge just upstream seems to be permanently looking for its other half and the men who dwelled here. The ruined wallsteads of fine houses they'd fought to save and the church exhale an atmosphere that lingers only in places that have been of special beauty. Those who study history with insight know that the past remains alive and that gallant people and their deeds never die.

Fast sailing at last with a brisk north wind. The old Goose seems to be smelling the stable. Arkady enjoys first time sailing at sea level. 'I am very exciting', he said, 'I very pleasure'

After lunch the stone buildings and boulevards of Rostov gradually envelop the river. We pass below the main bridge, go west of a grassy island and turn out of channel to tie up against a walled embankment by a statue of Maxim Gorky, a man of forbidding aspect. My eye was caught by this and the tall thin funnels of a Victorian steamer Spartak Volodarsky. So I failed to notice over-hanging branches until some hefty ones came crashing down on the deck. Anxious looks aloft. Our jumper struts and spreaders seem to have won.

Much wash from passing ships. I went straight with Vitali to get a room at Intourist Hotel for showers and phone calls; an exorbitant price of $40 for the night made us miss Jim Blair with his generous habit of picking up such bills.

194

Spent the evening checking and tuning the rig for open sea work while Arkady went off to buy charts of the Sea of Azov, once three roubles each, now four hundred. Still very cheap by western standards.

Back at 6pm. Great joy at post restante telegram from Larissa, Vitali's wife, to say all well and she would come and meet us at Novorossisk.

We should be out of Russian waters in two days!

Self and Arkady to Intourist Hotel for dinner, then swap over with Vitali. We moved off the wall for the night and anchor across the river where hoped for less swell.

Everything much more sophisticated now we are in the south. Rostov as a port is the southern equivalent of Murmansk, but Oh so much more cosmopolitan and colourful!

On Saturday 29th August we walked through city to see the Church of The Nativity, and shop in a wonderful market stocking everything from aubergines and runner beans to water melons. Water rats on promotion at 200 roubles! Good Caviar available so bought plenty; disregarding experience of the Supply Officer of a Royal Naval destroyer based here briefly about 1919. He invested in bulk supply but when the Officer of the Day came round the messdeck asking if there were any complaints the sailors said, 'Let's 'ave less of this bleedin' fish jam!'

A Cossack Hero

We visited the farm owned by Rita's grandfather of whom she had spoken so warmly. Now aged 75 he is gaunt, short, almost hairless and of striking bearing – the sort of man of whom John Buchan would have said that you'd like to have on your side in a scrap. His cavalry regiment had been at the harrying of Von Paulus' German army when they were encircled before Stalingrad. So he had a ringside seat at that turning point of Hitler's dreams of world conquest. Later captured, he had been sent to forced labour in Germany. Only one in ten survived the starvation and imprisonment there. Released by Soviet forces he had endured a worse captivity because it was anonymous and had no foreseeable end. That had been meted out by Stalin to each returned POW.

Ejected from this at last, he walked one day into the village where he had long been given up for dead. With incredible virility he took up family life, sired sons and daughters and was now working a small holding in the suburbs with pigs and cows. Said he'd never been really happy unless he was on horse; added something else about a woman we didn't quite catch. This heroic man and his wife made us welcome with tea and cakes and were looking forward to having Rita's children to live with them for Rostov schooling.

Quick end to breakfast as we spot swing bridge below us open-ing and ships heading towards it. Seven at once of the Volkskiy class. Up anchor and after them. As we passed River Control a heavy tug pulled out and headed straight towards us. We swerved inshore to avoid it and did a loop. Tug promptly steered straight for us again. It became clear that they were bulldozing us into the pier. This was not in the schedule. The bridge we were gruffly informed lifts only three times a day. An ugly bastard of a River Master with big pale blue rimmed spectacles and deeply cratered face talked of a twenty thousand rouble charge. Our funds were low. The Bridge slammed down and we were trapped again. We had to 'bout ship and motor back up river. Arkady went to see the Dispatcher. I gave him my last five thousand roubles and half a bottle of whiskey, and passed an anxious hour by scrubbing the dinghy which we had towed for so many thousands of miles. Then I painted deck silver work, varnished the bridge deck grating, and went aloft and double checked everything. Arkady came back after nearly three hours with a story to tell .

'Rostov on Don. I knew, is one of the most prosperous and crime ridden cities of the Russian south. The River Master, a crafty fellow with thick spectacles and a pock marked face had reckoned we were a soft touch.

'There will be 10,000 roubles for the mooring and another 10,000 for water sanitation and other facilities you have used,' he said, bar-ing a mouthful of gold without a hint of a smile. That was only £25 but we didn't want to be taken for suckers, and Milo was near skint.

I knew the River master was trying it on so I told him that Miles was a world famous writer with important connections at the Kremlin. I slapped him on the back metaphorically at least and told him that I could see he was a kindly old soul who could appreciate a young for-eigner's courage and resourcefulness. I flattered him on his hometown shamelessly saying Roscov's charming and colourful streets had been the undisputed high point of our voyage which was long and historic. Finally he got bored with me, shrugged his shoulders and muttered that he would agree on this one occasion to drop the usual charges and let us through free. Just to underline his generosity of spirit for having abolished river taxes as rapidly as he had invented them he placed Wild Goose at the head of a small flotilla of tugs and ferry boats as he raised the bridge and sent us all southwards.

'You write good things about Roscov', he leered.

And this time the gold teeth were bared in an unconvincing grin. *Arkady had pulled it off once more.*

196

Small tug urging us on past the bridge, gulls calling. As I write we are about to pass the third oldest Yacht Club in Russia and get ready to dip our Ensign in salute. Golden domes disappeared astern behind a bridge draped with hanging dip nets.

Vitali soon returned to essentials,

'Is it true that Britain has the most beautiful girls in the world?'

'No, Ireland.' I replied.

Asked what he had read in the newspapers Vitali said 'There was news but no knowledges. No direct information'.

Arkady continues:

I will never forget the moment when I first dipped my hand into the water racing below us and tasted salt. It was late in the evening of Saturday August 29th when we left the Don estuary and entered the choppy milky waters of the Sea of Azov, that shallow stretch of water that leads to the Black Sea.

A really spectacular sunset with a great orange fireball plunging into a straight line into the horizon helped us to recover from that encounter. We found ourselves in almost pitch darkness punctuated occasionally by the faint glow of a bonfire or a pier. Shortly before midnight the left bank mysteriously fell away, then minutes later Miles told me in a tone of weary exhilaration that we had left the last marks of the Russian river system. Forgetting his exhaustion for a moment he solemnly poured out a vodka for me and a Black Bush for himself, then gave the bow of Wild Goose a splash of whisky and said quietly, 'Here's to the engine and sails that have taken us this far and here's to the open sea'. For me too, a river man who had finally was going to sea, it was a great moment. I confess to loosing my few words of English under the effects of the Vodka, 'I am very exciting tonight'.

Fireball sunset. Ships which had passed us several times in past weeks honking and klaxoning greetings. Don't anyone tell me that the Brotherhood of the Sea is a myth. Huge reed beds to port glow under orangy pink light.

Can this really be the same sea that washes Ireland?

Xenophon, the Greek general, we used to read about in faded blue text books at Shrewsbury School, came vividly alive that night. After making so many stades a day for months across Anatolia at last like us they cried:

'Thalassa, Thalassa'!!

We make all secure on deck. Darkness is a somewhat daunting prospect with two crewmen who have never sailed the sea before, let alone at night, in shallow water and thick traffic. I plan to maintain speed so as to be well down to the Azov Sea by dawn. That

*should enable a daylight arrival two hundred miles away at its exit
through the Kerchenskiy Strait.*

*Wonderful luminous evening until sunset; then it became deepest
charcoal.*

*Suddenly our way was checked. A fishing line or net seemed to
be round the keel. Horrors! Our bow swung up into the wind facing
back the way we'd come. Waves started to throw spray over us but
after some anxious moments we came free. Line cut, I suppose, by
our blessed propeller shaft knives. Twisting lights of river boats
and pier at Azov town on east of river mouth. Then nothing but
shooting stars.*

*At midnight we left the Russian rivers and entered the Azov,
almost as big as the Irish Sea.*

*And nowhere deeper than 7 fathoms. A very great moment this –
Sunday 30th August 1992.*

'Life of life. This is the spirit of life!'

As the Sanskrit bard wrote two thousand years ago.

*Faces, dimly grouped together illuminated by the compass light,
discuss the likelihood that we are the first ever non-Russian to have
made the long traverse. It seemed certain that by the statement of
the head of the White Sea Canal Authority that we were the first
non Russian through it; hence, a fortiori as the lawyers say, the first
to make the full White to Black. What's more we've done more than
a third under sail. Could we become the first to sail round Europe?*

*It seems unlikely that any ship small enough to fit into the White
Sea Canal locks would have had occasion to make a return via the
long exposed coastal route. But a Russian Man o' War may have
done so. Records of that would, to put it mildly, be difficult of
access.*

*Arkady asked about phosphorescence of which very large lumps
appeared, saying, 'Stars in sky and stars in water'.*

*He turned in at two hours after midnight by last buoy in the
Channel. I began to plot a GPS route out through the shallows,
anchored ships and boats flashing torches. East wind good but
making present course little uncomfortable.*

*The stir and swing of sunlight air at dawn was even more wel-
come than usual.*

*We got the dinghy on board, shook out a reef in the main. The
water was muddy and unattractive. You could see why a well known
Royal Naval signal referred to this as the Putrid Sea.*

1000 – handed staysail, still making nearly five knots.

1130 – shortened route by taking Meteor course

*1200 – steel factory at Mauripol many miles away to the north
visible through haze. 'Water is now full salt', said Arkady as I
rigged the Autohelm 2000.*

He was soon gobsmacked by its efficiency. Levanter increasing all afternoon and blew a healthy six. 1640 – Handed reefed main; now running under jib alone making four knots. Arkady in good shape, Vit feeling a bit seasick but making tea and washing up. The old Goose having a ball. At midday a swarm of what looks like bees clustered on starboard side deck: horrible, but to make up for that we are being escorted by a large number of shearwaters. I wished they were bee eaters.

At last light wind up a bit and more breaking crests. At midnight I changed working jib to our tiny flax storm jib. Many more break-ing crests, Wild Goose beginning to surf in exhilarating fashion on the bigger waves. Several looked like coming onboard but all seemed to be smoothed out by our wake.

Sea remained very white all night. Lights of two ships, one far ahead, other on starboard quarter, taking a long time to pass, almost as if dogging us. Sometimes the breaking crests seemed so bright that they looked like flashing lights.

At 0400 it blew harder still and Wild Goose was rolling her decks under, but daylight brought its usual cheer with wind dropping. Milky water still looked pretty unfriendly with a few waves coming on board but none badly. Dad has only filled the cockpit once in almost forty seasons years and I didn't want to spoil his record. At 0810 we sighted land, the east side of the Straits away to south-ward. Tea, bread and jam for me and Arkady. Milky mogully sea, still lumpy.

1050 – still rolling our guts out, making five knots in brilliant sunshine.

The Strait itself is now open, ten miles wide but narrowed to five by a sandbank on the east side.

It is nowhere more than nine metres deep. A pod of dolphins gambol round us on the tideline where the brackish Azov water mingles with the strong Med. salt. The Russian chart we are using shows no less than ten wrecks in a row on a sandbank athwart entrance. Just after noon we tied up near the railway pier at Port Kavkaz. Quick eats, then all hands turned in.

Tuesday 1st September:
Port Kavkaz. Dozens of camari on the hunt. I had to wear a face net last night. 0920 – slipped
As we passed a formidable Genoese fortress on the Ukraine shore the exuberant dolphins were waiting for us again, breaching in unison and bow riding. Arkady says,
'Black Sea welcome Wild Goose. Those cormorants with wings out to dry are like ones we have on the Imperial Eagle.'
Big ship entering channel only just visible through haze. Wind

*steadily increasing, passed out through long lines of apparently
mown grass snaking down wind. Sea truly blue.*

Flecker's lines suited the day and our mood precisely

> *'The dragon green, the luminous, the dark, the serpent
> haunted sea.*
>
> *The snow besprinkled wine of earth, the white and blue flower
> foaming sea.'*

*2045 – Great discussion over the last of the dregs in the booze
locker. By the time we'd drunk it dry at a gentle pace Communism,
the Universe, life itself had all been in order stood. Set main to a
land breeze; time will tell it holds.*

George the Autohelm steering beautifully.

'George not drink', said Arkady.

*At midnight treated to a wonderful display of son et luminere by
the dolphins, one of the most fascinating moments of the voyage,
hypnotic and very appropriate for the last night. The Russians were
like schoolchildren. 'How far to St Helena?' they asked.*

Wednesday 2nd September:

*Wind increasing, rolling as we are on the dead run and quite
close to the jybe. Wild Goose was running too fast so I dowsed the
main and we ran again under jib alone.*

*First mountain scenery since Norway should start to appear to
port at dawn. Some fishing boats to seaward and great floodlights
along the shore which the Russians call projectors used by Frontier
Guards to check the coast.*

*0200 – wind still increasing and some sheet lightning to sea-
ward. 0240 – wind steady. More frequent fork lightening.
Sometimes three or four a minute; no sound and a shadow of the
highlands visible. Lightning kindled but cleared; we were on the
edge of somebody else's storm.*

*0325 – Very dramatic arrival as we passed a bright red ship
called Marshal Rokosovskiy; curious orange light effect, mingled
with thick cloud around the wall of the Varada mountains behind
the huge port of Novorossisk.*

*0800 – Tied up to alongside in most public part of the harbour
near the Sea Station and Passenger Terminal. Got a room in the
Hotel Novorosyssk for 450 roubles a night after helping the woman
to translate a registration document from a Turkish hotel. Vitali
waited for three hours for a phone call but no reply as to whether
Larissa his wife was at home or 150 miles down the coast in
Sukumi. Complete re-stow of the boat; dinner in a flying saucer
style tower on the water front. Tired cabaret being watched by a
tired audience of Phillipino and Middle East sailors and hookers.*

Filled up with water and diesel. All I need now is food and a crew.

Thursday 3rd September:

Stayed alongside. Arkady slept on deck to guard against pedestrians wandering home from restaurants and bars calling 'Hello, hello, are you sleeping?' Some might have been tempted to take an outboard with them. Rained heavily at 0230. 0700 – overcast and cold with a strong north east wind – a baby bora (depression).

It is clearly very difficult to travel to here. No plane seats for two weeks; no train seats for five days. How the hell can my crew make it? May have to wait here for days.

Had to move Wild Goose out and anchor with two picks in same place as before, mid harbour, where it is blowing a good seven, the first of the Black Sea gales we've heard so much about.

1300 – Great News! A whistle from the shore! It was Stass of the Adventure Club who had shepherded the recruits from Moscow. Mollie from Cork with shining chesnut hair, brown eyes and immaculate head to toe tan ; Calum with the stiff chin and the deep set pale blue eyes of his Montrose ancestors. Two bottles of champagne and two hours of continuous gassing followed. Arkady making final preparations for his last departure. I remitted via Stass to Nikita Schparo his final well-earned dividend, the last third on getting out of Russia!

We went to the same dreadful restaurant as last night, tits and bums and a fat singer, all for thirty pence each .

News that Vitali's wife and daughter are safe and well in Omsk. Much unpacking and stowing of food. To bed about midnight, foxed.

On Friday 4th September we woke to a howling northeaster. Wild Goose pulling hard on both anchors but she definitely has not moved. Motored in to pier where Immigration and Customs arrived with a great flourish and almost smothered us with friendliness and hospitality.

The Visitors Book records the mood. Vitali wrote:

> The words 'lucky voyage' and 'deep water under your keel' mean nothing without the people whom we love. So a toast to the our kids and wives who have waited while we were sailing. To you Good luck and Good Weather in the seas of Nature and Life.

Arkady, measured and sincere:

> 'I am sorry to say goodbye to Wild Goose – a remarkable yacht and to Miles, a wonderful man. I wish him a successful completion of this undertaking!'

The Harbour Master added:

On your departure from the territory of Russia we wish for you and all your crew and friends all over the world peace, love, and all the best for all your life.

A little maudlin perhaps but of the many ports from which Wild Goose has been cleared nothing has ever been written like this, so we accept the wishes at face value.

The overall impression of Russia, for all its contradictions, has been the friendly and helpful attitude of the ordinary man and woman.

At last after bear hugs and goodbyes to crewmen and officials alike we sailed out into the Black Sea in a haze of euphoria.

Wild Goose

CHAPTER SIXTEEN
Turkish Delight

By MILES and WALLACE

'Did you gaily, daily sail down the sunny Bosphorus!
It is grand to hear of your adventures and think that
perhaps postcards from The Wandering Albatross
started you or helped you start the urge to travel
and 'drink life to the lees'.
Letter from Miles Smeeton (The Wandering Albatross),
aged 79, to his godson Miles.

Milo Log:
A dram for the Novorossisk harbour heads as we drew beyond
the reach of any afterthoughts from officialdom. Wind dropping as
we set all plain sail on course for Inebolu in Turkey. Great salad
lunch by Mollie. Hot and sunny; siestas by turns, then lash up and
stow. hove-to and had a wonderful swim twenty miles offshore with
the Virada mountains a pale pastel line to the north. Watched sun
go down like a red ball with dolphins jumping clean out of the
water against the glow.
Wind building up and quite stiff by dusk. Russian courtesy flag
down; blue ensign up; half moon hangs above us.
By morning the southern Black Sea was living up to its reputa-
tion! Wind dead on nose. We had shifted to trysail and reefed the
staysail during the night. Now had them both sheeted in hard but in
very steep seas progress was minimal.
So decided to alter course 140 degrees for Sinope. Life became
more bearable with sun flashing on frequent breaking crests. Land
in sight by mid morning, probably Boztepe Burnu. At 1730 –
entered the Sinope fishing harbour and tied alongside two fishing
boats from Trabzon. I made effort to see customs but port police
said wait till morning. Went to find a hammam (Turkish bath)
whereupon seized by customs officials and threatened with fine of
one million lira for being ashore before clearance. So we moved
out, anchored and slept.

Monday 7th September:
Stayed on board well after breakfast for harbour master to arrive. He had craftily waited for our customs friends to leave before arriving with great smiles and bonhommie. We went through the first port formalities until he said, 'Whisky, whisky'. Upon response to this signatures by port health officer, port police and visa police followed swiftly.

Customs didn't even look at our boat but ashore later just took out a little rubber stamp and breathed on it before application.

Asking for forecast at NATO base we met a disagreeable Scotsman who rudely refused any help. So we telephoned to Bracknell, the UK weather centre and got a very clear picture. Dinner ashore in driving rain feeling very happy not to have left harbour and to be toasting Diogenes who was born here in BC 413 (I presume in a barrel).

Second toast to Xenophon's ten thousand who set sail from Samsun near here at the end of their long march.

We motored away from Sinope at 0715, getting our teeth round some of Mollie's adhesive porridge. Beating all day with lovely blue mountains to the south. By 1810 motor sailing into a steep sea.

1845:went forward to put cover on forehatch; fell back against the mast; cut my head'

Milo was surefooted as a cat, so at that moment either he was very tired, or seas exceptionally uneven. When he described that tumble it reminded me of an evening off Pasajes in Spain when we'd been caught carrying too much sail in a sudden blow. Milo went forward in a rush without a lifeline to dowse the big yankee. I said to Tony Traill, our shipmate, as we looked on from the cockpit, 'I feel like a hen with ducklings when I watch him'. 'You should hear what he says about you when you're up there!' was the memorable rely.

1940: wind and sea easing; tacked to seaward took second reef in main for the night; red sky in west, away to windward.

Milo's crews sometimes thought he was over careful but it was caution and watchfulness, combined with the efficiency of the various crews, that had brought the trip so far to successfully with nothing but minor mishaps.

He shared the view of Stormy Weather's skipper Hal Nossiter as stated in his classic *Southward Ho!* in 1935.

'I find it better not to have too much confidence in oneself, or think for a moment that there is no danger, for there is always danger at sea. Sudden squalls, reefs, floating debris, collision, fire, waterspouts may at any time annihilate the unwary, and it is generally in unguarded moments of over-confidence that accidents occur.'

By midnight wind backing, almost allowing us to lay a course for Kerempe.

Wednesday 9th:

0500 – Decided give Inebolu a miss because of lack of time. Tacked to seaward.

0930: Kerempe abeam, breakfast of eggie bread and fried kolbasa. Found our way into Gidero's Cove a rocky creek under mountains for lunch at 1445.

The Argo had called here a year or two back. That was Tim Severin's replica fifth Century BC galley, built to re-run Jason's Voyage of The Heroes in search of the Golden Fleece. I'd pulled an oar in her from her starting point in Greece but had left as we entered the Black Sea. As a serving soldier I wasn't allowed entry to their final destination in Georgia. This tiny inlet almost invisible from seaward, is the Turkish equivalent of Glas Uig on Islay where U boats landed spies unseen in the Hitler war.

We let go in deep blue water at 1445 and heard the anchor clank on a rocky bottom Then we swam ashore for beers, bread and 'bollochus' (sardine-sized fish) at a table by a tiny beach, among chickens, cats, ducks and cockerels. Mine Host Ahmad remembered Argo coming in and rowed the crew back to WG where I showed him the picture from Severin's Voyage of the Heroes book. Gidero is an idyllic landlocked anchorage, as big a contrast as could be imagined to the muddy banks of the rivers of Russia.

Amasra

1600 – Away again with fresh northeaster on the quarter, perfect sailing. Just after dark we cautiously noseyed into Amasra as lampero fishing boats hung with blinding flares were putting to sea.

Yellow house-lights flickered invitingly through screens of trees as we picked a berth and anchored. In the silence that followed came a feeling of timelessness as if armed Sallee Rovers lay inshore and the dimly lit boats in the shadows were gilded barges bringing out dark-eyed houris to solicit our custom.

'No such luck', said Calum,

Thursday 10th September

At dawn found ourselves secure in the lee of a forested bluff with red pantile roofs showing among tree tops, heard muezzins moaning from minarets and watched the rising sun strike fires of glass from the blue ripples at the mouth of the bay.

Morning shopping. We were in a NATO base with a Turkish submarine at anchor alongside us and Mel and Sal Jackson, an agreeable live aboard pair in an American Yacht called L'Affaire de Coeur. Ashore for hamams. Mollie was bruised in places she

refused to show us inflicted by the knuckles of over attentive atten-
dants, then lunch in a garden town of oleanders, hollyhocks and
geraniums. A lazy afternoon hoping wind would drop at dusk. This is
gentle cruising, as Calum later recorded in the Visitors Book, a
delightful contrast after the constant hurry of previous months. Spoke
by landline to Dad who was preparing our reception in Istanbul.

1830 – both reefs in main, got stowed, and away to north west
for rendezvous with him in Rumeli Ferrari. Great sailing as soon
as we were clear of the land:

For Miles to eat food of any sort he hadn't prepared himself was
luxury after three months as sole chef. Now lithe, bronzed, Mollie
who makes her living cooking for top people, set out to spoil him.
She dished up her special edition of Chicken Marsala and
Ratatouille as the Goose went rockin' and rollin' westwards at six
and a half knots. Calum, strong and stocky with twinkling wit, had
tales of farming in Rhodesia, a spell at Insiad, and his move to the
financial world of the City and selling its services on visits to many
overseas markets.

HOW THE BLACK SEA GOT ITS NAME

All day rockin' and rollin'. 1325 – sighted land to the south. These
were the ebony cliffs beside the mines of Eregli where the best
Turkish coal is found. It is from these that the Black Sea is said to
derive its name. Here was the point at which we had completed the
oft quoted White To Black.

Strange birds and unfamiliar coast revealed mile by mile. Grey
clouds over the Bosphorus, silver light on water ahead.

By 2 am wonderful bright moonlight showed dolphins leaping
vertically above the curl of breakers in phosphorescent pairs; a bit
like the Sarregoussets, the Breton water fairies who Dad once
thought he saw 'dance in the spume of the wave tops on the wings
of the wind' during a summer gale off Ushant. 2300 – picked up
Rumeli lights.

Friday 11th September:

'Running down at six knots for north entrance to Bosphorus.
Black bulk of land beginning to come out around the lights. Loom
of Istanbul against the south sky. Many jybes and jinks needed to
dodge fishing boats; warning flashes from some, but no outlying
nets to trap us, thank God.'

Identified at 0200 the winking red and greens of the harbour
entrance. Last time I was here was to jump ship from the Argo.

I now felt immense relief at entering somewhere with which I was
familiar, after the mental effort of avoiding mistakes while finding
a berth in hundreds of totally strange harbours. Sodium lights

revealed that it hadn't changed – a small rectangular man-made port, under cliffs at west side of Bosphorus entrance, its quays concealed by multicoloured hulls and masts festooned with nets.

We were thankful to turn in, but not so keen on turning out an hour later to let fishing boats inside us get to sea.. We'd half expected to find Dad asleep on the quay, in a flea bag or under an old boat but no sign yet.

At nine o'clock he arrived, armed with his usual large bottle of rum and larger appetite after a lengthy journey in a taxi. This had been most kindly provided by Ford Motor Agents in Istanbul. Vast hugs followed as we met on the hatch top of one of the trawlers which lay between Wild Goose and the quay.

Then an enormous breakfast of Mollie's special scrambled egg washed down with well spiked coffee; every one talking with mouths full – there was so much news to swap.

Wallace resumes narrative:

Wild Goose looked a dream of gleaming blue waterline, white deck and hull with shining brightwork unscarred by her farsailing, the mainsail stowed for my inspection with five exactly spaced robands, her raked varnished mast gleaming in the morning sun,the Royal Cruising Club Burgee fluttering the masthead to match the Blue Ensign at her taffrail.

I'd never seen her look smarter..

Milo sporting a leonine beard was in the exuberant mood of a man just released from penal servitude; bursting with his special brand of enthusiasm – that splendid word which comes from the Greek – en theos – the god within.

The happiest of happy ships Wild Goose slipped at 1030 to glide south before a fair north wind over a sparkling blue sea. The bonnie, bonnie banks of the Bosphorus reached out to embrace us between soft green arms.

There was a slight sense of awe at entering what is arguably the most historic waterway in the world and among the busiest. Its high sides are crammed with half revealed beauty in many forms. Bell-mouthed at first it soon tautened into a channel about a mile wide.

The Dardanelles, the Straits of Dover, of Gibraltar or of Hormuz. the Sound between Hong Kong and the Hudson river among p206 laces I've been afloat in might compete in interest. In terms of political importance and variety of craft The Bosphorus beats them all.

It is often described as dividing Europe and Asia which it now links. Its bridges have often been the sole way between the two when routes further north were blocked by Soviet xenophobia.

The shore lines are filled with interest; modern gun batteries mingle with forts and castles covering every epoch of the last thousand years. At Garipse, Buyuk Liman and later Buyukdere Cove there showed the masts of many yachts, ferries and coasters against a background of minarets, small houses and restaurants. Many of the latter had fronts of fretted woodwork so old that it had weathered to a dark chocolate brown.. Some had windows a-tilt, as piles had sunk, giving a pleasantly raffish appearance. Shore side buildings lay at the foot of verdant green slopes hundreds of feet high and occasional cliffs.

Half complete and abandoned housing estates disfigured some upper slopes; marks of a building slump ten years back. Yenikoy on the west side showed small warships at anchor against red cliffs.

Between the villages and small ports were many graceful private houses set among tall plane trees in seductive gardens.

A flight of snipe-like birds skimming low over the water caught my eye; grey with a few speckles but showing no white as they twisted and turned in exact unison There was nothing like them in my bird book.

Were these the ones I'd read about? Often seen but never identified, the souls of Byzantine Christians killed at the time of the Conquest by the Ottomans in 1453? Just one of the mysteries of the Bosphorus. The Turkish dead, according to ancient beliefs, have the best time of it, if a trifle exhausting, as a reward for killing Unbelievers. This was 'by the enjoyment on green carpets of women who are eternally virgin'.

Talk of the Conquest reminded us that after passing so many portages further north we were near the scene of the greatest portage in history. This was the final stage of the 53 day assault on Byzantium by Sultan Mehmet 11. He failed to break the chain across the mouth of the Golden Horn. Whereupon with 10,000 oxen and 50,000 men he hauled 70 ships overland to bypass the barrier and storm the walls at the Adrianople Gate.

The huge galley in which Mehmet crossed the Bosphorus to take possession of what had been for centuries Constantinople is preserved in a Naval Museum on the European side.

The next time a foreign warship entered the Golden Horn in anger was 500 years later when Nasmith came to periscope depth in Royal Naval Submarine E 11 in 1915. The munition ship Stamboul promptly fell a prey to his well aimed torpedo. We had on board the naval classic. 'By Guess and By God' about Royal Naval submarines in the Kaiser War and were able to locate the scenes of many adventures of E11 and her consorts as we voyaged further south.

No worry about masthead clearance as we passed under the two single span bridges carrying road and rail traffic a hundred feet over our heads. Soon the ornate rectangular Ortakoy Mosque and the six hundred foot frontage of the Dolmabache Palace lay to starboard.

Then we cut east in a brief gap between crowded passenger boats serving the sixteen ferry terminals.

The traffic thickened as we got further south. Low-lying rusty Volga-Dons heading south, gleaming white Cruise ships bound north for Odessa, a flotilla of dark grey gunboats, vicious with uncased quick-firers and loaded torpedo tubes.

High sided empty freighters 'flying light' and unmanageable as their propellers thrashed the surface, Ferry boats criss-crossing, yachts, deep sea trawlers and tiny open hand liners, rowing skiffs and canoes. At moments it was like the mad finale of a dream before waking. We were seldom on one course for more than a couple of minutes But the local understanding of the Rule of the Road was good and I recall no near misses. We arrived in the evening at Karima a little south of Istanbul on the Asian side to a marina berth specially provided for us by Otosan Otomobile, the Ford Agents. Beds too they had arranged in the unfortunately named Elsan Hotel but none the less comfortable for that.

Next day Mollie and I braved the sea traffic again while Milo took photographs of us from the flying bridge of a hired motor cruiser. As we circled the main features became familiar enough to have stuck ever since in my mind.

On the east the Leander Tower where the current runs swiftest; an evocative name indeed, although dull history says that the channel that lusty swimmer crossed nightly to see his lady love was not here but the Dardanelles, the Harem Ferry Station on the site where the Sultans kept their captive ladies. The swift hundred-oar galley used to bring the ladies across to Topkapi is preserved alongside that of Sultan Mehmets. On the west the sadly grotty and neglected inlet of Golden Horn; beside it the enchanting slim minarets of San Sophia and the Blue Mosque. It was late afternoon as we came abreast them and made many passes for Milo to catch the pointed pillars against the setting sun as the waters of the Bosphorus turned from vermilion to purple.

The Turks, perhaps due to their proximity, realised more than any other country the singularity of Milo's feat in a making a faultless transit of Russia. We appeared twice in colour on the front of *Milyet* the leading Istanbul daily. Pressed to stay an extra day; we were awarded a medal by the Minister of Sport and kissed in the cockpit by his representative and the Commodore of the Turkish Ocean Racing Club.

When Mehmet Batmanbek, the Managing Director, invited us to a Turkish dinner cooked by his stunning wife in the garden of his own marble floored house overlooking the Princess islands in Sea of Marmara our cup was full.

And that, I think, should be the end of the book.

POSTSCRIPT

Epilog

Calum carefully arranged to leave Istanbul before we were kissed by the sporting Minister.

Mollie, Milo and I sailed south at dusk on 13th September. A fair wind blew us in 18 hours across the calm and shining Sea of Marmara to the town of Gallipoli.

There was just time to visit by taxi the battlefields of 1915 and marvel at the bravery of the Australians, New Zealanders, Brits, Turks and Germans who fought so fiercely for that narrow ridge. Next day saw us through the famous Dardanelles to Chanak from where Mollie and I visited the ringing plains of windy Troy Milo was too busy with engine checks and ship's business to join us. In the Naval Museum we saw up on chocks the puny minelayer that put pain to the efforts of the French and English fleets to force the Narrows.

Next I remember the scent of pine trees at dawn as we approached the island of Lemnos. There Mollie s holiday time was up and she flew off to Athens. Milo and I had a triumphant sail before the meltemi wind between Andros and Tinos to Syros. There our wives, June and Sarah, flew out to join us.

We all partook of the generous hospitality of the Musgrave family in their unique hilltop called the House of the Winds. Their resourceful manager Janni helped us Wild Goose for the winter at Heraklion capital of Syros and the Cyclades.

Once home Milo picked up the threads of his freelance journalist career and began work on a book about the voyage. He was not in very good form but at first the writing went well. By November he had begun to have bad attacks of what seemed to be writer's block. I now believe that an organo-phosphate pollutant he had absorbed in the lower Volga was slowly poisoning his system but this was not apparent until later. During the spring he was hardly able to write at all.

Life had to go on and the plan for the summer was that I would sail Wild Goose as far west as Gibraltar, and Milo would skipper the Atlantic leg via the Azores to Ireland.

He and I flew out to Syros at the end of March an spent a happy week of 'paint till you faint' to get Wild Goose ready for the passage. Milo was his usual cheerful jocular self and returned home in apparent full health to work in Salisbury. Then Stephen, who as you may remember had crewed for us on the first leg to Barra, brought out his wife Johanna and the three of us had a sunny ten days of light weather, visiting neighbouring islands. Then came the inexpressibly sad news that Milo had suddenly died.

At the moment the devastating news reached us Wild Goose was in the care of the yacht club at Chalkidi on the island of Evvia. First family reaction was to sell her forthwith as the seat of our sorrow. Second thoughts soon settled for a sailing her home and taking time to reconsider.

Three stout crewmen of earlier voyages, my brother-in-law John Deane, John Fishbourne and Richard Butler dropped all commitments and flew out by turns to the Aegean to help June and me.

Through the Corinth Canal and the Straits of Messina, past the Aeolian islands and south of Sardinia we sailed her in ten days to Minorca. A few weeks later old shipmates Lewis Purser and Colin Gall joined me to take her on to Povoa de Varzim in Portugal. There the kindest of friends ashore saw her laid up free of charge in their Yacht Club for the winter.

Next year in 199 Chris Tinne and Billy Patterson from Donegal, Tony Harvey from New Zealand joined to take her across the Bay of Biscay to Ireland.

Wild Goose somehow saw to it that we were able to enjoy the sailing, with Milo of course uppermost in our minds. As he always will be. What of his trusty Russian crew?

Gallina and Vitali have visited us in Ireland. Nikolai and Arkady remain in touch and are just finishing an enormous and venturesome oceanic project. This has been to find and build a fifty footer named Apostle Andrew to sail round Europe and Asia, to mark the three hundredth anniversary of the founding of the Russian Navy by Peter the Great.

They postcarded me from the Kerguelen Islands in the Indian Ocean and wintered in Vladivostock. Then came the toughest leg in summer 1998 to penetrate the ice of Northern Asia and reach the White Sea from eastwards. In 1998 they reached Biki on the North coast of Russia and layed up there until 1999. Of this I have not yet heard details. Their deeds show that Milo was extraordinarily lucky in his Russian crew men who would never take no for an answer.

Not so lucky was Rory Peck who acted as adviser and courier. A bold recorder of the truth he was shot dead by a Russian sniper while photographing the fruitless assault the Moscow Parliamentarians had been tricked into making in 1995 on the Television Building.

Wild Goose soon got restless again and spent two summers in Brittany. Then we decided that June and I with stiffening joints and diminishing energy could manager her no longer. We would have to part company – but how?

Returning from France in July 1998 I made a careless mistake on a dark, but not particularly dirty night, off the entrance to our home port. The words came true of Harold Nossiter which I had included as a quote in Chapter 15 long before this happened: 'Accidents most often come when one is off one's guard in relatively easy conditions.'

She piled up on the beach just east of the River Bann mouth. My crewman and I stepped ashore unhurt. Wild Goose was bumping hard but was re-floated an hour or two later by the skill of the Portrush Lifeboat crew. Then after half a mile under tow she sank five fathoms.

A happy ending has however come as with co-operation of my insurers I was able to hand her over to The Causeway Coast Maritime Heritage Group. They salvaged her. So Wild Goose is being actively restored just now and will next year be on show to the public near the Giants Causeway among other classic craft, perhaps even sailing again. She seems as usual to have fixed things neatly for herself.

Of Milo, photographer, biographer, soldier, sailor, mimic, oarsman, climber, what can I say?

Oh were he and I together
Shipmates on the fleeted main
Sailing through the summer weather
To the spoil of France or Spain.

A. E. Housman

'There are three ways,' said the Ancients, 'in which a man can express his sorrow; man on the lowest level cries, man on the second level is silent but man on the highest level turns his sorrow into a song.'

This book is perhaps my song.

Acknowledgements

So many people helped with planning the sail round Russia, the voyage itself and putting this book together that it would almost take another book to fully record all their unselfish efforts.

Here is a list of those we have reason to remember most gratefully, with apologies for any accidental omissions.

My brother Henry for many suggestions.

Sponsorship and general: Brian Pilcher of Maber Associates, Fareham; Nigel Winser, Royal Geographic Society; British Telecom's Aeronautical and Maritime Services, Cimat UK (Autolink RT) and EB Communications (Skanti TRP 7200 transceiver); Peta Stewart-Hunt and Euro Marine Group (Garmin GPS); David Guthrie of Simpson Lawrence for life raft delta anchor and many items of chandlery; Keith Musto (for superb oilskins); Colin Ansty for a suit of Gowen Sails; Kelvin Hughes, Olympus, for Cameras; Fuji for films; Stowe Marine Electronics for echo sounder; The Meteorological Office; Autohelm, Portsmouth for self sterering.

Northern Ireland: Jim Mc Garry (see also under engine); Cunningham Covers, Tobermore, County Derry; Tobermore Concrete Products, and Walter Leacock, for towage; Bill McCourt of Bushmills Whiskey for putting us into good spirits; Hugh Elliot of McCreadys Belfast for paint and chandlery; Roy Barton, Barton Engineering Whitehouse for wires; Munster Simms, Bangor (Titan Pump for side deck); William Clark and Sons for storage and services of John Shiels for shipping food to Hammerfest and Blake Nelson for skilled welding; David Purvis and Archie Devennie for much Joinery; Jimmy Graham for painting.

Russia: Staff of British Embassy, Moscow; Nikolai Schparo of Adventure Club, Moscow.

Literary: Libby Purves, Jane Owens, and Lisa Eveleigh. The staff of *Yachting Monthly*, Tim Stampton (cover design); The staff of Maghera Library; Psion Ltd London; Euan Storey (proof reading).

Computer: Beverley Scott and Brian Scott for much patience and dealing with my computer crises!; Gavin Hill of Bite Back for much help installing my new PC.

Engine: Watermota Ltd and Hendy Lennox for engine and spares.

Otosan Otomobil (Ford Agents in Istanbul), for hospitality and great personal kindness from Managing Director Mehmet Barmanbek and his assistant Nurettan Arsan.

Jim McGarry, Crumlin, for a perfect installation at Upperlands.

Overseas: Layups, Sr. Neca, Arthur Cavallho, Peter Fishbourne and Ronnie Byford at Povoa De Varzim, Portugal.

The Musgrave family and Jannis at Syros.

Picture Credits:

All colour pictures by Miles Clark except where credited to Vitali Chankseliani, Hugh Clay (Royal Cruising Club), Jim Blair (National Geographic Society) and Wallace Clark.

Cover picture: Tim Stampton.

Line drawings: June Clark (p. 41); others and all maps by Ken Woods, Upperlands, County Londonderry.

Giving Something Back to Russia

THE MARY AND MARTHA COMMUNITY, MOSCOW

In the belief that every project involving Russia should give something back to that country, Bruce Clark and I have arranged to give a sum of at least £1 per copy (hardback) and 30 pence per copy (softback) to provide funds for a group of near saintly people who work in this remarkable community to alleviate suffering in times that are hard even by Russian standards.

Direct gifts may be made to:

> **Mary and Martha Account,**
> **Ulster Bank,**
> **Maghera,**
> **County Londonderry**
> **(Sort-code 981060).**
> **Account No. 26159408.**

APPENDIX ONE

Fitting Out

In addition to the jobs mentioned in the Introduction:

All keel bolts and rudder fastenings were drawn and checked.

Extra strong snugs were fitted for the dinghy to sit in when on deck.

Jackstays of terylene tape run from cockpit to bow for personal lifelines.

The sink drain was blanked off to eliminate a non essential hull opening.

A new Echo Sounder fitted.

And many similar safety matters attended to.

To be able to stay with the family through eras of school bills, house building and other such items for four decades Wild Goose has always had to be run on lines of considerable economy. Above this was our rule was that if a device (eg VHF radio, GPS Navigator) which contributed to safety appeared on the market it had to be promptly acquired.

Wild Goose was, except for one near disastrous year, fitted out by Wallace and Miles personally and progressively modernised.

PRINCIPAL SPARES FOR RUSSIAN TRIP

General: Steering compass, Tiller , Autohelm 2000, Dinghy oars, Navigation and riding lights.

Rope to replace all running rigging, wire for spare forestay and upper shrouds. Sheet anchor, mooring swivel and 20 fathoms of ½ inch chain.

For Engine: Diesel pump and piping, Injectors, Starter motor and solenoid, joints belts, exhaust hose complete mild steel exhaust assembly, propeller and many smaller items (as recommended by WaterMota).

Electrics: Petrol driven generator, jump leads, 12volt soldering iron, bulbs for all fittings. Spare 70 a/h Charged Battery in own box out of system.

REPAIR GEAR

A major tool kit including full set of socket, ring, tube, and open jaw spanners, Stillsons, gauges and Allen Keys.

Carpenters tools, cramps, wedges, caulking irons, seaming cotton, oakum and taper plugs.

Bottle screws, shackles, Jubilee clips, Bulldog grips and lengths of piping.

Legs to support hull when drying out.

А Т Л А С
ЕДИНОЙ ГЛУБОКОВОДНОЙ СИСТЕМЫ
ЕВРОПЕЙСКОЙ ЧАСТИ РСФСР

Т о м 3
ВОЛГО-БАЛТИЙСКИЙ ВОДНЫЙ ПУТЬ
имени В. И. ЛЕНИНА

От Ленинграда до Рыбинского водохранилища

Cover Page of Canal Atlas, Vol. 3.

APPENDIX TWO

Maps and Charts

Past Russian Governments deliberately suppressed the circulation of maps or charts, for security reasons and in1992 they remained hard to get. Best route planners were as the US Operational Navigation Charts, intended for fliers, scale 1:1,000,000. A pair of these Ref: ONC D3 and E4 were Milo's main route guide, also a Tactical Pilotage Chart 1:500.000 No.TPC D-3B.

A set of nine volumes, each 15" by 12", bears the awesome title of Atlas of the Single Deep Water System of European Russia. This Atlas, issued in numbered editions with a security rating, covers the entire route in detail from sea to sea. Plans of the ports show individual buoys and are accompanied by copious notes – wave heights, ice clearance dates and rates, temperatures and average winds. The set has the hawlmark of an efficient system. A friend by some means procured one which later came home with Wild Goose and is now in the Cruising Association Library.

The Onega Volume notes Rog Rushay where Wild Goose had her worst grounding as dangerous in winds from the north but makes no mention of a sunken pier.

Curiously enough a British War Office Map of 1955, 1:250,000, labelled Petrozavodsk (one of the few Wild Goose carried) shows a faint stroke indicating the pier protruding from the NW corner of Rog Rushay.

218

APPENDIX 3

Times and Distances (sea miles)

(Subject to the vagaries of Russian place names and their spellings)

Date		Sub Total	TOTAL
MAY			
12th/13th	Coleraine, Northern Ireland to Castlebay, Barra		140m
14th/15th	Castle Bay to Stornoway	70m	
16th/19th	Stornoway to Lerwick, Shetland	210m	
21st/24th	Shetland to Aalesund, Norway	230m	
29th	Harstad, Royal Marine Base	240m	
30th	Tromso	80m	
JUNE			
2nd	0230: Anchor Bradsfjord. 1230: Hammerfest	140m	
3rd	Anchor W. of Gjesvaer		
4th	Round North Cape		
6th/8th	Weatherbound in Vardo	180m	
9th	Murmansk	120m	
13th	Archangel	500m	
19th	Solovetsky Islands	200m	
22nd	Belomorsk	55m	2165m
25th	Shavan, S. end of first lake	50m	
26th	To Nadvoitsky at N. end of Lake Vyg	15m	
27th	Himpesky Island	30m	
28th	Povenets at N. end of Onega	45m	
	TOTAL WHITE SEA CANAL DISTANCE		140m
29/30th	Kizhi Island and on to Petrozavodsk	90m	
JULY			
2/3rd	Petrozavodsk to Rush Rogay Bay	55m	
	Lengthy grounding		
4th	Enter Volga – Baltic Canal	30m	
	Proceed via 6 locks to highest point on voyage,		
	370 feet and down by one lock to estuary on		
	N. shore of Lake Beloye	70m	
6th	Cross Beloye and by smaller lakes to Sheksna River	48m	
7th	Anchor close below lock at Pochino	22m	
8th	Anchor inshore by Cherepovets at N. end of Mologa	40m	
10th	First hot weather. Anchor at 0130 off Rybinsk barrage	65m	
	Reach Volga at midnight		415m
11th	Anchor off Tolga Monastery	45m	
12/13th	Yaroslavl		
14th	Kostroma	45m	
16th	Alongside Plyoss	42m	
17th	Anchor Yuryevets. Into Lower Volga	60m	
18th	Yacht Basin, Gorodets	50m	
19th	Anchor short of Gorky	35m	
20/21	Gorky (Nizhniy Novgorod)		22m
22nd	Off Makarief Monastery	40m	
23rd	Off Insect Island, Fukino	42m	
24th	Kozmodemyansk	38m	
25th	Yacht Club at Cheboksary	35m	

26th	Off Volshk	40m	
27th	Pass under Trans-Siberia Railway	50m	
28/29th	At Kazan		
30th	Shelango, Grebini		20m
31st	Confluence with R. Kama	30m	

AUGUST

1st	Anchor Staraya Mayna	58m	
2nd	Ulyanovsk	25m	
3rd	E. Bank	28m	
4th	Tolyatti	50m	
5/6th	Anchor 1745 (Disco camp)	40m	
7th	Samara	8m	
8th	Neck anchorage	50m	
9th		40m	
10th	Khvalynsk	40m	
11th	Barrage at Balakovo	40m	
12th	Balakovo		
13th	Marx	55m	
14th	Saratov	40m	
16th	Privoizhskoye	40m	
17th	Nizhnyaya Island	60m	
18th	Anchor Gorny	65m	
19th	Volgograd (Stalingrad)	65m	
	MILEAGE ON VOLGA		1276m
	Volga-Don Ship Canal		
	Built 1948 - 52, Length 63 miles 15 locks. Rise of 289 feet from the Volga, then descent 144 feet to the Don.		
21st	Anchor in channel S. of lock 5	25m	
22nd	2345 anchor in fairway, Lock 10	20m	
23rd	Anchor N. end Tsimlyanksoye Res.	40m	
24th	Anchor off bare earth cliffs	70m	
25th	1420 out of lock into Don proper. Rinskaya	65m	
26th	Just N. of Semikarakorski	40m	
27th	Bagayevsky	35m	
28th	Roscof on Don	35m	
31st	1245: Alongside, Port Kavkaz	180m	

SEPTEMBER

2nd	Enter Novorossiysk	80m	
4th	Slip for Inebolu, Turkey		
6th	Hove-to under trysail. Later arrive Sinop	200m	
9th	Amasra just after dark	150m	
11th	Tie up in Rumeli Ferrarri	180m	
12th	1800 Karima Marina, Istanbul	15m	

SUMMARY

Ireland to Belomorsk	2040m
(Minch, North Sea, Barents Sea, White Sea	2040m
White Sea Canal	140m
Onega and Volga-Baltic Canal to Rybinsk	415m
Volga	1276m
Volga-Don Canal and River Don	330m
Black Sea, Sea of Marmara, Aegean	1100m

GRAND TOTAL – SAY FIVE THOUSAND MILES

APPENDIX 4

YAOHT RENTAL
AGREEMENT BETWEEN
MILES CLARK & ADVENTURE CLUB, MOSCOW

INTRODUCTION

The expedition is a joint Russian-British voyage in a 80-year-old
11m wooden yacht from the White Sea to the Black Sea via the
White Sea Canal, Lake Onega, the Volga and the Don, to Istanbul.

CERTIFICATE

For the period within the Russian inland waterways (15 June -
1 September 1992), the yacht (WILD GOOSE) will be rented by
ADVENTURE CLUB, Moscow. The staff of ADVENTURE CLUB will be
responsible for navigation, conduct and maintenance of the yacht
and for all documentation relating to the voyage across Russia.

ADVENTURE CLUB is inviting three yachtsmen from Britain and one
from the United States to join the expedition.

Signed...................................... Date...............
                    ADVENTURE CLUB

Signed...................................... Date.. 29/4/92 ...
            Miles Clark, owner, WILD GOOSE

THE MAIN CENTER OF ELECTRO-MAGNETIC
COMPARTIBILITY OF RADIO-ELECTRONIC MEANS
8.05.92

The Main Center of Electro-Magnetic Compartibility of Radio-Electronic
Means gives the permition for the organizing of radiocommunication to the
"Adventur Club" between the yacht "Wild Goose" and Portishead Radio for
the period of Russian-British voyage in the Russia since 8.06 till 24.08 on the
rout Murmansk - Arkhangelsk - Solovets Islands - Belomorsk - Novorossiisk
- Istanbul aboard the yarcht with using of the double radiotelephone fre-
quinces, the type of radiation 2K80j3E:

The marine transmitter	Land transmitter (England)
with 200 Wt output	with 1 KWt output
Call-sign "MGBJ6"	Call-sign "GKA"
8249 KHz	8773 KHz
12323 KHz	13710 KHz
16402 KHz	17284 KHz

We do not have possibility to give the permision for 4MHz band.
This permition is valid till the end of the date mentioned above.
The alternative chief   V. M. Eliseev

221

RATHLIN – ITS ISLAND STORY

By

WALLACE CLARK

A5, 200 pages, five maps and thirty half tone illustrations.
Foreword by Richard Branson.

*The only book giving the full history of the L-shaped island
that lies in a key position in the tide-torn narrows
between Scotland and Ireland.*

Rathlin has survived eleven massacres and has a more
eventful story than other islands of its size in Europe.
The current fourth edition covers the construction of an
all-weather harbour in Church Bay.
Rathlin has previously had nowhere along its twenty mile
shoreline where a boat could be left safely afloat.
Now with a rock armoured Port and Ro-Ro ferry it has
become a positive link between its two neighbours.
Half the stars of Gaelic mythology appear in the book, as
well as latter-day names from Saint Columba to Robert the
Bruce, Queen Elizabeth, Marconi and Richard Branson.
Rathlin's tall stacks where tens of thousands of guillemots
and razorbills can be seen in May and June nest are arguably
the finest seabird nesting sites in Ireland.
The many wrecks at the base of its white cliffs make Rathlin
a fascinating hunting ground for divers.
Packed with interest for sailors, bird lovers and anyone who
likes to visit islands.

£9.50 from

WALLACE CLARK BOOK SALES

**115 Kilrea Road, Upperlands,
County Derry, BT 46 5SB
Telephone: 01648 42737**